YOUR
HOROS

NEIL SOMERVILLE

at the Year of the Ox Holds in Store for You

TO ROS, RICHARD AND EMILY

HarperElement
An Imprint of HarperCollins*Publishers*
77–85 Fulham Palace Road
Hammersmith, London W6 8JB

The website address is: www.thorsonselement.com

and *HarperElement* are trademarks of
HarperCollins*Publishers* Limited

Published by HarperElement 2008

10 9 8 7 6 5 4 3 2 1

A catalogue record for this book is
available from the British Library

ISBN-13 978-0-00-72644-5
ISBN-10 0-00-726444-5

Printed and bound in Great Britain by
Clays Ltd, St Ives plc

CONTENTS

ABOUT THE AUTHOR

Neil Somerville is one of the leading writers in the West on Chinese horoscopes. He has been interested in Eastern forms of divination for many years and believes that much can be learned from the ancient wisdom of the East. His annual book on Chinese horoscopes has built up an international following and he is also the author of *What's your Chinese Love Sign?* (Thorsons, 2000), *Chinese Success Signs* (Thorsons, 2001) and *The Answers* (Element, 2004).

Neil Somerville was born in the year of the Water Snake. His wife was born under the sign of the Monkey, his son is an Ox and daughter a Horse.

ACKNOWLEDGEMENTS

In writing *Your Chinese Horoscope 2009* I am grateful for the assistance and invaluable support that those around me have given.

I would also like to acknowledge Theodora Lau's *The Handbook of Chinese Horoscopes* (Harper & Row, 1979; Arrow, 1981), which was particularly useful to me in my research.

In addition to Ms Lau's work, I commend the following books to those who wish to find out more about Chinese horoscopes: Kristyna Arcarti, *Chinese Horoscopes for Beginners* (Headway, 1995); Catherine Aubier, *Chinese Zodiac Signs* (Arrow, 1984), series of 12 books; E. A. Crawford and Teresa Kennedy, *Chinese Elemental Astrology* (Piatkus Books, 1992); Paula Delsol, *Chinese Horoscopes* (Pan, 1973); Barry Fantoni, *Barry Fantoni's Chinese Horoscopes* (Warner, 1994); Bridget Giles and the Diagram Group, *Chinese Astrology* (HarperCollins, 1996); Kwok Man-Ho, *Complete Chinese Horoscopes* (Sunburst Books, 1995); Lori Reid, *The Complete Book of Chinese Horoscopes* (Element Books, 1997); Paul Rigby and Harvey Bean, *Chinese Astrologics* (Publications Division, South China Morning Post Ltd, 1981); Ruth Q. Sun, *The Asian Animal Zodiac* (Charles E. Tuttle Company, Inc., 1996); Derek Walters, *Ming Shu* (Pagoda Books, 1987) and *The*

Chinese Astrology Workbook (The Aquarian Press, 1988); Suzanne White, *The New Astrology* (Pan, 1987), *The New Chinese Astrology* (Pan, 1994) and *Chinese Astrology Plain and Simple* (Eden Grove Editions, 1998).

As we march into a new year
we each have our hopes, our ambitions and our dreams.

Sometimes fate and circumstance will assist us,
sometimes we will struggle and despair,
but march we must.

For it is those who keep going,
and who keep their aspirations alive,
who stand the greatest chance of securing what they want.

March determinedly,
and your determination will, in some way, be rewarded.

Neil Somerville

INTRODUCTION

The origins of Chinese horoscopes have been lost in the mists of time. It is known, however, that oriental astrologers practised their art many thousands of years ago and even today Chinese astrology continues to fascinate and intrigue.

In Chinese astrology there are 12 signs named after 12 different animals. No one quite knows how the signs acquired their names, but there is one legend that offers an explanation. According to this legend, one Chinese New Year the Buddha invited all the animals in his kingdom to come before him. Unfortunately, for reasons best known to the animals, only 12 turned up. The first to arrive was the Rat, followed by the Ox, Tiger, Rabbit, Dragon, Snake, Horse, Goat, Monkey, Rooster, Dog and finally Pig. In gratitude, the Buddha decided to name a year after each of the animals and that those born during that year would inherit some of the personality of that animal. Therefore those born in the year of the Ox would be hard working, resolute and stubborn, just like the Ox, while those born in the year of the Dog would be loyal and faithful, just like the Dog. While it is not possible that everyone born in a particular year can have all the characteristics of the sign, it is incredible what similarities do occur, and this is partly where the fascination of Chinese horoscopes lies.

In addition to the 12 signs of the Chinese zodiac there are five elements and these have a strengthening or moderating influence upon the signs. Details about the effects of the elements are given in each of the chapters on the 12 signs.

To find out which sign you were born under, refer to the tables on the following pages. As the Chinese year is based on the lunar year and does not start until late January or early February, it is particularly important for anyone born in those two months to check carefully the dates of the Chinese year in which they were born.

Also included, in the appendix, are two charts showing the compatibility between the signs for personal and business relationships and details about the signs ruling the different hours of the day. From this it is possible to locate your ascendant and, as in Western astrology, this has a significant influence on your personality.

In writing this book, I have taken the unusual step of combining the intriguing nature of Chinese horoscopes with the Western desire to know what the future holds, and have based my interpretations upon various factors relating to each of the signs. Over the years in which *Your Chinese Horoscope* has been published I have been pleased that so many have found the sections on the forthcoming year of interest and hope that the horoscope has been constructive and useful. Remember, though, that at all times you are master of your own destiny.

I sincerely hope that *Your Chinese Horoscope 2009* will prove interesting and helpful for the year ahead.

THE CHINESE YEARS

Rooster	22 January	1909	to	9 February	1910
Dog	10 February	1910	to	29 January	1911
Pig	30 January	1911	to	17 February	1912
Rat	18 February	1912	to	5 February	1913
Ox	6 February	1913	to	25 January	1914
Tiger	26 January	1914	to	13 February	1915
Rabbit	14 February	1915	to	2 February	1916
Dragon	3 February	1916	to	22 January	1917
Snake	23 January	1917	to	10 February	1918
Horse	11 February	1918	to	31 January	1919
Goat	1 February	1919	to	19 February	1920
Monkey	20 February	1920	to	7 February	1921
Rooster	8 February	1921	to	27 January	1922
Dog	28 January	1922	to	15 February	1923
Pig	16 February	1923	to	4 February	1924
Rat	5 February	1924	to	23 January	1925
Ox	24 January	1925	to	12 February	1926
Tiger	13 February	1926	to	1 February	1927
Rabbit	2 February	1927	to	22 January	1928
Dragon	23 January	1928	to	9 February	1929
Snake	10 February	1929	to	29 January	1930
Horse	30 January	1930	to	16 February	1931
Goat	17 February	1931	to	5 February	1932
Monkey	6 February	1932	to	25 January	1933

Rooster	26 January	1933	to	13 February	1934
Dog	14 February	1934	to	3 February	1935
Pig	4 February	1935	to	23 January	1936
Rat	24 January	1936	to	10 February	1937
Ox	11 February	1937	to	30 January	1938
Tiger	31 January	1938	to	18 February	1939
Rabbit	19 February	1939	to	7 February	1940
Dragon	8 February	1940	to	26 January	1941
Snake	27 January	1941	to	14 February	1942
Horse	15 February	1942	to	4 February	1943
Goat	5 February	1943	to	24 January	1944
Monkey	25 January	1944	to	12 February	1945
Rooster	13 February	1945	to	1 February	1946
Dog	2 February	1946	to	21 January	1947
Pig	22 January	1947	to	9 February	1948
Rat	10 February	1948	to	28 January	1949
Ox	29 January	1949	to	16 February	1950
Tiger	17 February	1950	to	5 February	1951
Rabbit	6 February	1951	to	26 January	1952
Dragon	27 January	1952	to	13 February	1953
Snake	14 February	1953	to	2 February	1954
Horse	3 February	1954	to	23 January	1955
Goat	24 January	1955	to	11 February	1956
Monkey	12 February	1956	to	30 January	1957
Rooster	31 January	1957	to	17 February	1958
Dog	18 February	1958	to	7 February	1959
Pig	8 February	1959	to	27 January	1960
Rat	28 January	1960	to	14 February	1961
Ox	15 February	1961	to	4 February	1962
Tiger	5 February	1962	to	24 January	1963
Rabbit	25 January	1963	to	12 February	1964

Dragon	13 February	1964	to	1 February	1965
Snake	2 February	1965	to	20 January	1966
Horse	21 January	1966	to	8 February	1967
Goat	9 February	1967	to	29 January	1968
Monkey	30 January	1968	to	16 February	1969
Rooster	17 February	1969	to	5 February	1970
Dog	6 February	1970	to	26 January	1971
Pig	27 January	1971	to	14 February	1972
Rat	15 February	1972	to	2 February	1973
Ox	3 February	1973	to	22 January	1974
Tiger	23 January	1974	to	10 February	1975
Rabbit	11 February	1975	to	30 January	1976
Dragon	31 January	1976	to	17 February	1977
Snake	18 February	1977	to	6 February	1978
Horse	7 February	1978	to	27 January	1979
Goat	28 January	1979	to	15 February	1980
Monkey	16 February	1980	to	4 February	1981
Rooster	5 February	1981	to	24 January	1982
Dog	25 January	1982	to	12 February	1983
Pig	13 February	1983	to	1 February	1984
Rat	2 February	1984	to	19 February	1985
Ox	20 February	1985	to	8 February	1986
Tiger	9 February	1986	to	28 January	1987
Rabbit	29 January	1987	to	16 February	1988
Dragon	17 February	1988	to	5 February	1989
Snake	6 February	1989	to	26 January	1990
Horse	27 January	1990	to	14 February	1991
Goat	15 February	1991	to	3 February	1992
Monkey	4 February	1992	to	22 January	1993
Rooster	23 January	1993	to	9 February	1994
Dog	10 February	1994	to	30 January	1995

Pig	31 January	1995	to	18 February	1996
Rat	19 February	1996	to	6 February	1997
Ox	7 February	1997	to	27 January	1998
Tiger	28 January	1998	to	15 February	1999
Rabbit	16 February	1999	to	4 February	2000
Dragon	5 February	2000	to	23 January	2001
Snake	24 January	2001	to	11 February	2002
Horse	12 February	2002	to	31 January	2003
Goat	1 February	2003	to	21 January	2004
Monkey	22 January	2004	to	8 February	2005
Rooster	9 February	2005	to	28 January	2006
Dog	29 January	2006	to	17 February	2007
Pig	18 February	2007	to	6 February	2008
Rat	7 February	2008	to	25 January	2009
Ox	26 January	2009	to	13 February	2010

NOTE

The names of the signs in the Chinese zodiac occasionally differ, although the characteristics of the signs remain the same. In some books the Ox is referred to as the Buffalo or Bull, the Rabbit as the Hare or Cat, the Goat as the Sheep and the Pig as the Boar.

For the sake of convenience, the male gender is used throughout this book. Unless otherwise stated, the characteristics of the signs apply to both sexes.

WELCOME TO THE
YEAR OF THE OX

Whether ploughing fields or carrying heavy loads, the Ox has served mankind well. Strong, hard working and reliable, he is a dutiful worker. This sense of duty will be very evident in the Ox's own year. A lot will happen in 2009 and while it may not always be an easy year, it will be one for steady growth and some often historic developments.

The emphasis in the Ox year is on effort and commitment and this will be reflected in many areas of life. In the political world the new American President, inaugurated just a few days before the Ox year begins, will be keen to establish their authority and introduce certain policy measures which, while not always popular, could have an impact on the economy, foreign policy and the environment as well as the number of troops serving overseas. Over the year decisions will be taken which could have far-reaching implications both in the US and overseas.

The Ox year is very much a time of conviction politics and many leaders, both new and well established, will be intent on change and improvement. This was illustrated in the Ox year of 1985 when President Reagan met the new Soviet leader Gorbachev, a meeting that marked a new era in Soviet–American relations. It was also at this time that President Gorbachev embarked on the policies of *perestroika* and *glasnost* which were to transform the Soviet

Union and later Eastern Europe. This Ox year is also likely to see a coming together of world leaders and some momentous decisions.

One area that will feature prominently over the year will be law, order and security, with many governments introducing further measures to counter criminal and terrorist elements. For those who do operate outside the law or embark on illegal protests or militant action, the consequences could be considerable. In the Ox year law and order reign supreme, and challenges to authority will be countered with considerable might.

Education and the environment will also be in the legislative programmes of many governments during the year. In education there will often be increased funding for further education as well as a greater emphasis on vocational and more specialist training. This could include large companies and organizations being encouraged to make more work-experience and job-training opportunities available, as well as a growth in apprenticeship and job-release schemes. And with the pressure on natural resources, many countries will see the introduction and enforcement of rigorous new environmental measures, some of which will have an impact on daily life.

This year will also see continuing advances in medicine and technology, some of which will be the culmination of many years of research, study and effort. Notable medical and technical breakthroughs in previous Ox years have included the use of insulin to control diabetes and lasers to clean out clogged arteries and the building of the world's first jet engine.

The Ox has a strong affinity with the land, and farming issues will also feature strongly this year. These could include assistance being offered to poorer regions to encourage a greater level of self-sufficiency as well as the introduction of hardier crops. It was an Ox year that saw the mammoth Live Aid concert, with a television audience of an estimated 1.5 billion, which was to raise so much for famine relief in Africa. Positive advances will again be made this year, but more ominously the year could also be marked by disease. It was the last Ox year that saw the killing of all the chickens in Hong Kong to stop the spread of avian 'flu, and while it is hoped there will be no recurrence of this or other diseases, the omens are not promising.

As far as the world stock markets are concerned, this will be a mixed year, with many markets sensitive to news and reacting quickly to events. As a result there could be wide fluctuations in prices and investors will need to remain vigilant throughout the year.

In the world of arts and culture, 2009 is likely to be marked by some often impressive and thought-provoking works. Harry Potter made his appearance in the last Ox year, with the publication of J. K. Rowling's first book, and that year also saw the release of some particularly ambitious films, including *Titanic* and *The Lost World: Jurassic Park*. Some new releases in the current Ox year could be equally impressive.

Although the British royal family is rarely far from the news, 2009 is also likely to be marked by some royal events that will attract worldwide comment.

For many, the Ox year will be a positive and constructive one, although it does call for commitment. Results will need to be worked for and time allowed for efforts to filter through. The Ox proceeds in a sometimes slow but always sure and measured way. His year favours traditional paths and values, and in consequence many people will decide to improve their domestic life over the year. The Ox year also has a strong practical edge to it and the emphasis will be on action. And as Henry David Thoreau, himself born under the sign of the Ox, once wrote, 'I know of no more encouraging fact than the unquestionable ability of man to elevate his life by a conscious endeavour.' In 2009 many will feel inspired to make that conscious endeavour and will reap the benefits.

I wish you good fortune and every success in the interesting year that lies ahead.

YOUR CHINESE
HOROSCOPE 2009

18 FEBRUARY 1912 ～ 5 FEBRUARY 1913	*Water Rat*
5 FEBRUARY 1924 ～ 23 JANUARY 1925	*Wood Rat*
24 JANUARY 1936 ～ 10 FEBRUARY 1937	*Fire Rat*
10 FEBRUARY 1948 ～ 28 JANUARY 1949	*Earth Rat*
28 JANUARY 1960 ～ 14 FEBRUARY 1961	*Metal Rat*
15 FEBRUARY 1972 ～ 2 FEBRUARY 1973	*Water Rat*
2 FEBRUARY 1984 ～ 19 FEBRUARY 1985	*Wood Rat*
19 FEBRUARY 1996 ～ 6 FEBRUARY 1997	*Fire Rat*
7 FEBRUARY 2008 ～ 25 JANUARY 2009	*Earth Rat*

THE
RAT

THE PERSONALITY OF THE RAT

To see,
and to see what others do not see.
That is true vision.

The Rat is born under the sign of charm. He is intelligent, popular and loves attending parties and large social gatherings. He is able to establish friendships with remarkable ease and people generally feel relaxed in his company. He is a very social creature and is genuinely interested in the welfare and activities of others. He has a good understanding of human nature and his advice and opinions are often sought.

The Rat is a hard and diligent worker. He is also very imaginative and is never short of ideas. However, he does sometimes lack the confidence to promote his ideas and this can often prevent him from securing the recognition he deserves.

The Rat is very observant and many Rats have made excellent writers and journalists. The Rat also excels at personnel and PR work and any job that brings him into contact with people and the media. His skills are particularly appreciated in times of crisis, for the Rat has an incredibly strong sense of self preservation. When it comes to finding a way out of an awkward situation, he is certain to be the one who comes up with a solution.

The Rat loves to be where there is a lot of action, but should he ever find himself in a very bureaucratic or restrictive environment he can become a stickler for discipline and routine. He is also something of an opportunist and is constantly on the lookout for ways in which he can improve his wealth and lifestyle. He rarely lets an opportunity go by and can become involved in so many plans and schemes that he sometimes squanders his energies and achieves very little as a result. He is also rather gullible and can be taken in by those less scrupulous than himself.

Another characteristic of the Rat is his attitude towards money. He is very thrifty and to some he may appear a little mean. The reason for this is purely that he likes to keep his money within his family. He can be most generous to his partner, his children and close friends and relatives. He can also be generous to himself, for he often finds it impossible to deprive himself of any luxury or object he fancies. He is very acquisitive and can be a notorious hoarder. He also hates waste and is rarely prepared to throw anything away. He can be rather greedy and will rarely refuse an invitation to a free meal or a complimentary ticket to a lavish function.

The Rat is a good conversationalist, although he can occasionally be a little indiscreet. He can be highly critical of others – for an honest and unbiased opinion, the Rat is a superb critic – and will sometimes use confidential information to his own advantage. However, as he has such a bright and irresistible nature, most people are prepared to forgive him his slight indiscretions.

Throughout his long and eventful life the Rat will make many friends and will find that he is especially well suited to those born under his own sign and those of the Ox, Dragon and Monkey. He can also get on well with those born under the signs of the Tiger, Snake, Rooster, Dog and Pig, but the rather sensitive Rabbit and Goat will find the Rat a little too critical and blunt for their liking. The Horse and Rat will also find it difficult to get on with each other – the Rat craves security and will find the Horse's changeable moods and rather independent nature a little unsettling.

The Rat is very family orientated and will do anything to please his nearest and dearest. He is exceptionally loyal to his parents and can himself be a very caring and loving parent. He will take an interest in all his children's activities and will see that they want for nothing. The Rat usually has a large family.

The female Rat has a kindly, outgoing nature and involves herself in a multitude of different activities. She has a wide circle of friends, enjoys entertaining and is an attentive hostess. She is also conscientious about the upkeep of her home and has good taste in home furnishings. She is most supportive to the other members of her family and, due to her resourceful, friendly and persevering nature, can do well in practically any career she chooses.

Although the Rat is essentially outgoing, he is also a very private individual. He tends to keep his feelings to himself and while he is not averse to learning what other people are doing, he resents anyone prying too closely into his own affairs. He also does not like solitude and if he is alone for any length of time he can easily get depressed.

The Rat is undoubtedly very talented, but he does sometimes fail to capitalize on his many abilities. He has a tendency to become involved in too many schemes and chase after too many opportunities at once. If he can slow down and concentrate on one thing at a time, he can become very successful. If not, success and wealth can elude him. But, with his tremendous ability to charm, the Rat will rarely, if ever, be without friends.

THE FIVE DIFFERENT TYPES OF RAT

In addition to the 12 signs of the Chinese zodiac there are five elements and these have a strengthening or moderating influence on the signs. The effects of the five elements on the Rat are described below, together with the years in which the elements were exercising their influence. Therefore those Rats born in 1960 are Metal Rats, those born in 1912 and 1972 are Water Rats, and so on.

Metal Rat: 1960
This Rat has excellent taste and certainly knows how to appreciate the finer things in life. His home is comfortable and nicely decorated and he likes to entertain and mix in fashionable circles. He has considerable financial acumen and invests his money well. On the surface the Metal Rat appears cheerful and confident, but deep down he can be troubled by worries that are quite often of his own making. He is exceptionally loyal to his family and friends.

Water Rat: 1912, 1972
The Water Rat is intelligent and very astute. He is a deep thinker and can express his thoughts clearly and persuasively. He is always eager to learn and is talented in many different areas. He is usually very popular, but his fear of

loneliness can sometimes lead him into mixing with the wrong sort of company. He is a particularly skilful writer, but he can get sidetracked very easily and should try to concentrate on just one thing at a time.

Wood Rat: 1924, 1984

The Wood Rat has a friendly, outgoing personality and is popular with his colleagues and friends. He has a quick, agile brain and likes to turn his hand to anything he thinks may be useful. His one fear is insecurity, but given his intelligence and capabilities, this fear is usually unfounded. He has a good sense of humour, enjoys travel and, due to his highly imaginative nature, can be a gifted writer or artist.

Fire Rat: 1936, 1996

The Fire Rat is rarely still and seems to have a never ending supply of energy and enthusiasm. He loves being involved in some form of action, be it travel, following up new ideas or campaigning for a cause in which he fervently believes. He is an original thinker and hates being bound by petty restrictions or the dictates of others. He can be forthright in his views but can sometimes get carried away in the excitement of the moment and commit himself to various undertakings without thinking through all the implications. Yet he has a resilient nature and with the right support can go far in life.

Earth Rat: 1948, 2008

This Rat is astute and very level headed. He rarely takes unnecessary chances and while he is constantly trying to improve his financial status, he is prepared to proceed slowly and leave nothing to chance. He is probably not as adventurous as the other types of Rat and prefers to remain in familiar territory rather than rush headlong into something he knows little about. He is talented, conscientious and caring towards his loved ones, but at the same time can be self conscious and worry a little too much about the image he is trying to project.

PROSPECTS FOR THE RAT IN 2009

The Year of the Rat (7 February 2008 to 25 January 2009) is a generally favourable one for the Rat himself and in the remaining months he can look forward to achieving a great deal.

At work the closing months of the year can see some important developments. For some Rats, there will be the chance to move to new duties, and those Rats who are keen to make a change in their work life or are seeking a position will often be able to benefit from the openings that arise at this time. Many Rats will be able to make good headway, with September and October seeing some particularly encouraging developments.

The Rat's finances can also see an improvement at this time, although to benefit the Rat would do well to keep watch over his outgoings. With the closing months of the year often being a time of increased spending, some restraint would be wise.

Being born under the sign of charm, the Rat sets great store by his relations with others, and many a Rat will play a leading role in making domestic arrangements and will enjoy the activities and get-togethers that take place. However, at such a busy time the Rat does need to consult others and discuss his hopes, plans and concerns. Good communication and planning *are* vital.

The Rat's social life could also enjoy a fillip at this time and for those enjoying new romance or who are hoping to meet new people, the closing months of the year can be exciting, with September and November bringing some especially good social opportunities.

In many respects the Rat year is supportive of the Rat and by being active and putting himself forward, he will find much going in his favour.

The Year of the Ox begins on 26 January and will be an encouraging one for the Rat, although it will call for effort. Should he slack or take situations for granted, problems could arise. The Rat does need to remember that the Ox is a hard taskmaster!

One of the more positive aspects of the year is the way in which the Rat will be able to develop both himself and his overall work situation. This is very much a year for furthering skills and during it the Rat should make the most of any opportunities to widen his experience. Knowledge acquired now can not only help him in the present but also open up new possibilities in the near future. The Ox year is no time for standing still, and by showing commitment and making the most of his chances to develop his skills, the Rat can make useful progress.

This also applies to those Rats who would welcome a change at work or are seeking work. By looking at their skills and strengths and considering other ways in which they can use them, they will find interesting possibilities starting to arise. If they are able to take advantage of training opportunities or refresher courses or set time aside for study and research, they are likely to find their efforts well rewarded. For work opportunities, March, June, October and November are particularly favourable, but such is the nature of the year that by showing commitment and putting in that extra effort the Rat could find opportunities arising at almost any time.

As well as making progress in his work, the Rat should also give some consideration to his own personal development over the year. This includes setting time aside for activities and interests he enjoys and looking to develop them or perhaps take up something new. By furthering his knowledge and using his time in purposeful ways, he can gain a lot of pleasure from his activities. Those Rats who lack regular exercise would also do well to consider ways in which they could remedy this and get medical advice on the most appropriate way to proceed. With the encouraging nature of the Ox year, positive action can be of great benefit.

As far as money matters are concerned, this is a year for careful control. Although many Rats will enjoy a rise in income, the Rat does need to keep watch on his outgoings and make provision for larger expenses as well as be wary of too much impulse buying, otherwise he could find he has to make cutbacks later. Although this is not a bad year financially, it is one for prudence and good management.

The Rat is usually popular and throughout the year he can look forward to a lot of support and encouragement from those around him as well as some pleasing domestic and social occasions. In his home life he will often benefit from the advice and assistance loved ones are able to give and whenever he has concerns, finds himself in a dilemma or would welcome more help, he should ask. Over the year the support of his family and those close to him can make a real difference to how he fares. In addition, the Ox year could give rise to some family highlights. Many a Rat household will have good reason to celebrate, perhaps due to a wedding, graduation, addition to the family or the success of a close relation. If he is able, the Rat should also ensure he takes a holiday with his loved ones over the year. The change of scene and time spent together can do everyone good. Domestically, this can be an active and pleasing year.

The Rat will also find himself in demand socially, with his interests often bringing him into contact with others. There will be good opportunities for him to make new acquaintances and his famous Rat charm will impress many. The period from April to early June and August and September could see the most social activity, and those Rats enjoying romance, especially with someone met during their own year (2008), will often find this becoming more significant as the Ox year progresses. For the unattached there will be excellent opportunities to meet others, including someone who could quickly become very special. The Ox year is supportive of the Rat and particularly encouraging to those who keep active and make the most of their talents.

Overall, this is a year of development and progress, and keen and willing Rats will find a great deal will go in their favour. The Rat will also benefit from the support and encouragement of others, and although this is a year for effort, it is also a positive one.

The Metal Rat

The Ox year, with its emphasis on commitment and effort, will suit the Metal Rat well. He is likely to make the most of the challenges and situations that arise and be satisfied with what he does. The Ox year may not always be plain sailing, but it can be rewarding.

In view of the changes many Metal Rats will have experienced in their work recently, quite a few will be content to remain where they are in the Ox year. Not only will this give them the chance to build on their skills, but by coping with an often heavy workload and meeting deadlines, as well as dealing with other pressures, the Metal Rat will not only impress others but also often be able to take on greater responsibilities. For many Metal Rats, this can be not only a year of consolidation but also one of steady progress.

In addition all Metal Rats, whether relatively new to their position or well established, should make the most of the training opportunities available to them. Keeping their skills up to date and taking any chances to further their knowledge can be to their present *and* future benefit.

For Metal Rats who are keen to move on or seeking work, again the Ox year can bring important developments.

Securing a new position will not be easy, especially as many people will often be competing for the same job. However, if he perseveres and emphasizes his skills and achievements, the Metal Rat can find doors opening up for him. March, June and mid-September to November are favourable for work opportunities.

The Metal Rat will also need to remain disciplined in financial matters. In view of his commitments, plans and possible support for others, he should keep watch over his level of spending and be particularly careful if tempted by too many impulse purchases. This is a year that requires good control over spending as well as budgeting for more expensive purchases and plans.

Although many Metal Rats will find their days are already full enough, it could also be to their advantage to consider taking up a new interest or challenge over the year. The Ox year does favour self-development and by trying something new and furthering their knowledge, many Metal Rats will feel reinvigorated.

In addition the Metal Rat should give consideration to his general level of exercise and diet. To be at his best, he does need to pay attention to his own well-being as well as keep his lifestyle in balance.

This will be a generally positive year for the Metal Rat's domestic life, with the progress and activities of a close relation often being a source of considerable pride. During the year many people will look to the Metal Rat for support and advice, and his good judgement and assistance will be valued. In domestic matters he will certainly play a central role. He will also derive a lot of pleasure from some of the joint activities that take place and, whether planning and carrying out home improvements or sharing interests with others, he will do a lot to encourage a good domestic rapport. Also, at times of pressure, if he or a loved one has concerns, he will find that being prepared to discuss matters can lead to better support and understanding.

In view of his busy life, the Metal Rat may be more selective in his socializing this year. However, it is important that he keeps his lifestyle in balance and whenever he has the chance to go out or there is an event that appeals to him, he should follow it up. Metal Rats who are lonely or keen to establish new contacts will find that involving themselves in interests and activities they enjoy will give them some good opportunities to meet others. For socializing and meeting new people, April, May and late July to September are particularly favourable times.

The Year of the Ox is a generally good one for the Metal Rat and while it will have its pressures and demands, by doing his best and rising to the challenges, he will not only have the chance to add to his skills but also to prepare the way for future progress. Parts of the year may be testing, but the Metal Rat can derive considerable benefit from these times and throughout the year his relations with others will bring him a great deal of pleasure.

TIP FOR THE YEAR

Do set aside time for recreation, relaxation and your personal interests. It is important that you keep your lifestyle in balance and preserve some time to enjoy the rewards you work so hard for.

The Water Rat

There is a Chinese proverb that is particularly apt for the Water Rat this year: *Diligence is the tool that brings one riches and frugality is the measure that helps keep them.* This is a year for effort and for care.

At work the Ox year can give rise to some important developments and whether the Water Rat is relatively new in his position or well established, there will often be the chance for him to make progress, either through more senior positions becoming available or through training that can lead to a greater role. Either way, the opportunities will be there and will enable many Water Rats to make headway.

The Ox year also holds encouraging prospects for those Water Rats seeking work or wanting to change what they do. To benefit, however, these Water Rats will need to remain active and persistent in their quest. As all Rats will find, the Ox year does require effort, but for those prepared to give this, the rewards can be substantial. In addition, with the Ox year favouring personal development, if these Water Rats are eligible for training or refresher courses or are prepared to study by themselves, they will not only help their prospects but also widen the scope of what is available to them. 'Diligence is the tool that brings one riches' and in 2009 this will be very true. For work opportunities, March, June and late September to November are especially favourable times.

Progress at work will, however, often bring new pressures for the Water Rat. Sometimes these will involve a change in his routine as well as learning new skills and coping with new demands. However, while such readjustments will ask a lot of the Water Rat, by rising to the challenge he will not only demonstrate his commitment but also find himself more inspired and motivated than he has been for some time. The opportunities of the Ox year can give many a Water Rat's career a real boost.

Another factor in the Water Rat's success over the year will be his willingness to develop his skills. This will not only help his current situation but also allow more to open up to him, both in his work and other areas of his life. In particular, by looking to develop an interest in some way, either by practising it or learning new skills or techniques, he will enjoy it all the more. Also, if there is a new interest or skill that appeals to him, he should set aside time to follow this up. Over the year developing his personal interests can do him a lot of good.

The progress the Water Rat makes in his work will help him financially, and many Water Rats will not only benefit from an increase in income but also receive money from another source. This could be a gift or, for some, the result of an enterprising idea. However, while this is a generally positive year money-wise, the Water Rat does need be careful with his outgoings. With his existing commitments, accommodation costs and the help he may want to give to others, as well as the plans he is keen to carry out, he will need to watch his spending and budget carefully. The more he is able to plan ahead and set funds aside for specific requirements, the better. Also, he needs to be wary of succumbing to too many impulse purchases. The Ox year does require careful financial control.

The year is, however, favourably aspected as far as the Water Rat's relations with others are concerned. Although in his home life there will often be competing demands on his time, if he ensures there is good communication and co-operation between family members and sets aside time for family activities, there will be many occasions for him to appreciate. Also, in giving support and encouragement to both younger and more senior relations, he will find his care and thoughtfulness especially valued. Time-wise, the Ox year may bring its pressures, but by balancing activities and commitments, the Water Rat will find his family life will be a very important and special part of his year.

As far as his social life is concerned, he is likely to be more selective in going out this year. However, if certain events appeal to him, he should try to attend. Not only will this help him to unwind and give him a welcome break, but he will often enjoy the chance to meet others. Some new acquaintances made during the year could soon become a part of his social circle. Late March to May, August and September could be the most active months socially, but generally, in view of the busy nature of the year, the Water Rat should try to make the most of his social opportunities.

The Ox year certainly has good possibilities for the Water Rat and will encourage him to make more of his skills and talents. Although it will bring its pressures, it will give him the chance to show his true qualities and reap some often considerable rewards. This is a year for moving forward.

TIP FOR THE YEAR
Look to develop your skills. Whether these are work-related or more personal, they can open up interesting opportunities and reward you handsomely for the effort you put in.

The Wood Rat

This will be a significant year for the Wood Rat and there could be some key developments, particularly in his personal life, while at work there will be good opportunities to make more of his skills. The Ox year will require effort and a willingness to take action, but the results *can* be substantial.

The Wood Rat's relations with others will be especially important and many Wood Rats will have cause for a personal celebration during the year. For some this could involve getting engaged or married, settling down with a partner, seeing an addition to the family or achieving a personal goal. The aspects are on the Wood Rat's side this year and someone very special will often make a difference to his life.

For those Wood Rats who are unattached and would welcome romance, this is also a year of encouraging developments. In many cases, someone met by chance in the early months of the year could quickly become important. Any Wood Rats who have had problems in a relationship and are currently alone will find that this is a time to look ahead. A key feature of the Ox year is that it is supportive of endeavour and if they are active and willing to move forward, these Water Rats will find that a lot can open up for them.

The Wood Rat will also value his social life over the year and with possible work changes as well as his own interests, there will be plenty of opportunities for him to get to know others. The months from April to early June and late July to September could see a great deal of social activity.

Another positive aspect of the year will be the level of support the Wood Rat enjoys and by being forthcoming and sharing his hopes and concerns with those he trusts, he will often be assisted in more ways than he anticipated. Indeed, sometimes just by mentioning a certain idea, he can obtain support and plans can be set in motion. Similarly, in his career or with his personal interests, if he gets to know others he can often gain assistance. This is a good year for networking and meeting others.

As far as work prospects are concerned, this is a year of steady progress. Results *will* need to be worked for, however, and the Ox year could present some stark warnings to any Wood Rat tempted to slack or take situations for granted. Wood Rats, do take note and be prepared to make the effort.

For those Wood Rats who are well established in their career, there will often be good opportunities to develop their role as new initiatives are introduced, changes in personnel lead to new openings or training is offered. By making the most of the chances that arise, the Wood Rat can do himself a lot of good. Also, by being an active member of any team he is involved with, he will get to impress many people and gain encouragement and advice from some more senior colleagues. March, June and late September to November could see some positive career developments.

For those Wood Rats who feel they could get more experience by moving on from their current position, the Ox year can again bring important developments. However, to benefit these Wood Rats need to remain focused and persistent. By contacting agencies and those with the knowledge and contacts to help, however, many Wood Rats will benefit from the advice and information they are given as well as be advised of possibilities to pursue. Even if initial applications do not go their way, by keeping alert and remaining persistent, many will find their efforts rewarded. As with so much this year, effort backed by the support of others will be a significant factor.

This also applies to those Wood Rats seeking a position. While securing one will take time, by being persistent and making the most of the information, support and any training and guidance available to them, many Wood Rats will be successful in their quest

The advances that so many Wood Rats will make in their work over the year will lead to an increase in income. However, the Wood Rat's outgoings will be considerable this year and could be made all the greater by new commitments. As a result, the Wood Rat will need to manage his finances very carefully and if entering into any new agreement, check the obligations he is taking on and make allowance for them in his budget. Financially, this is a year for careful control. Wood Rats, do take note.

The Ox year may be a busy one, but the Wood Rat should not let his interests, recreation or level of exercise suffer as a result. By setting time aside for recreation, he will not only derive pleasure from what he does but also be able to relax and bring balance to his lifestyle. Any interests that take him out of doors, give him the chance of additional exercise or allow him to meet others will be particularly beneficial.

In many respects the Ox year is encouraging for the Wood Rat, but to get the best out of it he will need to put himself forward. For the determined, what is achieved now can be an important foundation that can be built on in following years. Overall, the Wood Rat will benefit from the encouragement of those around him and many will enjoy some very special times in their personal life.

TIP FOR THE YEAR
Believe in yourself and be persistent. With your strengths and support, you can achieve a great deal this year, but it does rest with you to act determinedly and move forward.

The Fire Rat

The Ox year offers considerable scope for the Fire Rat and by making the most of his situation he can make this a satisfying and constructive time.

For Fire Rats born in 1996 this will be an important year with a lot being asked of them. There will be new challenges in their education as they move on to more complex work and they will sometimes feel daunted by all they have to do. However, the Fire Rat should realize he is not alone and those around often feel the same way as he does. By focusing on what needs to be done and giving his best, he will find himself mastering a great deal and making satisfactory progress. And, as so many have found, he will learn more by being challenged than by having things too easy. The emphasis of the Ox year is on commitment and effort, and by giving this, the Fire Rat will be helping his present situation and building the skills and knowledge he can use in following years.

The Fire Rat will enjoy a wide variety of recreational pursuits over the year. Whether in sport and outdoor activities or interests that allow him to express himself and draw on his ideas, by using the chances he has to develop and enjoy his skills, he can take much satisfaction in what he does. Also, if there are any after-school groups or local clubs he could join that could help him to try out more, he should make the most of them.

With his outgoing nature the Fire Rat will also enjoy a wide range of friendships, and by being involved in various interests, he can look forward to a great deal of fun. Over the year many Fire Rats will value one friendship in particular and will be especially grateful for the opportunity to share confidences. In addition the Fire Rat will often benefit from the help and encouragement he is given over the year and whenever he has concerns or is troubled over something, whether an academic matter or perhaps something else at school, it is important that he mentions this to others rather than keeps it to himself. By being forthcoming, he will find that others will be better able to assist and understand. Similarly, if there is any skill or interest he would like to take up or develop further, he should let others know. He does need to be open for his hopes to be realized.

There will also be opportunities for many Fire Rats to travel over the year and whether these involve short trips to places of interest or longer journeys, the Fire Rat will often enjoy the chance to see places new to him. His adventurous and enquiring spirit can be well satisfied this year.

For Fire Rats born in 1936 this can also be a satisfying time. As the Ox year starts, they would do well to give some thought to what they would like to do over the year and to discuss their ideas with others. With some clear aims, whether concerning household or garden projects, interests they are keen to pursue, travel or outings they would like to undertake, they will find they are not only able to direct their energies more profitably but that more will happen. As the Chinese proverb states, *well begun is half done*, and good planning early in 2009 can lead to a more fulfilling year. Also, the Fire Rat will be well supported by loved ones over the year.

The Ox year is a particularly encouraging one as far as the Fire Rat's personal interests are concerned and over the year many Fire Rats will enjoy furthering their knowledge and talents. Creative activities are especially favoured and those Fire Rats who enjoy art, craftwork, writing, photography or music will find their pursuits bringing much personal satisfaction. In addition, if they are able to meet others with similar interests, they will not only enjoy sharing their knowledge but also find this can lead to some special occasions. By making good use of their time, skills and opportunities, they will be well rewarded.

The Ox year will also bring some good travel opportunities, including invitations to visit those living some distance away. In addition, if there is a particular destination the Fire Rat has been promising himself that he will visit, he would do well to make enquiries and see what is possible.

As far as financial matters are concerned, however, the Fire Rat will need to be careful and thorough. This includes budgeting for commitments and plans as well as dealing with any financially related forms or correspondence promptly. If he is in any doubt over a financial matter, he would do well to seek advice. With care and attentiveness he will be pleased with how he fares, but this is a year for good financial management.

The Ox year is a generally positive one for Fire Rats and, whether born in 1936 or 1996, if he makes the most of his situation, he will often take much satisfaction in what he is able to achieve. Overall, the Ox year holds interesting prospects and fine opportunities for many.

TIP FOR THE YEAR
Embrace new challenges. By furthering your knowledge and skills you will find yourself gaining in a variety of ways.

The Earth Rat

This will be a pleasing year for the Earth Rat, giving him a good chance to concentrate on his plans and derive satisfaction from his activities.

Many of the Earth Rats in work will have been involved in recent change and in the Ox year they will often have more chance to focus on their particular duties and use their strengths to advantage. However, while this will be an often more fulfilling year, there will still be pressures and sometimes problems to be overcome. Nevertheless, the Ox year does bring out the best in people and it will give the Earth Rat the chance to draw on his often considerable experience. Over the year many colleagues will look to him for advice and some Earth Rats will be given the role of mentoring and training others. Work-wise, this may be a busy year, but it can be a satisfying one.

Many Earth Rats will remain with their present employer during the year, but for those keen to move on to greater responsibilities or alter their commitments, the Ox year can again bring good opportunities. However, these do need to be sought out and those Earth Rats intent on change will need to make enquiries as well as be active in seeking advice and information. Sometimes the changes they may be considering could have other implications, perhaps financial or involving alterations to their working pattern, and these do need to be carefully thought through. These Earth Rats' plans will take time and effort to achieve, but by remaining alert, they will find possibilities opening up for them. The period from March to mid-April and June, October and November could see some interesting developments.

This also applies to those Earth Rats seeking work. By widening the scope of what they are prepared to consider and persisting in their quest, many will secure a position that will prove an interesting way both to use and extend their experience.

Another benefit of the year will be the chance the Earth Rat has to add to his skills. In his work this could be through taking on new responsibilities, but as far as his personal interests are concerned, if there is a technique or skill that could help him get more from what he does, he should set time aside to acquire this. Whether through practice, study or enrolling on a course, by furthering his knowledge in some way the Earth Rat will derive much satisfaction from his interests. For some Earth Rats, new interests and skills could also open up some exciting possibilities. This is very much a time favouring personal development.

As far as financial matters are concerned, however, this is a year for careful management. With possible family and accommodation expenses and other plans, including travel, the Earth Rat does need to keep watch over his outgoings as well as set funds aside for forthcoming expenses. The more control he has, the more he will ultimately be able to do. He should also be careful when dealing with financial paperwork. To delay or not give matters sufficient attention could be to his detriment. Earth Rats, take note and do be thorough and careful in money matters.

Being born under the sign of charm, the Earth Rat always attaches a great deal of importance to his relations with others and this year he can look forward to some rewarding times. In his domestic life he will enjoy setting about various household activities and for quite a few Earth Rats the year will have a strong practical element, including possible home improvements. By carefully considering their options, these Earth Rats will often delight in what they are able to achieve. The Earth Rat will also find others supportive and will benefit from their ideas. In addition some ideas of his own, possibly concerning trips out, a holiday or a treat he thinks his loved ones may enjoy, can lead to some particularly appreciated occasions and his thoughtfulness and care will add a lot to the quality of his home life. Domestically, this will be an active but rewarding year.

This will also be a gratifying year on a social level, with the Earth Rat again enjoying spending time with his friends. Often both existing and new interests can bring him into contact with others, and enrolling on courses, undertaking training or joining in with local activities can lead to him getting to know quite a few new people. Those Earth Rats who would welcome new friendships will find their activities over the year can bring a real improvement in their situation. The months from mid-March to May and August to early October could see the most social activity.

In most respects this will be a positive year for the Earth Rat and it will bring some good opportunities for him to develop his skills and interests. His domestic and social life can also bring him much pleasure. However, the Ox year will not be without its pressures and many Earth Rats will find themselves with a heavy workload, challenges to meet or situations not changing as quickly as they would like. Parts of the Ox year will ask a lot of the Earth Rat, but it can bring out his strengths as well as add to his experience. With care, discipline and the goodwill and support of others, the Earth Rat will be generally pleased with what he is able to accomplish.

TIP FOR THE YEAR
The support of others will be an important and encouraging factor over the year. Although you may already do a great deal for your loved ones, make sure this is a two-way process and at times of pressure, do ask for help. It will make a considerable difference to your year and what you ultimately get to do.

FAMOUS RATS

Ben Affleck, Ursula Andress, Louis Armstrong, Lauren Bacall, Shirley Bassey, Kathy Bates, Irving Berlin, Silvio Berlusconi, Kenneth Branagh, Marlon Brando, Charlotte Brontë, Jackson Browne, George H. W. Bush, Glen

Campbell, David Carradine, Jimmy Carter, Aaron Copland, Cameron Diaz, David Duchovny, Noël Edmonds, T. S. Eliot, Eminem, Colin Firth, Clark Gable, Liam Gallagher, Al Gore, Hugh Grant, Geri Halliwell, Lewis Hamilton, Thomas Hardy, Prince Harry, Haydn, Charlton Heston, Buddy Holly, Mick Hucknall, Henrik Ibsen, Jeremy Irons, Samuel L. Jackson, Jean-Michel Jarre, Scarlett Johansson, Gene Kelly, Avril Lavigne, Jude Law, Gary Lineker, Lord Andrew Lloyd Webber, John McCain, Ian McEwan, Katie Melua, Claude Monet, Richard Nixon, Ozzy Osbourne, Sean Penn, Terry Pratchett, Ian Rankin, Lou Rawls, Burt Reynolds, Jonathan Ross, Rossini, William Shakespeare, Donna Summer, James Taylor, Leo Tolstoy, Henri Toulouse-Lautrec, Spencer Tracy, Carol Vorderman, the Prince of Wales, George Washington, the Duke of York, Emile Zola.

---

6 FEBRUARY 1913 ～ 25 JANUARY 1914   *Water Ox*

24 JANUARY 1925 ～ 12 FEBRUARY 1926   *Wood Ox*

11 FEBRUARY 1937 ～ 30 JANUARY 1938   *Fire Ox*

29 JANUARY 1949 ～ 16 FEBRUARY 1950   *Earth Ox*

15 FEBRUARY 1961 ～ 4 FEBRUARY 1962   *Metal Ox*

3 FEBRUARY 1973 ～ 22 JANUARY 1974   *Water Ox*

20 FEBRUARY 1985 ～ 8 FEBRUARY 1986   *Wood Ox*

7 FEBRUARY 1997 ～ 27 JANUARY 1998   *Fire Ox*

26 JANUARY 2009 ～ 13 FEBRUARY 2010   *Earth Ox*

THE
OX

THE PERSONALITY OF THE OX

The more considered the way,
the more considerable the journey.

The Ox is born under the signs of equilibrium and tenacity. He is a hard and conscientious worker and sets about everything he does in a resolute, methodical and determined manner. He has considerable leadership qualities and is often admired for his tough and uncompromising nature. He knows what he wants to achieve in life and, as far as possible, will not be deflected from his ultimate objective.

The Ox takes his responsibilities and duties very seriously. He is decisive and quick to take advantage of any opportunity that comes his way. He is also sincere and places a great deal of trust in his friends and colleagues. He is, nevertheless, something of a loner. He is a quiet and private individual and often keeps his thoughts to himself. He also cherishes his independence and prefers to set about things in his own way rather than be bound by the dictates of others or influenced by outside pressures.

The Ox tends to have a calm and tranquil nature, but if something angers him or he feels that someone has let him down, he can have a fearsome temper. He can also be stubborn and obstinate and this can lead him into conflict with others. Usually he will succeed in getting his own way, but should things go against him he is a poor loser and will take any defeat or setback extremely badly.

The Ox is often a deep thinker and rather studious. He is not particularly renowned for his sense of humour and does not take kindly to new gimmicks or anything too innovative. He is too solid and traditional for that and prefers to stick to the more conventional norm.

His home is very important to him and in some respects he treats it as a private sanctuary. His family tends to be closely knit and the Ox will make sure that each member does their fair share around the house. He tends to be a hoarder, but he is always well organized and neat. He also places great importance on punctuality and there is nothing that infuriates him more than to be kept waiting, particularly if it is due to someone's inefficiency. The Ox can be a hard taskmaster!

Once settled in a job or house the Ox will quite happily remain there for many years. He does not like change and he is also not particularly keen on travel. He does, however, enjoy gardening and other outdoor pursuits and he will often spend much of his spare time out of doors. He is usually an excellent gardener and whenever possible will make sure he has a large area of ground to maintain. He usually prefers to live in the country rather than the town.

Due to his dedicated and dependable nature the Ox will usually do well in his chosen career, providing he is given enough freedom to act on his own initiative. He invariably does well in politics, agriculture and in careers that need specialized training. He is also very gifted artistically and many Oxen have enjoyed considerable success as musicians or composers.

The Ox is not as outgoing as some and it often takes him a long time to establish friendships and feel relaxed in another person's company. His courtships are likely to be long, but once he is settled he will remain devoted and loyal to his partner. The Ox is particularly well suited to those born under the signs of the Rat, Rabbit, Snake and Rooster. He can also establish a good relationship with the Monkey, Dog, Pig and another Ox, but he will find that he has little in common with the whimsical and sensitive Goat. He will also find it difficult to get on with the Horse, Dragon and Tiger – the Ox prefers a quiet and peaceful existence and those born under these three signs tend to be a little too lively and impulsive for his liking.

The female Ox has a kind and caring nature, and her home and family are very much her pride and joy. She always tries to do her best for her partner and can be a most conscientious and loving parent. She is an excellent organizer and a very determined person who will often succeed in getting what she wants in life. She usually has a deep interest in the arts and is often a talented artist or musician.

The Ox is a very down to earth character. He is sincere, loyal and unpretentious. He can, however, be rather reserved and to some he may appear distant and aloof. He has a quiet nature, but underneath he is very strong willed and ambitious. He has the courage of his convictions and is often prepared to stand up for what he believes to be right, regardless of the consequences. He inspires confidence and trust and throughout his life he will rarely be short of people who are ready to support him.

THE FIVE DIFFERENT TYPES OF OX

In addition to the 12 signs of the Chinese zodiac there are five elements and these have a strengthening or moderating influence on the signs. The effects of the five elements on the Ox are described below, together with the years in which the elements were exercising their influence. Therefore those Oxen born in 1961 are Metal Oxen, those born in 1913 and 1973 are Water Oxen, and so on.

Metal Ox: 1961

This Ox is confident and very strong willed. He can be blunt and forthright in his views and is not afraid of speaking his mind. He sets about his objectives with a dogged determination, but he can become so involved in his various activities that he can be oblivious to the thoughts and feelings of those around him, and this can sometimes be to his detriment. He is honest and dependable and will never promise more than he can deliver. He has a good appreciation of the arts and usually has a small circle of very good and loyal friends.

Water Ox: 1913, 1973

This Ox has a sharp and penetrating mind. He is a good organizer and sets about his work in a methodical manner. He is not as narrow minded as some of the other types of Ox and is more willing to involve others in his plans and aspirations. He usually has very high moral standards and is often attracted to careers in public service. He is a good judge of character and has such a friendly and persuasive manner that he usually experiences little difficulty in securing his objectives. He is popular and has an excellent way with children.

Wood Ox: 1925, 1985

The Wood Ox conducts himself with an air of dignity and authority and will often take a leading role in any enterprise in which he becomes involved. He is very self confident and is direct in his dealings with others. He does, however, have a quick temper and has no hesitation in speaking his mind. He has tremendous drive and willpower and an extremely good memory. He is particularly loyal and devoted to the members of his family and has a most caring nature.

Fire Ox: 1937, 1997

The Fire Ox has a powerful and assertive personality and is a hard and conscientious worker. He holds strong views and has very little patience when things do not go his own way. He can also get carried away in the excitement of the moment and does not always take into account the views of those around him. He nevertheless has many leadership qualities and will often reach positions of power, eminence and wealth. He usually has a small group of loyal and close friends and is very devoted to his family.

Earth Ox: 1949, 2009

This Ox sets about everything he does in a sensible and level headed manner. He is ambitious but also realistic in his aims and is often prepared to work long hours in order to secure his objectives. He is shrewd in financial and business matters and is a very good judge of character. He has a quiet nature and is greatly admired for his sincerity and integrity. He is also very loyal to his family and friends and his views and opinions are often sought.

PROSPECTS FOR THE OX IN 2009

The Year of the Rat (7 February 2008 to 25 January 2009) will have been a constructive one for the Ox and he will be able to build on his achievements in his own year.

In the remaining months of the Rat year, the Ox should make the most of any chances to further his experience. Whether by taking on more responsibilities or changing his duties in some way, by showing initiative, he can do a lot to help his prospects. September and early December could see some interesting work developments.

As far as relations with others are concerned, however, the closing Rat months are a time for care. The determined Ox does like to hold sway and has a tendency to speak his mind. However, if he appears unaccommodating or speaks without consideration, tensions could arise. As the Chinese proverb reminds us, *a word, once spoken, can't be retrieved*, and the Ox does need to think before he speaks. However, if he keeps this in mind and pays attention to the views of others, there will be many domestic and social occasions that will please him, with December and early January likely to be an active and meaningful time.

In view of the pressures the Ox will often be under, it is also important that he makes the most of his chances to relax and unwind. This could be by spending time on interests and recreational pursuits, but for many Oxen there will be chances to travel towards the end of the year. If the Ox receives an invitation to visit others or sees a travel opportunity that appeals to him, he should consider taking it up. A change of scene could do him considerable good.

Generally, the Ox can fare well in the closing Rat months and if he takes care with his relations with others and makes the most of his opportunities to develop his skills, what he accomplishes can pave the way for the more auspicious times that await in his own year.

The Year of the Ox begins on 26 January and the general nature of the year will suit the Ox. This is a year for steady growth and some pleasing personal developments.

One of the most promising areas of the Ox's life concerns his relations with others, and whether spending time with family, enjoying romance or making new friends, many an Ox will find himself in demand and benefiting from the company of others. Those who have experienced problems or tensions in the Rat year will also find these can often be eased, with this being a more settled year.

The Ox's home life is particularly well aspected and many Oxen will have some good news to celebrate – perhaps an addition to the family, an engagement, marriage, academic success or personal achievement. Also, while his various commitments will often keep the Ox busy, by making sure quality time is spent with others, he can add a lot to his home life, with his thoughtfulness and care being appreciated. With the emphasis this year on joining with others, some Oxen could also be tempted to take up a new hobby or interest with a loved one or tackle a specific home or garden project together. This could not only make the undertaking more satisfying but also help build rapport. The Ox will also give valuable support to those around him and many will be grateful for his time, care and judgement.

Travel is also well aspected this year and the Ox should try to go away for a holiday or break with his loved ones. The rest and change of routine can do everyone good. The second half of the year could see some particularly good travel opportunities.

For unattached Oxen their own year holds exciting possibilities. Love and romance are very much in the air and while the Ox usually takes his time forming relationships, this year many Oxen will realize very quickly that they have met their soul mate. With the aspects as they are, such a meeting could occur at almost any time, but March to May, August and September could see the most social activity. For those Oxen already enjoying a relationship, this can be a year for getting engaged or married or settling down together. As far as the Ox year's relations with others are concerned, this can be a special time.

The Ox will also appreciate the social occasions the year can bring. Such is the nature of the year that new contacts could turn out to be very helpful to him.

As far as the Ox's work is concerned, this can be a positive and often satisfying year. Rather than look to change, many Oxen will decide to remain in the type of work they are already engaged in and to build on their expertise. As the year progresses, these Oxen will often have the opportunity to take on greater responsibilities or concentrate on a more specialist role. This is a year of steady progress.

For those who are keen to move on or are seeking work, the year holds interesting prospects. However, securing a new position may not be a swift process and these Oxen will need to persevere. This may be the Ox's own year, but results *will* need to be worked for. With effort and time, however, many Oxen will secure an interesting new role and, importantly, one that could have considerable potential. March, June, September and November could see some good opportunities.

The progress the Ox makes in his work can lead to a rise in income and some Oxen may also benefit from a bonus or extra funds from another source. However, while the Ox's hard work will be recognized and rewarded, he does need to manage his finances well. If he is able, it would be worth him reducing any borrowings and adding to his savings as well as setting money aside for specific requirements. With the exciting prospects that are in store for him, he may be keen to set money aside for personal plans, and financially this can be an improved year.

The Ox year is certainly full of potential for its own sign. At work this can be a year of steady progress, with the Ox being able to make good use of his skills and strengths. Interesting possibilities can open up but these will need to be worked for, as this is very much a time for effort and application. However, it is the Ox's relations with others that can make his own year so special. Over the year there could be good cause for a special celebration, and for the unattached, this is a year when love can blossom. For the Ox, his own year is a good, full and rewarding one.

The Metal Ox

This will be a constructive year for the Metal Ox, allowing him to build on his recent achievements. He will also be well supported by those who know him well and his domestic and social life will bring some pleasing times. However, while the aspects may be on his side, he does need to be realistic in his objectives. This is very much a year for concentrating on the areas he knows and drawing on his considerable knowledge.

In his work there will be some interesting opportunities that will often give him the chance to take on greater responsibilities as well as encourage him to make more of particular strengths. Work-wise, this can be a satisfying year. Those Metal Oxen who have been with their present employer for some time could also find their in-house knowledge an asset, particularly if they are being considered for a further role or helping with the training of new staff. Many a Metal Ox will find his skills, experience and contacts serving him well this year.

There will, of course, be some Metal Oxen who are keen to use their skills in other ways and for these Oxen, as well as those who are looking for work, the Ox year can bring significant opportunities. Time and persistence will be required, but many Metal Oxen will eventually secure a position that can mark a significant stage in their career. March, June, September and November could see some interesting work developments.

A key feature of the Ox year is that it encourages the development of skills, and many Metal Oxen will decide to add to their knowledge at this time. This could be through training at work, studying by themselves or deciding to learn a recreational skill. Whatever they do, by giving themselves something purposeful to achieve, these Metal Oxen will find their actions not only benefiting them but also reinforcing the constructive nature of the year.

The Metal Ox will also be encouraged by the support and goodwill of those around him. Colleagues, including some influential ones, can often be helpful, sometimes in ways the Metal Ox might not know about, including putting in private recommendations on his behalf. Also, the people he meets at work or through his interests will often be impressed by his straightforward manner, and new contacts and friendships will result. Although the Metal Ox can have an independent streak to his nature, by making the most of his chances to get to know others he not only stands to gain a great deal but also to enjoy himself more. The months from March to early June and August and September could be the most active socially and those Metal Oxen who are unattached and would welcome new friendships will find that going out, pursuing interests and joining social groups can bring results and, for some, an important new romance.

Domestic life is also favourably aspected and many Metal Oxen will enjoy some significant family news. Those close to the Metal Ox can make him especially proud this year.

The Metal Ox will also value the support of those around him and if at any time he feels under pressure or is in a dilemma, it is important that he talks this over with them. He may be willing to take on a lot by himself, but he must not forget that others are keen to assist. Domestically, this may be a busy year, but with good communication and a willingness to share and help out, it can be a special one.

As far as money matters are concerned, many Metal Oxen will benefit from an extra sum over the year. However, with all the Metal Ox's commitments, plans and domestic expenses, he does need to manage his money carefully and, if in receipt of extra funds, consider his options carefully. The Metal Ox is usually cautious and disciplined and this approach will serve him well. Financially, this is a year for planning and control.

Generally, the Ox year will contain some interesting opportunities for the Metal Ox, particularly in terms of making more of his strengths and developing certain skills and interests. Also what he achieves during the year can often bring him a great deal of satisfaction and be something he can take further in the future. Personally, this can be a special year, with good news to celebrate as well as the love and support of those around him to enjoy. Overall, a rewarding and fulfilling year.

TIP FOR THE YEAR

In this promising year you would do well to watch your independent Metal Ox tendencies and be more forthcoming with others. They can often give useful support, advice and encouragement, but to benefit you do need to be active, listen and consult.

The Water Ox

Gary Player once said, 'The harder I work, the luckier I become,' and the Water Ox will find this very true this year. By putting in the effort and acting determinedly, he can look forward to making headway as well as benefiting from some good fortune.

The Water Ox's domestic life can be especially pleasing this year, with some personal as well as family news to look forward to. Those Water Oxen who are parents will find the achievements of their children can mean a great deal, and encouraging their progress and sharing in their delights can often make home life all the more rewarding. The Water Ox will also be encouraged by the support he is given for his own activities and when he has decisions to take, especially relating to work and possibly involving a change in routine, it is important that he talks these through with his loved ones. With consultation and co-operation, a lot can turn out in his favour.

With the encouraging aspects of the year, many Water Oxen will also be tempted to carry out projects on their home, perhaps improving décor, replacing equipment or deciding to move to accommodation better suiting their requirements. Again, much can be achieved this year, but major undertakings should not be rushed. Although the aspects may be positive, this is not a year for haste. By proceeding steadily, the Water Ox will find the results more satisfying.

With family expenses, possible accommodation plans and, for some, a move, the Water Ox's outgoings will be quite considerable. However, if possible, he should still try to take a holiday with his loved ones over the year.

A change of scene will do everyone good and visits to new areas, even if not too far away, can often be interesting.

In view of their commitments and plans over the year, some Water Oxen will decide to keep their social life relatively low key. However, while they may not go out as much as usual, they should still try to keep in regular contact with friends as well as go to events that appeal to them.

For those who are unattached or have experienced recent problems in their personal life, the Ox year can bring major change. To benefit, though, these Water Oxen must be careful not to withdraw into themselves and should resolve to go out and enjoy their spare time as well as take part in activities that appeal to them. Again, the more effort the Water Ox makes, the luckier he can become. The months from March to May and August to early October could be promising for meeting others and socializing.

Another benefit of the year will be the way in which many Water Oxen will be able to develop certain interests. With the element of Water giving the Ox a more expressive and creative nature, Water Oxen can derive considerable pleasure from exploring their ideas and talents. For some, work they put forward or skills they display could bring forth an encouraging response and lead to interesting developments. For the aspiring and creative Water Ox, the Ox year can turn out to be a personally rewarding one.

This will also be an encouraging year as far as the Water Ox's work is concerned. While many Water Oxen will remain with their present employer, they will often benefit from the chance to make more of their position and knowledge, possibly through openings that arise as others move on or through taking on new responsibilities. The Ox year will certainly give many Water Oxen the opportunity to build on their experience and make pleasing headway. In addition, what they accomplish this year can often be instrumental in their success in the future.

For Water Oxen who feel openings are limited where they are currently, this can also be a time of interesting possibilities. By giving some thought to the way in which they can progress and areas of work they would now like to concentrate on, many will find the enquiries and applications they make opening up interesting possibilities. Even if some applications do not go their way, feedback they are given or information they gain can often prove useful. Results may not always come quickly, but with persistence the Water Ox will prevail.

This also applies to those Water Oxen seeking work. By remaining determined, being prepared to draw a line under past disappointments and looking to move on, they will often be successful in securing an ideal opening. This is a year which is very rewarding of effort. March, June, September and November could see some interesting developments as far as the Water Ox's work prospects are concerned.

The progress the Water Ox makes in his work can bring an increase in income and some Water Oxen may be able to supplement this in other ways or benefit from a bonus or gift. The Water Ox's good work and diligence can certainly be well rewarded, although to benefit fully he does need to remain disciplined in his spending and plan his major purchases in advance. This is a year for careful control and should he have uncertainties over any financial matter, it is important that he seeks appropriate advice.

Overall, the Year of the Ox holds encouraging prospects for the Water Ox and by setting about his activities in his usual determined way, he will enjoy some positive results as well as benefit from some moments of good fortune. The year will especially favour his personal life and he can look forward to good support and some often special times with his loved ones, while for those who are alone and would welcome new friends and possibly love, the Year of the Ox could mark a transformation in their situation. For many Water Oxen, this can be a very fortunate year.

TIP FOR THE YEAR

Be persistent and have faith in yourself. The aspects *are* on your side, but you do need to allow time for results to filter through. Do not let any initial setbacks or delays deter you. Persevere, believe and you *will* prevail.

The Wood Ox

The Wood Ox will have seen a lot happen in recent years and in 2009 he will have an excellent chance to build on his achievements and make important headway. This will be a year of steady progress.

One of the most meaningful aspects of the year will be the Wood Ox's relations with others. For those with a partner this could be a time of significant developments, including a possible addition to the family, new accommodation or some personal success. These Wood Oxen will be encouraged by the love and support they receive and this will spur them on. For many, this will be a special and often personally important year.

The aspects are also auspicious for the unattached, with many Wood Oxen meeting their future partner over the year. Such a meeting could come about by chance and seem as if it was meant to be. And for those Wood Oxen who have had recent disappointments in their personal life, the Ox year will allow them to move forward and build up a new social circle. As far as relations with others are concerned, this is a splendidly aspected year. Late February to May, August and September could see the most social activity as well as bring excellent chances for meeting new people, whether through work, friends or other interests.

Many Wood Oxen will also enjoy the way in which they are able to pursue their personal interests this year. Setting themselves certain objectives or challenges will give them something to aim towards and also allow them to gain more enjoyment from what they do. This could be through making more of a certain skill, tackling a particular project or, for some, gaining a new qualification. Whatever they do, by taking their interests and recreational pursuits further, Wood Oxen can benefit from their actions.

This will also be an interesting year as far as work is concerned. Many Wood Oxen will find their recent work has made them a strong candidate for a greater role, and when promotion opportunities arise or they see a position that interests them, they should put themselves forward. By showing commitment and a desire to progress, many will not only make what will be an important career advance but also gain valuable experience and, in the process, greatly help their future prospects. This is a year when effort and a genuine desire to make more of themselves will be recognized *and* rewarded.

For Wood Oxen who are not satisfied in their present position or are seeking work, again the Ox year can have some interesting possibilities in store. By seeking advice from employment and career advisers and following up any vacancies that interest them, these Wood Oxen will find doors opening for them. It may take time and persistence, but the opportunities that come in the Ox year can often have long-term significance, particularly in terms of gaining skills and experience. While results *will* need to be worked for, the Ox year is supportive of its own sign and what is achieved now can have both present and future value. March, June, September and late October to November could see some interesting work developments.

As far as money matters are concerned, however, this will be an expensive year for the Wood Ox. In addition to a full and often lively social life, there will be accommodation outgoings, including possible deposits to put down, as well as other plans and purchases. To do all he wants, he will need to remain disciplined. This is not a year to succumb to too many impulse purchases. Also, if entering into any new agreement, the Wood Ox would do well to compare the terms being offered by different companies and check the implications. The more care he takes, the better. His good work can lead to a rise in income, but money-wise this is a year for good management. Wood Oxen, do take note.

Throughout the year the Wood Ox should also remember that he can always turn to others for advice. More senior members of his family in particular are often willing to help, but to benefit the Wood Ox does need to be forthcoming.

The Year of the Ox certainly holds excellent opportunities for the Wood Ox. In his work he will have the chance to make progress, with what he achieves often being important in the longer term. But it is in his relations with others that the year can be so special. In 2009 many a Wood Ox will find himself in demand, with the chance to make new friends and to enjoy the love and support of his partner or someone met during the year. For the Wood Ox, the Ox year can be a special one. It is a time to enjoy.

TIP FOR THE YEAR
Two tips. First, add to your skills and experience, both in your work and your interests. By furthering your knowledge you can gain a lot of value from what you do. Secondly, make the most of your chances to meet others. You will be in impressive and often sparkling form this year and the support and friendship of others will help you to get far more out of the year.

The Fire Ox
The Year of the Ox holds good prospects for the Fire Ox and generally he will fare well. However, central to this will be his attitude. This is a year for concentrating on the tasks before him and putting in the effort. If he does not, chances could slip by and his results not turn out as satisfying as they otherwise might.

For Fire Oxen born in 1997, the year will offer considerable scope. In their schoolwork they will become involved in new subjects and activities and will often welcome the chance to find out more. If the Fire Ox makes the effort, he will sense in himself the progress he is making, and this can be an important and encouraging factor in his success.

Another beneficial aspect of the year is that the Fire Ox will be able to learn about himself. By being willing to try things out, he will discover new strengths. This could apply to certain subject areas or more recreational pursuits, but for many Fire Oxen the Ox year will see the emergence of new talents.

In addition to the progress the Fire Ox makes in his schoolwork and other pursuits, he will often enjoy the company of those around him. Over the year there will be fun, shared interests and confidences and also the forging of one or two strong and enduring friendships.

The Fire Ox will also benefit from the encouragement he is given by those around him and whether at home or school, if there is something he finds difficult or, alternatively, would like to try out or take further, it is important that he asks for assistance. This way others can better help and advise him.

Generally, the Year of the Ox is a favourable one for Fire Oxen born in 1997, particularly in the progress they make in their education and in identifying emerging talents. For many this can be a year of discovery and, with effort, they can make it a satisfying and successful time.

For Fire Oxen born in 1937 the Ox year also holds promising prospects. However, to benefit, they should give some thought to their activities for the year and decide on what they want to do. That way they will not only make better use of their time but also benefit from some good opportunities. As the Chinese proverb reminds us, *well begun is half done,* and a good beginning to the year can get it off to an encouraging start.

In considering his hopes for the year, the Fire Ox would do well to discuss them with others. The pooling of ideas and support can make some of what he wants to do a lot easier to accomplish. The Fire Ox may have a tendency to keep his thoughts to himself, but in 2009 a greater openness on his part will be to the advantage of all concerned.

Some of the Fire Ox's thoughts are likely to concern his accommodation. They could include improving certain areas and sorting out items he has accumulated – something that will appeal to his methodical Ox nature. Also, he may decide to buy new equipment or home comforts which will make certain aspects of his life easier. Again, time spent considering his options and discussing them with others will lead to better choices.

The Fire Ox will also derive considerable pleasure from his various interests over the year, especially those that allow him to extend his knowledge in some way. For some Fire Oxen this could involve improving their computer or technical skills, while others may prefer more expressive pursuits, but by setting themselves rewarding objectives they can help to make this a satisfying time. The Ox year does encourage the Fire Ox to make the most of his interests.

Given the favourable aspects, the Ox year can also give rise to some unexpected opportunities and the Fire Ox would do well to make the most of these. Some could be travel opportunities or invitations to visit others or go to social events. Although some may come at short notice, by taking them up the Fire Ox will often enjoy himself as well as appreciate the spontaneity of the process.

The Fire Ox will also find certain interests he has bringing him into contact with others and may enjoy the chance to share his knowledge and ideas. Any Fire Ox who would welcome more company would find it well worth considering joining a local interest group or club this year. March to May, August and September could be the busiest periods socially.

As far as money matters are concerned, this can be a reasonable year, although, as with all Oxen, it is a case of keeping a watchful eye over spending. By making provision for his plans in advance and keeping good control over his budget, the Fire Ox will not only help his current situation but ultimately be able to achieve a lot more.

The Ox year can be a highly satisfying one for the Fire Ox and, whether born in 1937 or 1997, with careful planning, good support and a certain amount of effort, he will be pleased with his achievements.

TIP FOR THE YEAR
With a positive attitude and the goodwill of others, you can achieve a lot this year. New ideas or emerging talents can open up some interesting possibilities. This is very much a year for making the most of your chances.

The Earth Ox

This is the Earth Ox's own year and promises to be a special one. By setting about his activities in his usual purposeful way, he can look forward to some pleasing times. And in a lot of what he does he will be encouraged by the support of others.

The Earth Ox's domestic life is especially well favoured and there will be some special occasions to look forward to. These will not only include the possible marking of his own sixtieth year – and here there could be some surprises lined up – but there could also be some pleasing family news, particularly involving the achievements of a younger relation. There will certainly be times during the year that will make the Earth Ox feel proud and special.

The Earth Ox will also be satisfied by the way that he is able to advance many of his plans. These can include projects to improve his home and garden as well as other ideas he is keen to pursue. For many Earth Oxen their own year can see a great deal of practical activity and by planning this out carefully and in consultation with others, the Earth Ox will be pleased with what he gets to do and the benefits that will often follow on. Shared interests can also lead to some special occasions and can add to the pleasure and value of the year.

Travel can also figure strongly during the year and those Earth Oxen who are keen to visit a particular destination or who see a travel offer that appeals to them would do well to follow it up. This is very much a year for making the most of opportunities.

The Earth Ox will also value his social life and even though some Earth Oxen may have kept this relatively low key in recent times, this year could see an increasing number of opportunities to go out. These could come as a result of work, friends or interests, but certainly many an Earth Ox will find his social life enjoying a revival. Those Earth Oxen who are alone and would welcome new friends or something extra in their lives would do well to take up their chances to go out and become involved in new activities. Their actions can definitely make a difference to their situation this year. Not only will they get to meet others with similar outlooks and interests, but for some the year could mark the start of a special friendship. The months from March to May and August to mid-October could see the most social activity.

Another encouraging feature of the year will be the opportunities the Earth Ox has to try out new activities. These could involve a subject he wants to find out more about, a course run locally or a new fitness discipline. By getting advice and making the most of his opportunities, he will find this adding an interesting element to the year.

As far as work matters are concerned, many Earth Oxen will be content to remain in their current position, where they can use their skills and knowledge. However, they should not let this prevent them from taking advantage of training opportunities or chances to add to what they do. By furthering their skills and keeping themselves informed of new developments they will not only help their current situation but also enhance their prospects should they decide to move on.

For Earth Oxen who are already eager for change, their own year can be important, but they do need to think matters through carefully. Some will be keen to take on a greater role, while others may decide to retire or reduce their working commitments and look for something nearer to where they live. Although they may know in their own mind what they want, there will often be other implications to consider. The Ox year may be encouraging, but the right opportunity may not always be swift in coming. Over the year, however, many Earth Oxen can help their situation by consulting those in a position to give advice, as well as colleagues and other contacts. With help, backed by their own efforts, their hopes can often be realized, but this is a year for patience and persistence. May and June could see interesting developments, but it is in the second half of the year that many Earth Oxen will reap the rewards of their efforts, notably September and November.

In money matters the Earth Ox can look forward to some good fortune in his own year, possibly through a bonus, the fruition of a policy or a gift. For some, an enterprising idea or interest they have could bring in something extra. However, while this can be a favourable year for money matters, the Earth Ox still needs to manage his situation well. With family activities and the plans he wants to carry out, possibly including travel and changes to his accommodation, he does need to budget carefully. Also, if he is able, he should try to use any financial upturn to reduce any borrowings he may have. The attention he is able to give to money matters can make a noticeable difference to his situation as well as allowing him to do more over the year. With care, this can be a positive and often fortunate year financially.

In almost all respects the aspects are on the Earth Ox's side this year and if he acts on his ideas and seizes his opportunities, he will be pleased with how he fares. The support of those around him can also help him in a great deal and there will be some enjoyable times in his domestic and social life. This is the Earth Ox's own year and his determined nature and positive actions can help to make it very special.

To mark your sixtieth year it could be worth considering taking up a new interest or challenge or setting yourself a particular project. Also, be forthcoming with your plans and ideas. This is your own year and it is a time to enjoy.

FAMOUS OXEN

King Abdullah of Jordan, Lily Allen, Hans Christian Andersen, Johann Sebastian Bach, Warren Beatty, Kate Beckinsale, David Blaine, Napoleon Bonaparte, Albert Camus, Jim Carrey, Charlie Chaplin, George Clooney, Natalie Cole, Bill Cosby, Tom Courtenay, Tony Curtis, Diana, Princess of Wales, Marlene Dietrich, Walt Disney, Patrick Duffy, Jane Fonda, Edward Fox, Michael J. Fox, Peter Gabriel, Elizabeth George, Richard Gere, Ricky Gervais, Handel, King Harald V of Norway, Adolf Hitler, Dustin Hoffman, Anthony Hopkins, Billy Joel, King Juan Carlos of Spain, B. B. King, Keira Knightley, Mark Knopfler, Burt Lancaster, Jessica Lange, Leona Lewis, Kate Moss, Alison Moyet, Eddie Murphy, Paul Newman, Jack Nicholson, Leslie Nielsen, Barack Obama, Gwyneth Paltrow, Oscar Peterson, Paula Radcliffe, Robert Redford, Lionel Richie, Wayne Rooney, Tim Roth, Rubens, Meg Ryan, Jean Sibelius, Sissy Spacek, Bruce Springsteen, Meryl Streep, Lady Thatcher, Alan Titchmarsh, Scott F. Turow, Vincent van Gogh, Minette Walters, Zoë Wanamaker, Sigourney Weaver, the Duke of Wellington, Arsène Wenger, W. B. Yeats.

26 JANUARY 1914 ～ 13 FEBRUARY 1915   *Wood Tiger*

13 FEBRUARY 1926 ～ 1 FEBRUARY 1927   *Fire Tiger*

31 JANUARY 1938 ～ 18 FEBRUARY 1939   *Earth Tiger*

17 FEBRUARY 1950 ～ 5 FEBRUARY 1951   *Metal Tiger*

5 FEBRUARY 1962 ～ 24 JANUARY 1963   *Water Tiger*

23 JANUARY 1974 ～ 10 FEBRUARY 1975   *Wood Tiger*

9 FEBRUARY 1986 ～ 28 JANUARY 1987   *Fire Tiger*

28 JANUARY 1998 ～ 15 FEBRUARY 1999   *Earth Tiger*

THE

TIGER

THE PERSONALITY OF THE TIGER

It's
the zest,
the enthusiasm,
the giving the little bit more,
that makes the difference.
And opens up so much.

The Tiger is born under the sign of courage. He is a charismatic figure and usually holds very firm views. He is strong-willed and determined, and sets about most of his activities with tremendous energy and enthusiasm. He is very alert and quick-witted and his mind is forever active. He is a highly original thinker and is nearly always brimming with new ideas or full of enthusiasm for some new project or scheme.

The Tiger adores challenges and loves to get involved in anything that he thinks has an exciting future or that catches his imagination. He is prepared to take risks and does not like to be bound either by convention or the dictates of others. He likes to be free to act as he chooses and at least once during his life he will throw caution to the wind and go off and do the things he wants to do.

The Tiger does, however, have a somewhat restless nature. Even though he is often prepared to throw himself wholeheartedly into a project, his initial enthusiasm can soon wane if he sees something more appealing. He can also be rather impulsive and there will be occasions in his life when he acts in a manner he later regrets. If he were to think things through or be prepared to persevere in his various activities, he would almost certainly enjoy a greater degree of success.

Fortunately the Tiger is lucky in most of his enterprises, but should things not work out as he hoped, he is liable to suffer from severe bouts of depression and it will often take him a long time to recover. His life often consists of a series of ups and downs.

The Tiger is, however, very adaptable. He has an adventurous spirit and rarely stays in the same place for long. In the early stages of his life he is likely to try his hand at several different jobs and he will also change his residence fairly frequently.

The Tiger is very honest and open in his dealings with others. He hates any sort of hypocrisy or falsehood. He is also well known for being blunt and forthright and has no hesitation in speaking his mind. He can be rebellious at times, particularly against any form of petty authority, and while this can lead him into conflict with others, he is never one to shrink from an argument or avoid standing up for what he believes is right.

The Tiger is a natural leader and can invariably rise to the top of his chosen profession. He does not, however, care for anything too bureaucratic or detailed, and he does not like to obey orders. He can be stubborn and obstinate and throughout his life he likes to retain a certain amount of independence in his actions and be responsible to no one but himself. He likes to consider that all his achievements are due to his own efforts and he will not ask for support from others if he can avoid it.

Ironically, despite his self confidence and leadership qualities, the Tiger can be indecisive and will often delay making a major decision until the very last moment. He can also be sensitive to criticism.

Although the Tiger is capable of earning large sums of money, he is rather a spendthrift and does not always put his money to its best use. He can also be most generous and will often shower lavish gifts on friends and relations.

The Tiger cares very much for his reputation and the image that he tries to project. He carries himself with an air of dignity and authority and enjoys being the centre of attention. He is very adept at attracting publicity, both for himself and for the causes he supports.

The Tiger often marries young and he will find himself best suited to those born under the signs of the Pig, Dog, Horse and Goat. He can also get on well with the Rat, Rabbit and Rooster, but will find the Ox and Snake a bit too quiet and serious for his liking, and he will be highly irritated by the Monkey's rather mischievous and inquisitive ways. He will also find it difficult to get on with another Tiger or a Dragon – both partners will want to dominate the relationship and could find it difficult to compromise on even the smallest of matters.

The Tigress is lively, witty and a marvellous hostess at parties. She takes great care over her appearance and is usually most attractive. She can be a very doting mother and while she believes in letting her children have their freedom, she makes an excellent teacher and will ensure that her children are well brought up and want for nothing. Like her male counterpart, she has numerous interests and likes to have sufficient independence and freedom to go off and do the things she wants to do. She has a most caring and generous nature.

The Tiger has many commendable qualities. He is honest, courageous and often a source of inspiration to others. Providing he can curb the wilder excesses of his restless nature, he is almost certain to lead a fulfilling and satisfying life.

THE FIVE DIFFERENT TYPES OF TIGER

In addition to the 12 signs of the Chinese zodiac there are five elements and these have a strengthening or moderating influence on the signs. The effects of the five elements on the Tiger are described below, together with the years in which the elements were exercising their influence. Therefore those Tigers born in 1950 are Metal Tigers, those born in 1962 are Water Tigers, and so on.

Metal Tiger: 1950
The Metal Tiger has an assertive and outgoing personality. He is very ambitious and while his aims may change from time to time, he will work relentlessly until he has obtained what he wants. He can, however, be impatient for results and become highly strung if things do not work out as he would like. He is distinctive in his appearance and is admired and respected by many.

Water Tiger: 1962

This Tiger has a wide variety of interests and is always eager to experiment with new ideas or satisfy his adventurous nature by going off to explore distant lands. He is versatile, shrewd and has a kindly nature. He tends to remain calm in a crisis, although he can be annoyingly indecisive at times. He communicates well with others and through his many capabilities and persuasive nature usually achieves what he wants in life. He is also highly imaginative and is often a gifted orator or writer.

Wood Tiger: 1914, 1974

The Wood Tiger has a friendly and pleasant personality. He is less independent than some of the other types of Tiger and is more prepared to work with others to secure a desired objective. However, he does have a tendency to jump from one thing to another and can easily become distracted. He is usually very popular, has a large circle of friends and invariably leads a busy and enjoyable social life. He also has a good sense of humour.

Fire Tiger: 1926, 1986

The Fire Tiger sets about everything he does with great verve and enthusiasm. He loves action and is always ready to throw himself wholeheartedly into anything that catches his imagination. He has many leadership qualities and is capable of communicating his ideas and enthusiasm to others. He is very much an optimist and can be most generous. He has a likeable nature and can be a witty and persuasive speaker.

Earth Tiger: 1938, 1998

This Tiger is responsible and level-headed. He studies everything objectively and tries to be scrupulously fair in all his dealings. Unlike other Tigers, he is prepared to specialize in certain areas rather than get distracted by other matters, but he can become so involved in what he is doing that he does not always take into account the opinions of those around him. He has good business sense and is usually very successful in later life. He has a large circle of friends and pays great attention to both his appearance and his reputation.

PROSPECTS FOR THE TIGER IN 2009

The Year of the Rat (7 February 2008 to 25 January 2009) will have been a mixed one for the Tiger. While he will have enjoyed some success, the Rat year could also have brought its frustrations and in the remaining months the Tiger will need to keep his wits about him. This is not a time for hasty action or being too independent.

In his work the Tiger should aim to work as part of a team. Not only can more be achieved that way but the Tiger himself will be able to benefit from the support of others. For those Tigers interested in changing their job or seeking work, October could see some interesting possibilities. However, this is a time for working with others and concentrating on the tasks that need to be done.

The closing months of the year could also be expensive, with the Tiger making quite a few seasonal and other purchases. As far as possible, he should try to make early provision for this extra outlay as well as take his time in making decisions. Too much haste could lead to him spending more than is necessary.

The Tiger's domestic and social life is also set to become busier as the year draws to a close and could also benefit from some early planning. The more organized he is, the more he will be able to spread out his activities rather than having too much concentrated in a very short space of time. Domestically and socially, September and the closing weeks of the Rat year will be especially favourable times.

The Ox year begins on 26 January and can be a demanding one for Tiger. However, while he will face problems and pressures, there is good reason for him to take heart. The following year is his own year and what he experiences now can prepare the way for the better times ahead.

Also, while the Ox year may not always suit the Tiger's personality, there are ways in which he can counter some of its more awkward aspects. In particular he does sometimes have a rebellious streak to his nature and, if he is not careful, this could lead to an undermining of his position or leave him lacking the support he needs. In addition, in any tense or awkward situation, he does need to watch his words. However, while the year does call for care, progress is still possible, with the Tiger often having excellent chances to add to his experience. And he will be able to profit from it in his own, more favourable year that follows.

This year, however, the Tiger needs to remain disciplined in his work and concentrate on his own particular duties and objectives. This is not a time for getting distracted or embroiled in less helpful matters. He should also take full advantage of any opportunities to add to his knowledge and skills, whether through training at work or undertaking a course or other studies by himself. By developing his skills he will be investing in himself and his future.

Throughout the Ox year, however, problems could suddenly arise. When they do, the Tiger will need to deal with them as quickly and competently as he can. Although some situations may be challenging, they will also be a good test of his abilities and will give him the chance to prove himself and enhance his reputation. For many Tigers, the Ox year will prove both instructive and instrumental in their later progress.

Overall, although the aspects may be mixed, many Tigers will be able to advance their position over the year, either through taking on greater responsibilities in their existing place of work or moving elsewhere. April, July, August and November could see some interesting developments, but the main value of the Ox year will come from the experience and skills the Tiger can gain.

For Tigers seeking work, whether at the start of the Ox year or during it, this can also be a significant time. Although obtaining a position will not be easy, by widening the scope of what they are prepared to consider many Tigers will be successful in getting a new job and in many cases, what is accomplished in the Ox year will be of considerable value in 2010.

The Tiger will need to be cautious, however, in financial matters. Although many Tigers will enjoy a modest rise in income, they still need to keep watch over their spending and make allowances for their plans and obligations. In addition the Tiger should be wary about acting on impulse, whether in making spontaneous purchases or taking hurried decisions. This is a year for careful control.

As far as the Tiger's social life is concerned, this can be an interesting year. With the various activities he is involved in and the many people he knows, there will be good chances for him to go out and meet others. As a result many Tigers will find their circle of acquaintances growing over the year and any who move to a new area or are keen to get to know others can find their activities leading to a significant improvement in their social lives. February, April, July and December could be the busiest months socially.

However, while the Tiger will often enjoy his social life, he must not forget the prevailing aspects of the year. He does need to be wary about being drawn into potentially difficult situations and should he find himself in any disagreement, he should watch his words. Any arguments, flare-ups or indeed loss of temper could sour relations with others and cause difficulties. Tigers, *do* take note.

This also applies to the Tiger's domestic life. When tired or under pressure, he could find his patience wearing thin. Again he needs to be careful and rather than allow frustrations to build up, he should be open about his concerns. Not only can talking over any worries often help to ease them, but it will also enable others to understand him better. Also, at busy times, others may be able to assist by doing more around the home.

In view of the often busy nature of his home life, the Tiger would also find it helpful to spread out his various activities. If there are any projects he would like to proceed with, possibly concerning his accommodation, he should allow plenty of time for them and tackle one at a time. Again, this is a year for patience and planning.

The Tiger should also make sure quality time is set aside for sharing with loved ones. Sometimes, with the pressures of everyday life, such time is put off, and the Tiger does need to watch this and plan accordingly.

In view of the demanding nature of the year the Tiger would also do well to give some consideration to his own well-being and make sure he has both sufficient exercise and a nutritious diet. He could also benefit from going away for a break or holiday during the year. A change of routine could be especially beneficial.

In general, the Year of the Ox may contain its awkward moments, but with patience and care there is much that the Tiger can do to minimize some of its more troublesome aspects. In particular he does need to watch his sometimes stubborn and rebellious tendencies and be tactful and discreet, especially in any fraught situation. However, while the Ox year will not always suit the Tiger's style, it will have its benefits. Not only will the Tiger have the chance to add to his skills but what he achieves now can prepare him for the excellent opportunities that await in 2010. And by balancing out his activities, sharing his thoughts and spending time with those around him, he will enjoy a lot of his activities. Overall, though, a year for care, patience and awareness.

The Metal Tiger

The Metal Tiger has a keen and resourceful nature and uses his abilities well. He is not one who gives up easily, and with his personality and determination, he often gets his way. He could, though, find parts of the Ox year frustrating. Sometimes results will be slow in coming, sometimes the attitude of others be annoying and sometimes delays will occur which he can do little about. However, he can still emerge from the year with gains he can build on in the Tiger year that follows.

For now, the key message for the Metal Tiger is to show greater flexibility. This is no year to be intransigent or unyielding in the face of change. Instead, the Metal Tiger should be prepared to adapt.

At work this will be a year of interesting developments. Although many Metal Tigers will be content to remain where they are, they could still be affected by change. In some cases this could involve having to learn new working methods as well as adapt to changes brought in by new personnel or management. Some of what happens could be unsettling for the Metal Tiger, but in 2009 it is very much a case of making the best of his situation. Also, some of the changes that occur will require training and if he is prepared to embrace this and add to his skills, other opportunities could open up later. Developments in the Ox year can often have future benefit, even if this may not always be apparent at the time.

For Metal Tigers who are keen to progress in their career, feel frustrated where they are or are seeking work, the Ox year can be tricky. There could be few opportunities in the type of work they want and the applications they do make may not get taken up. However, the Metal Tiger is tenacious and by having faith in himself and widening the scope of positions he is prepared to consider, in time he will find an opportunity opening up. Also, once in a new position, many Metal Tigers will find it can lead to other possibilities, especially next year. April, July to mid-September and November could see some opportunities, but as far as work matters are concerned, this is a year to be flexible.

This need for care also applies to financial matters. In 2009 the Metal Tiger should keep a close watch on his spending and if considering a new agreement or large purchase, check the terms and implications. To proceed too hurriedly or without making sure everything is in order could cause problems later. The Ox year is a time for increased vigilance and should the Metal Tiger have doubts over any matter, financial or otherwise, it is important that he gets clarification.

A more positive aspect concerns the Metal Tiger's personal interests and he should make sure he sets time aside for these. Not only can they bring him pleasure and be a good source of relaxation, but they often allow him to meet others too, and in this frequently demanding year he does need to keep his lifestyle in balance. He should also make the most of travel opportunities, as a break can do him a lot of good.

With his outgoing nature, the Metal Tiger will also enjoy many of the social opportunities that come his way. He will be in demand but, as is the way in the Ox year, problems could still loom. In some cases disagreements could occur or the Metal Tiger could find himself in an awkward situation. At such times he does need to watch his words and remain tactful, discreet and aware. Metal Tigers, do take note. For the most part this will be a pleasing year socially, but it is still a time to be alert.

The Metal Tiger's domestic life will be busy and, with possible changes to his own working routine or that of a loved one, is likely to require good co-operation between family members. In addition, in view of the general activity of the year, the Metal Tiger will need to show some flexibility when making plans. Certain home projects may need to be deferred or take longer than anticipated and the Metal Tiger will need to show patience – not always his strong point! However, there will still be much for the Metal Tiger to appreciate, including shared interests, trips, other forms of entertainment and a possible holiday. The Ox year can certainly have its pleasing moments, even though it is one for care and mindfulness.

Overall, to get the best from the year the Metal Tiger will need to be accommodating in his approach and show greater patience than usual. However, by adapting and doing his best, he can still accomplish and learn a great deal and he will often be able to build on this in the more rewarding Year of the Tiger.

TIP FOR THE YEAR
Be cautious. This is not a year for risk or haste. Also, although it may not always suit your style, a slightly lower profile may sometimes be wise. In the face of change, do be prepared to adapt. This may not always be a comfortable year, but it can be instructive.

The Water Tiger
There is a Chinese proverb that reminds us *constant effort yields certain success* and this is very appropriate for the

Water Tiger. By nature he is determined and keen to make the most of his abilities and over the years he will have achieved a great deal. In 2009 his efforts may not always produce immediate or obvious results, but they can be significant in the longer term. The legacy of the Ox year can be far-reaching and should not be under-estimated.

In his work this is a year for focusing on the tasks before him. Many Water Tigers will face increased pressures or be set challenging objectives. However, by showing commitment, using their skills well and putting in that all-important effort, they will not only add considerably to their experience but also help their reputation. Over the year the Water Tiger's talents and conscientious nature will impress many but the real gains will come next year.

For Water Tigers who are anxious to change their job or are seeking work, finding a position will not be easy. There could be a lack of openings and fierce competition. However, with persistence, initiative and time, many Water Tigers will be successful in obtaining a position which they can build on in the future. Again, what is achieved now can leave a significant legacy. April, mid-June to August and mid-November to December could see some interesting developments.

Another important factor in how the Water Tiger fares over the year will be his relations with colleagues. During the year he should make the most of any chances to meet others and become better known. Contacts made now can often be helpful later. However, with the prevailing aspects, he will still need to be on his guard. A *faux pas* or ill-judged remark could cause problems.

This need for care also applies to financial matters. During the year many Water Tigers could find themselves spending heavily on family activities as well as making home purchases, and though they may enjoy a modest rise in income, this is a time for careful management.

Although the Water Tiger will often have many demands on his time, it is also important that he sets some aside for his own recreational pursuits. Not only can these help him unwind but sometimes they can also give him the chance to get out of doors or take some additional exercise. In this busy year the Water Tiger does need to make sure his lifestyle has balance.

As far as his domestic life is concerned, this will often be conducted at a fast pace, and family members will need to co-operate well with each other. Amid all the activity, home projects that can be tackled together and an occasional treat can do everyone good. During the year there could also be news of someone's achievements that will particularly delight the Water Tiger and the encouragement he is able to give can be an important factor in what takes place.

The Ox year can also bring some interesting social occasions for the Water Tiger, including the opportunity to add to his circle of acquaintances. February, April, July and December could see the most activity. However, the Water Tiger does still need to be careful, alert and discreet. This is a year when minor differences of opinion could get blown out of proportion or unguarded comments cause problems. Water Tigers, do take note.

Overall, the Ox year will ask a lot of the Water Tiger, but by meeting its challenges he can gain a lot from it. Pressures and problems can reveal new strengths, give him the chance to add to his experience and prepare him for the opportunities that await in the Tiger year. And amid all the activity and demands of the year there will be many times that he will value.

Your relations with others will be key this year and while they can go well, you do need to be careful in potentially awkward situations. Also, be realistic in your expectations. This is no year for risks or major breakthroughs. Rather, it is a time for preparing for the often considerable rewards next year.

The Wood Tiger

This will be a busy and often challenging year for Wood Tiger. Not only will he face many demands on his time, but some of his plans could be subject to delay or not proceed in the manner he wants. The year may bring its frustrations, but mixed in with this will be more favourable times. An important feature of the year is what the Wood Tiger can take from it. Not only will he have the chance to further his skills, but he will also learn from the situations he has to deal with and can emerge from the Ox year wiser, stronger *and* well placed for the excellent opportunities that await next year.

In his work this is a year for proceeding carefully and steadily. As an ambitious Wood Tiger he may be keen to advance, but this is no year for throwing caution to the wind. Instead he should concentrate on doing his best *in his present situation.* Although this may not always be ideal, particularly as pressures increase or changes take place, by showing commitment he will find his efforts will be noted and stand him in good stead when other responsibilities become available. In addition, all Wood Tigers should make the most of any training they may be offered or any chance to learn other duties, including perhaps covering for absent colleagues. The more experience they can gain, the more they will help their prospects.

During the year the Wood Tiger will also need to take care in his relations with colleagues. This includes co-operating well with those around him as well as being aware of their viewpoints. With the aspects as they are, the Wood Tiger does need to be careful not to be drawn into office politics, petty feuds or other time-consuming matters. This is no year to jeopardize his good work by getting embroiled in unhelpful distractions.

Over the year many Wood Tigers will have the chance to take on additional duties, but for those who are interested in changing their job or are seeking work, this can be a challenging time. To make headway these Wood Tigers will need to be persistent and not too restrictive in the type of work they are prepared to consider. Also, they should take careful note of any feedback they are given after an interview or application. By taking advice and building on it, rather than sticking to their own ways, they can not only improve their chances but in many cases succeed in gaining a position which will have potential for the future. The Ox year may not always be easy for the Wood Tiger, but his achievements during it can often be of value later. April, July, August and November could see the best work opportunities.

The Wood Tiger will also need to remain disciplined in his financial dealings. Many Wood Tigers will be keen to make purchases connected to their interests and accommodation, but these will need careful planning. Rather than proceeding too hurriedly, the Wood Tiger could save himself some outlay by being prepared to wait for sales or other favourable buying opportunities. The Ox year favours patience and deliberation. Should the Wood Tiger take on any new financial commitment, he also needs to check the terms and that all the paperwork is in order. All forms of paperwork do need careful attention this year.

In view of the pressures of the year it is also important that the Wood Tiger gives some consideration to his well-being and he should aim to have a balanced diet as well as regular exercise. He may consider starting a new fitness programme, but before beginning any new activity, or should he feel under par at any time during the year, it would be a good idea for him to seek medical guidance.

The Wood Tiger should also make sure he takes a proper holiday over the year. A break and change of scene can do him considerable good. Also, despite his many commitments, he should keep in regular contact with his friends as well as follow up any social opportunities that arise. These can give him the chance to unwind as well as allow him to meet others. February, April, July and December could see the most social activity, although when in company the Wood Tiger does need to remain attentive and aware. With the prevailing aspects, misunderstandings and disagreements can all too easily arise. Wood Tigers, take note. Enjoy your social life, but do be careful.

This will be a busy year as far as the Wood Tiger's domestic life is concerned, with loved ones often looking to him for advice, support and assistance. Although the Wood

Tiger may sometimes be anxious about all he has to do, if he can give some of his time to his partner, children or more senior relations, they will have good reason to be grateful to him over the year. In turn, he should also avail himself of the help others can give and if he is under strain at any time it is important that he gets any problems off his chest. Communication will be very important this year. Amid all the activity, however, there will also be moments that will be particularly special to the Wood Tiger. These could include a token of love or surprise he is given and the achievements of a loved one. The year may be demanding, but it will certainly not be without its more treasured times.

Overall, in the Ox year the Wood Tiger will need to keep his wits about him. This includes taking note of the prevailing situations and the opinions of those around him. This is not a year for risk, rush or being too independent, but the Wood Tiger can make steady progress. The real gains, however, will come from the experience he gains. This can often strengthen him as a person as well as prepare the way for the opportunities that await next year.

TIP FOR THE YEAR
Be careful in your relations with others. Remain aware and attentive and listen well. Also, be patient. Although some situations may be frustrating and your plans may not always proceed as you may want, in time things *will* move. For now, however, it is a case of waiting, watching developments and doing what you can.

The Fire Tiger

The element of fire gives the Tiger an added exuberance and the Fire Tiger is enthusiastic, determined and sets about his activities with considerable energy. With this drive and his ability to get on well with others, he is often destined to lead a rich, rewarding and interesting life. However, as he himself recognizes, progress is not always easy and on life's long and varied path there will inevitably be challenging times. This year will be one of these. However, although the Ox year can be a demanding one, the Fire Tiger's efforts will certainly not be without reward.

Fire Tigers who are established in a career will find the Ox year can teach them a great deal and many will have the chance to take on greater duties. However, what is asked of them will not only increase their workload but also often involve learning new techniques and adapting to new ways of working. The Ox year can be demanding – sometimes daunting – but the Fire Tiger will recognize that he needs to rise to the challenge and show what he is capable of. As a result, there will be many chances for him to impress and his work over the year will be an important factor in his subsequent progress.

For Fire Tigers who are dissatisfied in their present situation and those who are seeking work, the year can also be significant. However, to make progress they will need to draw on the assistance of others. This includes being prepared to register with various employment agencies as well as discussing their situation and hopes with those who have the knowledge and experience to advise. This way they could learn of possibilities worth considering and ways in which they could develop their particular strengths. If any training is suggested, these Fire Tigers would do well to follow it up. Action taken in the Ox year can often be instrumental in later progress, but to benefit the Fire Tiger does have to make the most of his opportunities. April, July, August and November could see some positive work developments.

With his outgoing nature, the Fire Tiger will have the chance to meet many new people over the year and in work situations his personality, varied interests and keen manner will impress. However, he does need to keep in mind the more cautionary aspects of the year and be wary of any petty jealousies, office politics or negative attitudes. While relations with his colleagues can mostly be constructive, this is still a year when he will need to keep his wits about him.

The Fire Tiger should also be careful in money matters. Over the year he will have many outgoings and will need to keep watch on his spending. If he is entering into any new agreement, he should compare the terms being offered by various companies and check the obligations he may be taking on, and if he has doubts or problems over any financial matter, he should seek advice. This is not a year for risks or making assumptions in matters that could have important implications.

The Fire Tiger can, though, look forward to an active social life. Those Fire Tigers who move to a new area will quickly get to meet others and make some good friends. February to April, July and December could see the most social activity. However, while the Fire Tiger will often thoroughly enjoy himself, differences of opinion, misunderstandings or an unguarded comment could all too easily cause problems and undermine friendships. This also applies to romantic situations. These can develop well, but the Fire Tiger *does* need to be attentive and mindful of the views of others. Fire Tigers, do take note and do take care.

Also if at any time the Fire Tiger has problems or is worried over certain decisions, he would find it helpful to talk to others. In some cases senior relations could be especially helpful. In this sometimes tricky year he should remember he is not alone.

With his active lifestyle the Fire Tiger often gets a good deal of exercise, but he should not be neglectful of his wellbeing this year. In particular he should try to ensure he has a balanced diet rather than rely too much on convenience foods and, at busy times, that he has sufficient rest. To drive himself hard as well as sometimes keep long hours can leave him susceptible to minor ailments or lacking his usual sparkle. He may want to fit a lot into a day, but he does need to strike a sensible balance.

The Year of the Ox will bring its challenges and progress will not always be easy. But the Fire Tiger knows he has it within him to achieve a great deal and what he gains in experience will be to his future benefit. Also, the year can give him new insights into his strengths and the direction he wants to follow, especially work-wise, and he will be able to build on this in the following and more auspicious Tiger year.

TIP FOR THE YEAR

Although you like to take responsibility for your actions and set about things in your own way, this year you should be wary of adopting too independent an attitude.

You will not only fare better with support and advice but also find more possibilities beginning to open up for you. Do be receptive to the help and encouragement others can give.

The Earth Tiger

This will be a mixed year for the Earth Tiger and while it will have its more rewarding moments, there could also be frustrations. This is a time for care and patience.

Those Earth Tigers born in 1938 would do well to start the Ox year by giving some thought to what they want to accomplish over the next 12 months, otherwise opportunities could slip by and they could start to feel dissatisfied. The aspects may be variable, but all Earth Tigers should aim to have some sort of direction for the year.

To help in this, the Earth Tiger should draw on the opinions and support of those around him. Combined effort will not only lead to more being achieved but will also help rapport and understanding. This is no year for the Earth Tiger to be too independent or rigid in what he sets out to do.

Quite a few Earth Tigers will decide to make improvements to their home over the year and it is important that changes should not be rushed. It is better to talk through plans and spend time comparing options. In addition, by waiting for favourable buying opportunities, many Earth Tigers could save themselves considerable outlay as well as be fortunate in certain acquisitions. Practical activities over the year can go well but will require time and patience.

Earth Tigers who have gardens will also find these bringing them a great deal of pleasure. For many, gardening, or just being outside and appreciating their surroundings, can be a particular joy over the year.

As always, the Earth Tiger will follow the activities of family members with keen interest and there could be a family event or get-together that will be especially meaningful. Younger family members could be particularly grateful for the support, time and advice the Earth Tiger is able to give. For the most part domestic life will go well, but the prevailing aspects do call for care. Throughout the year the Earth Tiger will need to be thorough, mindful of others and avoid haste. Difficulties can arise all too easily in the Ox year, but can often be prevented by discussion, co-operation and allowing more time. Earth Tigers, *do* take note.

This need for care also applies to finance and paperwork. Over the year the Earth Tiger does need to keep watch on his position and set money aside for larger purchases and plans, including travel. The earlier he can do this, the better. Also, he should take care when dealing with financial paperwork and seek advice if necessary. A mistake or delay could be to his detriment. In financial matters, this is a year for vigilance.

More positively, the Earth Tiger will very much appreciate meeting up with his friends and attending social occasions. Any Earth Tiger who is feeling lonely would find it worth joining a local social or interest group. This can brighten his situation as well as give an additional interest to the year.

For those Earth Tigers born in 1998, this can be a challenging time. Quite a few will change their school and as well as settling into a new environment will have new subjects to learn. As a result there could be some particularly daunting weeks and it is important that the Earth Tiger is prepared to talk over any concerns with others.

Also, while the Earth Tiger has a keen nature and is eager to do what is asked of him, he needs to be realistic. Certain activities, subjects or skills may take longer to master than he may think and over the year he should not put pressure on himself by expecting swift results. This is a year for application, steady effort, patience and laying a solid foundation for later on.

With his wide interests and genial nature, the Earth Tiger will have good chances to get to know others over the year and in the process will often add to his close band of friends. In addition, interests that can be shared can often provide a good deal of fun. However, while there will be many good times to be had, the year still calls for care. Sometimes differences of opinion, even over minor matters, can escalate and views may clash. At such times the Earth Tiger should avoid exacerbating any situation. The more quickly any disagreements can be sorted out, the better for all. The Earth Tiger should also remember that there are many people he can turn to for advice and help. Fortunately, such difficult moments will be few and, with care, can often be avoided, but the Ox year does call for greater awareness as well as a willingness to talk to others.

For all Earth Tigers, whether born in 1938 or 1998, it is very much a case of rising to the challenges the year will bring. The Earth Tiger also needs to be realistic and to have patience. This is not a year for swift results, but for good planning, co-operation and steady effort.

Do involve others in your activities and plans. Also, be open to new challenges, particularly those that allow you to add to your skills and knowledge. By stretching yourself and being prepared to work on what you enjoy, you will be able to draw much personal satisfaction from your achievements.

FAMOUS TIGERS

Paula Abdul, Debbie Allen, Kofi Annan, Sir David Attenborough, Queen Beatrix of the Netherlands, Victoria Beckham, Beethoven, Tony Bennett, Tom Berenger, Chuck Berry, Jon Bon Jovi, Sir Richard Branson, Emily Brontë, Garth Brooks, Mel Brooks, Isambard Kingdom Brunel, Agatha Christie, Charlotte Church, Helen Clark, Phil Collins, Robbie Coltrane, Sheryl Crow, Tom Cruise, Penelope Cruz, Charles de Gaulle, Leonardo DiCaprio, Emily Dickinson, David Dimbleby, Dwight Eisenhower, Queen Elizabeth II, Enya, Roberta Flack, Frederick Forsyth, Jodie Foster, Crystal Gayle, Buddy Greco, Germaine Greer, Ed Harris, Hugh Hefner, William Hurt, Amir Khan, Ray Kroc, Stan Laurel, Jay Leno, Matt Lucas, Groucho Marx, Karl Marx, Marilyn Monroe, Demi Moore, Alanis Morissette, Jeremy Paxman, Marco Polo, Beatrix Potter, Renoir, Kenny Rogers, the Princess Royal, Dame Joan Sutherland, Dylan Thomas, Liv Ullman, Jon Voight, Julie Walters, H. G. Wells, Oscar Wilde, Robbie Williams, Dr Rowan Williams, Tennessee Williams, Sir Terry Wogan, Stevie Wonder, William Wordsworth.

14 FEBRUARY 1915 ⁓ 2 FEBRUARY 1916   *Wood Rabbit*

2 FEBRUARY 1927 ⁓ 22 JANUARY 1928   *Fire Rabbit*

19 FEBRUARY 1939 ⁓ 7 FEBRUARY 1940   *Earth Rabbit*

6 FEBRUARY 1951 ⁓ 26 JANUARY 1952   *Metal Rabbit*

25 JANUARY 1963 ⁓ 12 FEBRUARY 1964   *Water Rabbit*

11 FEBRUARY 1975 ⁓ 30 JANUARY 1976   *Wood Rabbit*

29 JANUARY 1987 ⁓ 16 FEBRUARY 1988   *Fire Rabbit*

16 FEBRUARY 1999 ⁓ 4 FEBRUARY 2000   *Earth Rabbit*

THE
RABBIT

THE PERSONALITY OF THE RABBIT

Whenever
Wherever
With whoever.
Always I try to understand.
Without this one flounders.
But with understanding,
at least you have a chance.
A good chance.

The Rabbit is born under the signs of virtue and prudence. He is intelligent, well mannered and prefers a quiet and peaceful existence. He dislikes any sort of unpleasantness and will try to steer clear of arguments and disputes. He is very much a pacifist and tends to have a calming influence on those around him. He has wide interests and usually a good appreciation of the arts and the finer things in life. He also knows how to enjoy himself and will often gravitate to the best restaurants and nightspots in town.

The Rabbit is a witty and intelligent speaker and loves being involved in a good discussion. His views and advice are often sought by others and he can be relied upon to be discreet and diplomatic. He will rarely raise his voice in anger and will even turn a blind eye to matters that displease him just to preserve the peace. He likes to remain on good terms with everyone, but he can be rather sensitive and takes any form of criticism very badly. He will also be the first to get out of the way if he sees any form of trouble brewing.

The Rabbit is a quiet and efficient worker and has an extremely good memory. He is very astute in business and financial matters, but his degree of success often depends on the conditions that prevail. He hates being in a situation which is fraught with tension or where he has to make sudden decisions. Wherever possible he will plan his various activities with the utmost care and a good deal of caution. He does not like to take risks and does not take kindly to change. Basically, he seeks a secure, calm and stable environment, and when conditions are right he is more than happy to leave things as they are.

The Rabbit is conscientious and because of his method-ical and ever watchful nature he can often do well in his chosen profession. He makes a good diplomat, lawyer, shopkeeper, administrator or priest, and he excels in any job where he can use his superb skills as a communicator. He tends to be loyal to his employers and is respected for his integrity and honesty, but if he ever finds himself in a position of great power he can become rather intransigent and authoritarian.

The Rabbit attaches great importance to his home and will often spend a lot of time and money maintaining and furnishing it and fitting it with all the latest comforts – the Rabbit is very much a creature of comfort! He is also something of a collector and there are many Rabbits who derive much pleasure from collecting antiques, stamps, coins, *objets d'art* or anything else which catches their eye or particularly interests them.

The female Rabbit has a friendly, caring and considerate nature, and will do all in her power to give her home a happy and loving atmosphere. She is also very sociable and enjoys holding parties and entertaining. She has a great ability to make the maximum use of her time and although she involves herself in numerous activities, she always manages to find time to sit back and enjoy a good read or a chat. She has a great sense of humour, is very artistic and is often a talented gardener.

The Rabbit takes considerable care over his appearance and is usually smart and well turned out. He also attaches great importance to his relations with others and matters of the heart are particularly important to him. He will rarely be short of admirers and will often have several serious romances before he settles down. The Rabbit is not the most faithful of signs, but he will find that he is especially well suited to those born under the signs of the Goat, Snake, Pig and Ox. Due to his sociable and easy-going manner he can also get on well with the Tiger, Dragon, Horse, Monkey, Dog and another Rabbit, but he will feel ill at ease with the Rat and Rooster, as both these signs tend to speak their mind and be critical in their comments and the Rabbit just loathes any form of criticism or unpleasantness.

The Rabbit is usually lucky in life and often has the happy knack of being in the right place at the right time. He is talented and quick witted, but he does sometimes put pleasure before work and wherever possible will opt for the easy life. He can at times be a little reserved and suspicious of the motives of others, but generally will lead a long and contented life and one which – as far as possible – will be free of strife and discord.

THE FIVE DIFFERENT TYPES
OF RABBIT

In addition to the 12 signs of the Chinese zodiac there are five elements and these have a strengthening or moderating influence on the signs. The effects of the five elements on the Rabbit are described below, together with the years in which the elements were exercising their influence. Therefore those Rabbits born in 1951 are Metal Rabbits, those born in 1963 are Water Rabbits, and so on.

Metal Rabbit: 1951

This Rabbit is capable, ambitious and has very definite views on what he wants to achieve in life. He can occasionally appear reserved and aloof, but this is mainly because he likes to keep his thoughts to himself. He has a quick and alert mind and is particularly shrewd in business matters. He can also be very cunning in his actions. The Metal Rabbit has a good appreciation of the arts and likes to mix in the best circles. He usually has a small but very loyal group of friends.

Water Rabbit: 1963

The Water Rabbit is popular, intuitive and keenly aware of the feelings of those around him. He can, however, be rather sensitive and tends to take things too much to heart. He is very precise and thorough in everything he does and has an exceedingly good memory. He tends to be quiet and at times rather withdrawn, but he expresses his ideas well and is highly regarded by his family, friends and colleagues.

Wood Rabbit: 1915, 1975

The Wood Rabbit is likeable, easy-going and very adaptable. He prefers to work in a group rather than on his own and likes to have the support and encouragement of others. He can, however, be rather reticent in expressing his views and it would be in his own interests to become a little more open and let others know how he feels on certain matters. He usually has many friends, enjoys an active social life and is noted for his generosity.

Fire Rabbit: 1927, 1987

The Fire Rabbit has a friendly, outgoing personality. He likes socializing and being on good terms with everyone. He is discreet and diplomatic and has a very good understanding of human nature. He is also strong willed and provided he has the necessary backing he can go far in life. He does not, however, suffer adversity well and can become moody and depressed when things are not working out as he would like. He has a particularly good manner with children, is very intuitive and there are some Fire Rabbits who are even noted for their psychic ability.

Earth Rabbit: 1939, 1999

The Earth Rabbit is a quiet individual, but he is nevertheless very astute. He is realistic in his aims and is prepared to work long and hard in order to achieve his objectives. He has good business sense and is invariably lucky in financial matters. He also has a most persuasive manner and usually experiences little difficulty in getting others to fall in with his plans. He is held in high esteem by his friends and colleagues and his views are often sought and highly valued.

PROSPECTS FOR THE RABBIT IN 2009

The Year of the Rat (7 February 2008 to 25 January 2009) will have been an active one for the Rabbit and the pace will quicken further in the closing months.

In his work the Rabbit will often find himself with increased demands as well as possible changes to adapt to. Although he may not always feel at ease with developments and, being conscientious, he does like to keep on top of his situation, he can make useful progress in the closing months of the year, with September to November seeing some interesting developments.

This is a time for vigilance in financial matters, however, and the Rabbit will need to be his careful self if he is to prevent mistakes or spending more than is necessary.

His social life is set to become busier as the Rat year draws to a close, with invitations to go out and chances to meet others, including some he does not often see. However, while the Rabbit will often enjoy himself at social gatherings, he does need be wary of rumour or believing all he is told. The Rat year requires him to be circumspect and on his guard.

There will also be a lot of activity in the Rabbit's domestic life at this time and the Rabbit himself will often enjoy making arrangements and helping others. Many a Rabbit will greatly value the time he spends with his loved ones and the various occasions that take place. To add to the activity, there could be also travel opportunities in the closing weeks of the year.

The Year of the Ox begins on 26 January and will be a challenging one for the Rabbit. Progress may be slow and results will need to be worked for. This is a year for effort, resolve and patience. However, by remaining persistent and doing his best, the Rabbit can emerge f om the year with some useful gains to his credit.

At work, many Rabbits prefer to specialize. That way they can always draw on and add to their skills and their career can be a progression of carefully considered stages. For those Rabbits who have been involved in change in the preceding Rat year, this is a time for consolidation. Also, whether relatively new to their current role or well established, all Rabbits should make the most of any training opportunities they may be offered. By showing commitment and adding to their knowledge and skills, they can lay the foundation for future progress.

For Rabbits who are anxious to move on from their present position or are seeking work, the Ox year can be a frustrating time. Many a Rabbit will despair, but while the wheels of fortune may be slow moving, they *do* move, and opportunities will eventually open up. Also, the Rabbit should not be too restrictive in what he is prepared to consider. Something he may not have thought of before can often be significant and have the potential for further development. April, May, October and November could see some key opportunities.

Although the progress Rabbits make in the Ox year may be modest, many Rabbits will enjoy a rise in income, with some also finding ways to supplement their earnings, perhaps through overtime or putting an interest or skill to profitable use. Other Rabbits may benefit from a gift or a maturing policy. Any upturn in the Rabbit's financial position is likely to tempt him to go ahead with plans and purchases for his accommodation, but again he should not rush. To make the best decisions and get the best value, he should consider options, costs and what most suits his requirements. As in so much this year, it is a case of proceeding steadily and cautiously. Fortunately, the Rabbit's good sense and financial acumen can serve him well.

As well as a financial boost, the Ox year will also bring several travel opportunities. Some of these may be connected with the Rabbit's work, but he should also try to go away for a holiday over the year. Getting away from his everyday routine can do him a lot of good. Again, though, to get the best from it, he should proceed carefully, giving some thought to where he wants to go as well as reading up about his destination before he leaves. This will allow him to enjoy his time away all the more.

As always, the Rabbit's home life will mean a great deal to him in the Ox year and he will be grateful for the support of his loved ones. He may have a busy schedule, but by setting time aside for shared activities, he will find home life will generally go well. Also, if he feels under pressure at any time, it is important that he lets others know. Not only will they be able to help and advise, but sometimes just the process of talking can clarify thoughts in his own mind. In this demanding year, good communication can make an important difference.

With his creative nature and fine taste the Rabbit will often have projects he wants to carry out in his home, but as with so much this year, these will require patience and good planning.

The Rabbit will value his social life and interests over the year and both are good ways for him to unwind and enjoy himself. In this busy year he does need to keep his lifestyle in balance. Rabbits who would like to build up their social life should make an effort to go out rather than keep themselves to themselves. This way some valuable friendships could be made. April, June, September and November could see the most social activity.

With the demands and strains of the year, the Rabbit also needs to look after himself. If he feels he is lacking his usual energy, has any concerns or does not tend to get regular or sufficient exercise, it would be worth him seeking medical advice.

The Ox year will ask a lot of the Rabbit and progress will often be slow. The conscientious and caring Rabbit may worry greatly about his situation. However, he should remember those around him are often willing to support and advise. Also, this can be an instructive time and will allow him to further his experience as well as alert him to strengths or possibilities that he can build on, particularly in the more progressive Tiger year that follows. The Ox year will require effort, but it will not be without its pleasurable aspects, including an often rewarding home life and the satisfaction personal interests and friendships can bring.

The Metal Rabbit

There is a Chinese proverb that is especially apt for the Metal Rabbit this year: *Slow and steady wins the race.* By proceeding carefully and keeping his expectations realistic, he will fare reasonably well.

In his work the Metal Rabbit will often find himself with increased pressures. These could result from additional work as well as new initiatives and procedures. Some parts of the year may be tricky and the Metal Rabbit may be uncomfortable about what is being asked of him. However, by rising to the challenge he will not only have the chance to prove himself but also to further his experience. Work-wise, the Ox year may not always be easy, but it can prepare the way for opportunities either later in 2009 or in the more favourable Tiger year ahead.

Another quality that will help the Metal Rabbit this year is his ability to relate well to others. Working closely with colleagues will not only help his own position but often make his work more satisfying, especially if he is involved in training or mentoring.

Many Metal Rabbits will remain with their current employer over the year, but for those intent on change or seeking a position, the Ox year can be challenging. Obtaining a new position may not be easy and many Metal Rabbits will need to widen their views about the type of work they are prepared to consider. However, while progress may be slow in coming, steady and consistent effort *will* deliver. Generally, the last quarter of the year will see the best work developments, but opportunities could also arise in April and May.

The Metal Rabbit can look forward to some money luck during the year, perhaps through a gift or bonus. In addition some Metal Rabbits could find a hobby or spare-time interest bringing in something extra. However, to benefit from any improvement the Metal Rabbit does need to manage his resources well and, if he is able, use any financial upturn to reduce borrowings or set something aside for the longer term. Also, where more substantial purchases are concerned, he would do well to take his time rather than proceed too hastily. This way he will not only have more chance to compare items and prices but could also benefit from some advantageous buying opportunities.

The Metal Rabbit should also aim to go away for a holiday during the year, as well as take up any invitations to visit others. A break can do him a lot of good.

With his tendency to specialize, the Metal Rabbit often has very particular interests which he has pursued for a long time. Over the year some Metal Rabbits will decide to share their knowledge, perhaps by meeting other enthusiasts or by writing and passing on their ideas. Here the Metal Rabbit's excellent communication skills can be a real asset. Some Metal Rabbits may also decide on a new project or activity for the year. By using their time well, they will be pleased with what they do, even if it does take time before results begin to filter through.

With his interests and wide circle of friends the Metal Rabbit will have some good social opportunities and in view of the pressures of the Ox year, his social life can do him a lot of good. April, June, September and November could be the busiest months socially, and those Metal Rabbits who would welcome new friends will find that their interests will bring them some excellent chances to meet others.

The Metal Rabbit's home life will be especially important to him this year and by making sure time is spent with loved ones and sharing activities and interests, he can make it richly rewarding. He will do much to assist and encourage others, including both younger and more senior relations, and his advice and ability to empathize will be truly valued. Some Metal Rabbits could find themselves being rewarded in an unexpected way, either through a gift or some splendid family news. Certainly the Metal Rabbit's domestic life can be particularly special to him during this busy year.

In view of all the activity of the year the Metal Rabbit would also do well to give some consideration to his well-being. This includes eating a balanced diet as well as taking regular exercise, and if he does have concerns at any time, he should seek medical advice.

The Year of the Ox will certainly contain its pressures. The changes it brings can often have later value, but for the Metal Rabbit, it is a case of adapting to the situations that arise and doing his best. Also, he does need to be patient, for this is no year to rush or expect fast results. The greatest pleasures of the year will come from his relations with others, and his domestic and social life and personal interests will all bring him considerable satisfaction.

TIP FOR THE YEAR
Persevere. Your plans may not always proceed as quickly as you would like, but this is no time to give up too easily. Steady effort will allow you to prevail. Also, your family, friends and close contacts will often be able to help you.

The Water Rabbit

The Water Rabbit is able to gauge situations well and this will be very useful to him this year. By being prepared to adapt, he can often benefit from the Ox year, and its lessons can be far-reaching.

In the Water Rabbit's work it is very much a case of concentrating on his specific duties and dealing with situations as they occur. Although some weeks could be demanding, with problems and new pressures suddenly arising, by dealing with these and drawing on his considerable experience, the Water Rabbit can do his standing and prospects considerable good. Some of the Ox year will test his skills and fortitude, but in the process it will prepare the way for later opportunities.

During the year the Water Rabbit should make the most of any opportunities that come his way. These could include training as well as chances to learn about other aspects of his work, take on further duties or assist colleagues. The Ox year is very much a time when effort and commitment are noticed and rewarded.

Many Water Rabbits will remain with their present employer over the year and benefit from in-house opportunities. However, for those who are keen to make a change or seeking work, the Ox year can be important, particularly as it will often give the Water Rabbit the chance to reassess what he wants to do. He will find it useful to talk to employment agencies and obtain information from professional organizations and companies. By getting as much guidance as he can, he may be alerted to other possibilities worth considering. To make headway will require persistence, effort and advice, but some Water Rabbits will be able to set their career on a new and more fulfilling path. April, May and mid-September to November could see some important chances.

In addition to the career developments, many Water Rabbits will feel the time is right for the challenge of taking up a new interest or developing an existing one. By setting aside time for this, these Water Rabbits will often be satisfied with what they do. The Ox year is one for using time and opportunities to advantage. Some Water Rabbits may also give some consideration to their general well-being and decide to enrol on a keep-fit programme, start a discipline such as tai chi or yoga or take up regular exercise. By seeking medical advice on the best way to proceed, these Water Rabbits can again benefit from their actions.

The progress the Water Rabbit makes in his work will bring a rise in income, but with accommodation and other expenses likely, he will need to manage his situation well. This is a year for planning and budgeting ahead and if entering into any new agreement, the Water Rabbit should check the terms carefully. The Ox year does favour thoroughness.

The Water Rabbit can look forward to an interesting but busy domestic life over the year. Some of those around him could have important decisions to take or be heavily involved in certain activities and here the Water Rabbit's encouragement and understanding can be a real asset.

In view of his own commitments and the generally busy nature of home life, however, he does need to make sure that everyone does their fair share around the home. Also, while he may be keen to carry out certain home improvements, he would do well to allow ample time for them. This is no year for rush or over-committing himself.

In view of his various commitments, the Water Rabbit may be selective in his socializing this year, but when he does go out he will often thoroughly enjoy himself. It is important that he does not allow his social life to fall away in this busy year. April to mid-July, September and November could see the most social activity.

Also, if during the year the Water Rabbit finds himself in a dilemma, talking to a close friend could bring some helpful advice or assistance. With the active nature of the year, the Water Rabbit should not forget that there are many people who would be glad to help or advise him.

The Ox year can bring some good travel opportunities, some work-related, but the Water Rabbit should try to take a holiday as well and so benefit from the change and rest this can bring. However, before leaving, he would do well to check that his documentation is in order and allow sufficient time to make any connections. As with so much this year, the more care and attention he can take, the better.

The Year of the Ox will be a busy one for the Water Rabbit and he will need to work hard for results. However, what he achieves now can leave a significant legacy that he will often be able to build on in the more encouraging Tiger year that follows. He will also derive much pleasure from his domestic life and from developing his interests and this will help him to cope with some of the more demanding aspects of the year.

You will do a great deal for others over the year, but make sure this is a two-way process Also, do keep your lifestyle in balance and allow time to relax.

The Wood Rabbit

This will be a busy year for the Wood Rabbit, but by setting about his activities in his usual conscientious way and being realistic in his undertakings, he can make steady progress. Although this will not be an easy or smooth year, what the Wood Rabbit takes from it can be instrumental in his later success.

A valuable aspect of the year will be the support the Wood Rabbit receives from those around him, and if at any time he has concerns or is in a dilemma, he should remember that he does know people who have the experience to help. In some cases, senior relations could be especially helpful.

With this being a year that could see a lot of practical activity it is also important that the Wood Rabbit takes the time to talk his ideas through and involve others. The Ox year favours a steady and methodical approach rather than a rush. Quite a few Wood Rabbits will consider moving over the year and the process could be protracted, but the main thing is to be patient and to allow time for plans to come to fruition.

In addition to the often considerable practical activity, this can also be an eventful year in the Wood Rabbit's domestic life. For those who are parents or become parents this year, a lot of time will be spent tending to the needs of children and supporting their progress. For many there will be some very special moments during the year, although there will also be times when the Wood Rabbit will feel tired and even despair of all he has to do. When possible, he should try to share some of the domestic activities and be willing to draw more readily on the help that is available. With good co-operation and joint effort, domestic life can be easier and smoother. Also, it is important that mutual interests do not get sidelined and that amid all the activity there is still time for fun and recreation. In 2009 the Wood Rabbit does need to keep his lifestyle in balance and communicate well with others.

Although the Wood Rabbit will have many financial commitments over the year, he would do well to take advantage of any travel opportunities that arise and aim to take a break or holiday during the year. A change will do him considerable good.

The Wood Rabbit will also value his social life and over the year he could well find his social circle widening. Those Wood Rabbits who are lonely, perhaps having experienced some recent personal problems, will find that some new friends they make could soon become important. April, June, September and November could see the most social activity.

It is also important that the Wood Rabbit takes good care of himself over the year. With his busy lifestyle and the long hours he sometimes keeps, he does need to make sure he has a good diet and regular exercise. Driving himself too hard could leave him prone to minor ailments or lacking his usual energy and sparkle. Wood Rabbits, do take note.

As far as the Wood Rabbit's work is concerned, this will be another busy year. With the experience he has built up in recent times, he will often be well placed to take on further responsibilities. With these, though, will come new pressures and some Wood Rabbits could have a considerable workload. However, the Wood Rabbit is both thorough and diligent, and by concentrating on what he has to do and familarizing himself with the various aspects of his work, he will not only be getting excellent experience but also becoming more established in a particular area. This may be a demanding year, but it can mark an important stage in the Wood Rabbit's career development.

For Wood Rabbits who are seeking work or anxious to move from their present position, the Ox year can again be significant. To secure an opening will require time, effort and persistence, but by showing initiative and obtaining advice from professional organizations or employment agencies, many Wood Rabbits will succeed in gaining a position that can be an important platform on which to build for the future. A key value of the Ox year is that it can prepare the Wood Rabbit for later success. April, May and mid-September to November could see some interesting work possibilities.

The progress the Wood Rabbit makes in his work will bring a rise in income, but with accommodation and other costs likely, he does need to keep a close watch on his outgoings. Also if entering into any new agreement, he needs to check the small print and any implications. Financially, this is a year for care and thoroughness.

The Year of the Ox will demand a great deal of the Wood Rabbit and there will be occasions when he will feel tired and daunted as well as sometimes frustrated by the length of time certain plans may take. However, this is a year for patience and steady effort and the Wood Rabbit will learn a lot from it. And throughout the year he will be assisted by those close to him, with his personal life giving rise to some often special moments.

TIP FOR THE YEAR
This is not a year to expect swift developments. Be patient and take your time. Results *will* be worth waiting for, especially as many can have later significance. Also, do communicate well with those around you. If you share your hopes, plans and concerns, others will be better able to help and encourage you.

The Fire Rabbit

The Fire Rabbit has a keen and ambitious nature and will fare reasonably well this year. By being prepared to adapt, he can not only add to his experience but also learn a lot about himself and his strengths. For many Fire Rabbits, the Ox year is one of personal discovery as well as preparation for future success.

In the Fire Rabbit's work this will be a busy and occasionally frustrating year. Sometimes the Fire Rabbit could find projects he is working on delayed or beset by problems. Some parts of the Ox year will ask a lot of him, but by rising to the challenge he can gain a lot of useful experience. In addition, as he sets about his duties and deals with some of the problems that arise, he will often discover new strengths that he will be keen to develop further. The Ox year may not be an easy one, but it can be illuminating.

The Fire Rabbit should also make the most of any training he may be offered and could also be alerted to other possibilities worth considering. In many cases, what he learns over the year will be instrumental in the progress he will enjoy in the Tiger year and beyond.

For Fire Rabbits who are keen to change their job, as well as those seeking work, the Ox year can be significant. Finding an opening will not be easy and there will be disappointments in their quest. However, by considering a wide range of possibilities these Fire Rabbits could, with the help of others, find a type of work that not only suits their skills but also has potential for the future. Again, what is achieved now can often be important in the longer term.

Another positive side of the year will be the chances the Fire Rabbit will have to meet colleagues, particularly those in similar positions to his own. By making the most of such opportunities and working well with others, he will not only get himself better known but could forge some new friendships. The Fire Rabbit will impress many over the year, not only in the way he handles pressure and certain situations but also with his manner and approachability. April, May, October and November could see the best opportunities, but what he does in the Ox year can be very much to his future benefit.

This will also be an important year for those Fire Rabbits studying for qualifications. With many approaching the end of their course, there will often be exams to prepare for and work to complete. The pressures may be considerable, but by remaining organized and keeping in mind the possibilities that can open up following qualification, these Fire Rabbits will find what is achieved now of lasting value. This is, though, a year when it is worth putting in that extra effort.

In addition to any qualifications and work skills the Fire Rabbit is able to acquire, it would also be worth him furthering his personal interests. By setting himself some objectives, he can take great satisfaction from what he is able to do. Those Fire Rabbits who enjoy expressive and creative pursuits will particularly enjoy exploring ideas as well as discovering talents or aspects of their interests they are keen to develop. Again, the Ox year can be illuminating.

As far as financial matters are concerned, with the Fire Rabbit's existing commitments and various activities, he will need to keep a close watch on his outgoings. Also, if there are particular purchases he wants to make or he has plans that could involve considerable outlay, it would be worth him saving up in advance. The more disciplined he is, the more he will be able to do.

Throughout the year the Fire Rabbit will value his social life and particularly the support and camaraderie of good friends. In view of some of pressures and decisions of the year, talking matters over with those he trusts can often give him the help and reassurance he needs.

The Fire Rabbit will also appreciate many of the social occasions the Ox year can bring and will often have something to look forward to. April, June, September and

November could be the most active months for socializing. Many Fire Rabbits will find their interests and work will give them good opportunities to meet others and important friendships can be made. Such are the long-term implications of the Ox year that some Fire Rabbits who are unattached could meet their future partner.

For those who are settled in a relationship, this can also be an important year, with certain plans and hopes being moved forward. However, throughout the year, there does need to be good communication and a willingness to adapt to situations. Sometimes this will involve compromise or being more flexible with certain plans, but by talking through his thoughts and the possibilities available, the Fire Rabbit can make this an often special time.

As with all Rabbits this year, the Fire Rabbit should also keep an eye on his general well-being. This includes making sure he does not skimp on healthy or nutritious food as well as having sufficient rest, particularly during busy periods. To be at his best, he does need to look after himself.

The Ox year will ask a lot of the Fire Rabbit, but he can gain a lot from it. In particular it will give him excellent opportunities to add to his experience and sometimes gain important qualifications, as well as discover strengths that he can build on in following years. And throughout the year he will benefit from the support and friendship of others, with those close to him being of particular assistance.

TIP FOR THE YEAR
Make this a year for extending your knowledge and skills. What you do will not only be satisfying but could also have considerable future value.

The Earth Rabbit

This year marks the 10th or 70th birthday of the Earth Rabbit, and for both it can be an interesting and constructive one.

For Earth Rabbits born in 1939, this is a year when good planning and concentrated effort can be well rewarded. With some specific aims in mind, the Earth Rabbit will not only make more effective use of his time but also derive much satisfaction from his activities. However, he should remember that this is no year for rush and certain plans will take longer to realize than he may anticipate. The Ox year does call for patience and persistence.

With his fertile mind the Earth Rabbit enjoys creative activities and in 2009 he will not only delight in what he sets out to do but also in the way that he is able to further his knowledge and skills. This could be by setting himself a more ambitious project or enrolling on a course, but by challenging himself in some way, he will often be pleased by his progress. Even though new undertakings may bring initial frustrations or take time to get under way, with patience and perseverance the Earth Rabbit will see his efforts paying off.

Also, if the Earth Rabbit has let a personal interest lapse or feels in need of a new challenge or occupation, this is a year for action. The Ox year encourages personal development and by doing something that has purpose and meaning, the Earth Rabbit can derive much satisfaction from his activities.

This can also be a special year as far as family matters are concerned. Not only will the Earth Rabbit enjoy the possible marking of his 70th year, but also the love, affection and esteem others show him. Family and close friends will mean a lot to him in 2009. He will often find himself doing a great deal to help younger relations, whether through giving his time or offering advice and encouragement.

However, while the Earth Rabbit will do a lot for others, this must not prevent him from speaking openly about any plans or hopes of his own. Keeping his thoughts to himself could lead to possible frustration and disappointment. In the Ox year it is important that the Earth Rabbit is communicative and does not hold back from expressing what he wants or is considering carrying out.

There will be chances for the Earth Rabbit to go away during the year and whether he is visiting relatives or going on holiday, he will often appreciate the travel opportunities the year can bring. Some Earth Rabbits will find their travels having a good social element and some interesting new friendships can be formed.

On a social level this can also be a pleasing year and any Earth Rabbits who are feeling lonely would do well to consider joining a local society or interest group. April, June, September and November could see some interesting social opportunities.

In money matters, this is a year for care and good planning. When making expensive purchases the Earth Rabbit does need to take his time and fully consider what best meets his requirements. To rush could lead to disappointment. Similarly, when entering into an agreement or completing financial forms, he should read the terms carefully and check anything that may be unclear. As with so much, this is a year for remaining vigilant.

For Earth Rabbits born in 1999 this can be an interesting year, especially as they will get to do and learn more. If they put in the effort, many of them can look forward to making good progress. However, one important feature of the year is that it is a time for patience, and if certain activities or subjects do not go well, the young Earth Rabbit should not lose interest and give up too easily. By asking for extra help or recognizing that more time is needed, valuable headway can be made. This is not a year for the Earth Rabbit to be too hard on himself, especially when tackling anything new.

In addition the young Earth Rabbit does need be forthcoming. If he has concerns or there are certain activities he would like to try out, he should talk these over with others. During the year those around him can make a real difference to how he fares. Also, he will particularly enjoy joint pursuits this year, especially the camaraderie and fun that come from being with others.

For the Earth Rabbit, whether born in 1939 or 1999, this is a year of opportunity and progress. However it does require him to put himself forward. By seizing his opportunities and drawing on the support of others, he can make this a satisfying time. Results may not always be immediate, but they *will* come. And many Earth Rabbits will celebrate the start of a new decade in their life in fine style.

Set yourself some aims for the year and particularly look at areas or interests you could expand on. With good use of your time, you can make this a personally rewarding year.

FAMOUS RABBITS

Margaret Atwood, Drew Barrymore, David Beckham, Harry Belafonte, Pope Benedict XVI, Ingrid Bergman, St Bernadette, Jeff Bezos, Gordon Brown, Nicolas Cage, Lewis Carroll, Fidel Castro, John Cleese, Confucius, Marie Curie, Johnny Depp, Albert Einstein, George Eliot, W. C. Fields, James Fox, Sir David Frost, Cary Grant, Edvard Grieg, Oliver Hardy, Seamus Heaney, Tommy Hilfiger, Bob Hope, Whitney Houston, Helen Hunt, John Hurt, Anjelica Huston, Chrissie Hynde, Enrique Inglesias, Clive James, Henry James, Sir David Jason, Angelina Jolie, Michael Jordan, Michael Keaton, John Keats, Lisa Kudrow, Ralph Lauren, Gina Lollobrigida, George Michael, Colin Montgomerie, Sir Roger Moore, Andrew Murray, Mike Myers, Brigitte Nielsen, Graham Norton, Jamie Oliver, George Orwell, Edith Piaf, Sidney Poitier, Romano Prodi, Ken Russell, Elisabeth Schwarzkopf, Neil Sedaka, Jane Seymour, Neil Simon, Frank Sinatra, Sting, Quentin Tarantino, J. R. R. Tolkien, KT Tunstall, Tina Turner, Luther Vandross, Queen Victoria, Muddy Waters, Orson Welles, Hayley Westenra, Walt Whitman, Robin Williams, Kate Winslet, Tiger Woods.

3 FEBRUARY 1916 ∼ 22 JANUARY 1917   *Fire Dragon*

23 JANUARY 1928 ∼ 9 FEBRUARY 1929   *Earth Dragon*

8 FEBRUARY 1940 ∼ 26 JANUARY 1941   *Metal Dragon*

27 JANUARY 1952 ∼ 13 FEBRUARY 1953   *Water Dragon*

13 FEBRUARY 1964 ∼ 1 FEBRUARY 1965   *Wood Dragon*

31 JANUARY 1976 ∼ 17 FEBRUARY 1977   *Fire Dragon*

17 FEBRUARY 1988 ∼ 5 FEBRUARY 1989   *Earth Dragon*

5 FEBRUARY 2000 ∼ 23 JANUARY 2001   *Metal Dragon*

THE
DRAGON

THE PERSONALITY OF THE DRAGON

I like giving things a go.
Sometimes I succeed,
sometimes I fail.
Sometimes the unexpected happens.
But it is the giving things a go
and the stepping forward
that make life so interesting.

The Dragon is born under the sign of luck. He is a proud and lively character and has a tremendous amount of self confidence. He is also highly intelligent and very quick to take advantage of any opportunities. He is ambitious and determined and will do well in practically anything he attempts. He is also something of a perfectionist and will always try to maintain the high standards he sets himself.

The Dragon does not suffer fools gladly and will be quick to criticize anyone or anything that displeases him. He can be blunt and forthright in his views and is certainly not renowned for being either tactful or diplomatic. He does, however, often take people at their word and can occasionally be rather gullible. If he ever feels that his trust has been abused or his dignity wounded, he can sometimes become very bitter and it will take him a long time to forgive and forget.

The Dragon is usually very outgoing and is particularly adept at attracting attention and publicity. He enjoys being in the limelight and is often at his best when he is confronted by a difficult problem or tense situation. In some respects he is a showman and he rarely lacks an audience. His views are highly valued and he invariably has something interesting – and sometimes controversial – to say.

He also has considerable energy and is often prepared to work long and unsocial hours in order to achieve what he wants. He can, however, be rather impulsive and does not always consider the consequences of his actions. He also has a tendency to live for the moment and there is nothing that riles him more than to be kept waiting. The Dragon hates delay and can get extremely impatient and irritable over even the smallest of hold ups.

The Dragon has an enormous faith in his abilities, but he does run the risk of becoming over confident and unless he is careful he can sometimes make grave errors of judgement. While this may prove disastrous at the time, he does have the tenacity and ability to bounce back and pick up the pieces again.

The Dragon has such an assertive personality, so much willpower and such a desire to succeed that he will often reach the top of his chosen profession. He has considerable leadership qualities and will do well in positions where he can put his own ideas and policies into practice. He is usually successful in politics, show business, as the manager of his own department or business, and in any job that brings him into contact with the media.

The Dragon relies a tremendous amount on his own judgement and can be scornful of other people's advice. He likes to feel self sufficient and there are many Dragons who cherish their independence to such a degree that they prefer to remain single throughout their lives. However, the Dragon will often have numerous admirers and many will be attracted by his flamboyant personality and striking looks. If he does marry, he will usually marry young, and will find himself particularly well suited to those born under the signs of the Snake, Rat, Monkey and Rooster. He will also find that the Rabbit, Pig, Horse and Goat make ideal companions and will readily join in with many of his escapades. Two Dragons will also get on well together, as they will understand each other, but the Dragon may not find things so easy with the Ox and Dog, as both will be critical of his impulsive and somewhat extrovert manner. He will also find it difficult to form an alliance with the Tiger, for the Tiger, like the Dragon, tends to speak his mind, is very strong willed and likes to take the lead.

The female Dragon knows what she wants in life and sets about everything she does in a determined and positive manner. No job is too small for her and she is often prepared to work extremely hard to secure her objectives. She is immensely practical and somewhat liberated. She hates being bound by routine and petty restrictions and likes to have sufficient freedom to go off and do what she wants to do. She will keep her house tidy, but is not one for spending hours on housework – there are far too many other things that she prefers to do. Like her male counterpart, she has a tendency to speak her mind.

The Dragon usually has many interests and enjoys sport and other outdoor activities. He also likes to travel and often prefers to visit places that are off the beaten track rather than head for popular tourist attractions. He has a very adventurous streak in him and providing his financial circumstances permit – and the Dragon is usually sensible with his money – he will travel considerable distances during his lifetime.

The Dragon is a very flamboyant character and while he can be demanding of others and in his early years rather precocious, he will have many friends and will nearly always be the centre of attention. He has charisma and so much confidence that he can often become a source of inspiration to others. In China he is the leader of the carnival and he is also blessed with an inordinate share of luck.

THE FIVE DIFFERENT TYPES OF DRAGON

In addition to the 12 signs of the Chinese zodiac there are five elements and these have a strengthening or moderating influence on the signs. The effects of the five elements on the Dragon are described below, together with the years in which the elements were exercising their influence. Therefore those Dragons born in 1940 and 2000 are Metal Dragons, those born in 1952 are Water Dragons, and so on.

Metal Dragon: 1940, 2000
This Dragon is very strong willed and has a particularly forceful personality. He is energetic, ambitious and tries to be scrupulous in his dealings with others. He can also be blunt and to the point and usually has no hesitation in

speaking his mind. If people disagree with him or are not prepared to co-operate, he is more than happy to go his own way. The Metal Dragon usually has very high moral values and is held in great esteem by his friends and colleagues.

Water Dragon: 1952

This Dragon is friendly, easy going and intelligent. He is quick witted and rarely lets an opportunity slip by. However, he is not as impatient as some of the other types of Dragon and is prepared to wait for results rather than expect everything to happen at once. He has an understanding nature and is willing to share his ideas and co operate with others. His main failing is a tendency to jump from one thing to another rather than concentrate on the job in hand. He has a good sense of humour and is an effective speaker.

Wood Dragon: 1964

The Wood Dragon is practical, imaginative and inquisitive. He loves delving into all manner of subjects and can quite often come up with some highly original ideas. He is a thinker and a doer and has the drive and commitment to put many of his ideas into practice. He is more diplomatic than some of the other types of Dragon and has a good sense of humour. He is very astute in business matters and can also be most generous.

Fire Dragon: 1916, 1976

This Dragon is ambitious, articulate and has a tremendous desire to succeed. He is a hard and conscientious worker and is often admired for his integrity and forthright nature. He is very strong willed and has considerable leadership qualities. He can, however, rely a bit too much on his own judgement and fail to take into account the views and feelings of others. He can also be rather aloof and it would certainly be in his own interests to let others join in more with his various activities. He usually enjoys music, literature and the arts.

Earth Dragon: 1928, 1988

The Earth Dragon tends to be quieter and more reflective than some of the other types of Dragon. He has a wide variety of interests and is keenly aware of what is going on around him. He also has clear objectives and usually has no problems in obtaining support and backing for any of his ventures. He is very astute in financial matters and is often able to accumulate considerable wealth. He is a good organizer, although he can at times be rather bureaucratic and fussy. He mixes well with others and has a large circle of friends.

PROSPECTS FOR THE DRAGON IN 2009

The Year of the Rat (7 February 2008 to 25 January 2009) has a considerable vitality about it and suits the Dragon personality well. It is a time for going ahead with plans and looking to make changes, and the closing months of the year can be encouraging ones for the Dragon.

In his social life the Dragon will have many chances to go out and this can be a pleasing time. For Dragons who are enjoying romance or who are unattached and would welcome the chance to meet someone, November and December are particularly favourably aspected.

The Dragon's domestic life will also see a lot of activity at this time and the Dragon will immerse himself in much that takes place and enjoy himself. He does, however, need to watch his spending and be wary of too many impulse purchases. He will fare much better by planning ahead and deciding on purchases (including any seasonal items) in advance.

The Dragon's work prospects are encouraging in the closing months of the Rat year and his skills and often enterprising approach will be well received. If there are ideas he is keen to explore, he could find some interesting possibilities arising in October and early January.

The Rat year is a generally positive one for the Dragon and by setting about his activities in his usual enthusiastic way he can look forward to achieving a great deal. His relations with others at this time will also mean a lot to him.

The Ox year starts on 26 January and during it the Dragon may be frustrated by the time some activities or plans take – the Ox year *can* be slow moving – but by remaining persistent and steady, he will eventually prevail. This is not a year for haste or quick results, but it can still be a reasonable one for him.

In his work the Dragon will fare best by concentrating on the areas with which he is most familiar. For those Dragons who are keen to move their career forward, there will often be chances to pursue in their existing place of work, especially as more senior colleagues move on. However, by concentrating on his area of expertise, the Dragon will be generally pleased with how he fares. This may not be a year of swift progress or radical change, but the Dragon's work can be an often fulfilling outlet for his talents.

While many Dragons will remain with their current employer over the year, there will be some who are keen to move on, and for these Dragons, as well as those seeking work, the Ox year can present some good openings. Again, however, these Dragons should concentrate on positions that draw on their experience rather than look to switch to something completely different. Although there will be times when these Dragons will be frustrated by a lack of opportunities, by remaining persistent, many will be given the chance they want. March, May, July and September could see the best opportunities.

Although the Dragon's progress in his career may be of a modest rather than substantial nature this year, many Dragons can still look forward to a noticeable rise in income. In addition some could also benefit from a bonus or gift. To make the most of this upturn the Dragon should, though, manage his money well and, if possible, give some thought to the longer term. Savings or investments made now could build into a useful asset in years to come. Also, by setting money aside for specific requirements rather than proceeding in too ad hoc a manner, the Dragon can make a real difference to his financial situation.

Another encouragingly aspected area of the year is travel and if there is a particular destination that appeals to the Dragon or he sees a tempting travel opportunity, he should find out more. His travels could be one of the highlights of the year.

With his outgoing nature, the Dragon knows a great many people and he may find his social circle widening even further as the year develops. Many a Dragon will find himself in demand this year and enjoying his social life. February, April, August and December could be the liveliest months for socializing and meeting others.

This can also be a significant time for those Dragons enjoying romance, with relationships often becoming more meaningful and some Dragons settling down or getting married. However, while a lot can go well, the Dragon does need to be wary of rumour or getting drawn into what could be a complicated situation. In his dealings with others, he does need be open, aware and his honourable self. Indiscretions or lapses could cause problems. Dragons, do take note.

The Dragon's domestic life is particularly well aspected and by giving time to others he can make this a rewarding year. It is one when enjoying activities together can do a lot to strengthen relationships and good communication can make a real difference to home life.

Overall, the Ox year may lack the activity of some and the Dragon may feel frustrated by the time it takes for his plans to come to fruition, but by proceeding steadily, he can fare well. This may not be a year for major breakthroughs, but it can be a satisfying one, with his relations with others often being significant.

The Metal Dragon

The Metal Dragon has a very strong will and when he sets himself an objective he pursues it determinedly. As the Ox year starts, many Metal Dragons will have ideas about what they want to accomplish over the next 12 months. Although a lot will be possible, the Metal Dragon does need to allow plenty of time to carry out his plans. The Ox year can be slow moving and requires patience – not always a Metal Dragon strong point!

In his planning the Metal Dragon should also consult others and listen to what they have to say. Not only can they give useful encouragement, but they can sometimes indicate where plans can be improved. Throughout the Ox year the Metal Dragon must not close his mind to the suggestions of others. He may be determined, but greater flexibility will often lead to him achieving more.

One area that many Metal Dragons will give attention to over the year is their home. They may have had ideas in mind for some time and this year many will set about them in earnest. Here again, however, they do need to allow time for practical undertakings as well as regularly consult others. This is no year for rush or for having too many activities underway at once.

Also, should the Metal Dragon be involved in any strenuous activity, whether in the home or garden, he does need to be careful, follow recommended procedures and, where necessary, seek the help of others. A strain could cause him considerable discomfort. Metal Dragons, do take note.

In addition to the satisfaction home projects and improvements can bring, the Metal Dragon will generally delight in the family activities that take place over the year. He will follow the progress of loved ones with keen interest and his care and affection will be particularly valued. For those Metal Dragons who are grandparents or great-grandparents, this can be a special year, with some key achievements taking place.

There will also be some excellent travel opportunities in the Ox year and the Metal Dragon should make the most of them. If there is a particular destination he is keen to visit, he should make enquiries and talk his ideas over with others. Once again, however, he does need to allow ample time for his plans to take shape. This is not a year to leave arrangements to the last moment.

Another rewarding aspect of the year will be the Metal Dragon's interests and if he can share these or get to meet other enthusiasts, this can add to the pleasure. Similarly, if there is a subject that appeals to him or he is keen to further a particular skill, he should follow it up. By acting on his ideas, possibly including enrolling on a local course or joining a local group, he can make this a satisfying time.

The Metal Dragon will also value the very good friends he has and will enjoy attending a variety of social occasions. Lonely Metal Dragons will find that by going out more and becoming involved in interest-related pursuits, they can see a real improvement in their social life over the year. Some Dragons may also decide to give some of their free time to help a good cause or another person and this can not only be personally satisfying but also of value to others.

The Metal Dragon is generally thorough by nature and this will stand him in good stead this year, as he will need to manage his finances and paperwork well. In view of some of his plans for the year, he will need to budget carefully. He also needs be attentive with paperwork, returning any financially related forms promptly as well as making sure insurance and other policies are kept up to date. The more vigilant he is, the better.

Generally, the Metal Dragon can fare well in the Ox year, even though some plans may take longer to realize than anticipated. However, as with all years, problems will arise and it is important that the Metal Dragon talks these through and, if appropriate, seeks professional advice. This is not a year to keep his worries to himself. Also, he does need to be wary of rumour or becoming involved in matters that are not really his concern. There will be occasions in 2009 when he will need to be on his guard as well as prepared to check the facts for himself. If he has misgivings at any time, he needs to be careful and aware.

For Metal Dragons born in 2000 this can be an interesting year, especially as they will get to learn more and try out new activities. However, sometimes they will need to show greater patience than usual. As the saying reminds us, *you can't run before you can walk,* and the young Metal Dragon should learn carefully and thoroughly rather than be over-ambitious or rush. This can be a constructive and satisfying year for him, but he does need to allow time for results to filter through.

For all Metal Dragons, this can be a generally positive year. Their relations with others will mean a great deal, but they do need to show patience. The Ox year proceeds at a slow but steady pace and, frustrating though this may sometimes be for the eager Metal Dragon, he does need to adapt to the rhythm of the year.

TIP FOR THE YEAR
Listen to the advice of those around you. There will be much wisdom in what they say. Also, show greater patience. You may face delays and frustrations, but the results will often be worth waiting for.

The Water Dragon

This will be a satisfying year for the Water Dragon and while it may lack the activity of some, he will generally be pleased with how his plans develop.

At work many Water Dragons will be content to remain with the work they know and do well. As a result many will find this a fulfilling time. There could be the chance to take on more specialist duties or become involved in new projects and the Water Dragon may well be able to add to his often considerable expertise.

For Water Dragons who are feeling staid and would welcome a new challenge, or those who are looking for work, this can be a significant time. Obtaining a position will be neither easy nor swift, but by showing initiative in their applications and at interview, many will be given what can be an excellent new opportunity. It will take time but, as the Water Dragon has so often shown, persistence and self-confidence *will* eventually bring results. An interesting new challenge will also give him the incentive to prove himself – something he may feel has been lacking in recent years. March, May, July and September could see some interesting developments.

The Water Dragon's financial prospects are encouraging this year and in addition to a rise in income some Water Dragons may benefit from a gift or be able to supplement their earnings through a particular interest or skill. The Water Dragon's enterprise can stand him in good stead, although to benefit from any financial upturn he does need to manage his situation well. Rather than spend his money too readily, he should set funds aside for specific requirements and, if he is able, consider making provision for the longer term. With careful control, he can do a lot to improve his financial position.

Travel is also favoured this year and all Water Dragons should try to take a holiday or break at some time. Even if it is not always possible to travel far, the change of scene will do them a lot of good. Many Water Dragons will also receive invitations to visit relations or friends and such visits can turn out well.

The Water Dragon's domestic life can also bring him a lot of pleasure. Although he will often be busy, sharing activities can make this a rewarding year and some family occasions will be particularly appreciated. Over the year the Water Dragon will also do a lot to help both younger and more senior relatives, and here his caring nature and sound judgement will count for a great deal. Water

Dragons who decide to tackle practical projects, however, especially around the home, do need to allow ample time to complete them. The Ox year is not one for swift results.

A positive aspect of the year will be the way the Water Dragon is able to develop some of his interests, and if he involves others in his activities, this can often add to the fun. Some Water Dragons may consider enrolling on a course or learning a new skill with a loved one and this can bring both pleasure and often personal benefit.

With the Water Dragon's circle of friends, his work and his interests, he will also have some good social opportunities during the year. For Water Dragons who are alone and would welcome the chance to get to know others, the Ox year could mark the start of a significant friendship and, for some, possible romance. As many will find, personal interests can be good ways to meet others over the year. February, April, August, December and early January could see some particularly interesting social opportunities.

Generally, the aspects are on the Water Dragon's side this year but, as with any year, there will be more awkward elements. In 2009 the Water Dragon does need to be wary of rumour or being drawn into unhelpful and time-consuming matters. If he has doubts over anything, he should check it out himself or seek appropriate advice. This is not a year for taking risks or jeopardizing his good standing by some lapse. Water Dragons, do take note. However, if you are careful and rely on your instincts, you can do a lot to minimize the trickier aspects of the Ox year.

This may not be a year of major developments for the Water Dragon, but it can be a satisfying one and by using his skills, seizing his opportunities and spending time with others and on interests he enjoys, he will be happy with how the year unfolds. Overall, a pleasant if sometimes slow-moving year.

TIP FOR THE YEAR
Rather than setting your sights too high, simply enjoy what you do and the people you have around you. These are real treasures in your life and this is a year when you can really appreciate them.

The Wood Dragon

There is a Chinese proverb that is especially apt for the Wood Dragon this year: *Follow proper procedures and enjoy success in whatever you do.* This is a year for the Wood Dragon to concentrate on what he does best. If he does, he can look forward to making good progress. However, should he venture into unfamiliar areas, be less than thorough or take risks, problems could occur.

At work this can be a constructive year and many Wood Dragons will have the chance to make more of their particular skills. In some cases their specialist knowledge will make them ideal candidates for a greater role. Their progress may not be substantial this year, but they may well have the chance to gain further experience and this can stand them in good stead for later on.

Throughout the Ox year the Wood Dragon will be helped by the good working relationships he enjoys. Not only will he benefit from the support of others (including the encouragement of some senior to him) but also from networking and becoming better known. Contacts made now can help his prospects in the future. However, if at any time he has doubts about any information he hears, it would be to his advantage to check things out for himself. Without extra care, there is a risk that he could be misled and sometimes worried unnecessarily. Wood Dragons, take note and be on your guard.

The majority of Wood Dragons will remain with their present employers over the year, but for those who are frustrated by their current situation or are seeking work, the Ox year can be significant. By giving careful thought to what they now want to do and getting advice from organizations and employment agencies, they can find their determination and initiative leading to a new opportunity. March, May, July and September could see some interesting work developments, but the best results will come from the areas in which the Wood Dragon already has knowledge and skills rather than from something completely new.

The Wood Dragon's financial prospects are encouraging this year and many Wood Dragons will enjoy some good fortune. To benefit from any upturn, though, the Wood Dragon does need to manage his resources well, including setting sums aside for specific requirements and, if he is able, for the longer term. Savings or investments made now could develop into a useful asset in the future. The Wood Dragon also needs to be thorough when completing financial forms and should ensure that insurance and other policies are up to date and kept safely. Again, it is a case of 'following proper procedures' and being attentive.

In view of his various commitments the Wood Dragon will also need to manage his time well, otherwise there is a danger that certain recreational pursuits may be ignored or not enough time allowed for rest or exercise. Wood Dragons who lead particularly active lifestyles will need to watch this and ensure they set aside time for themselves. Any who lack regular exercise or are reliant on convenience food would do well to look at ways in which they can rectify this. Medical advice can make a real difference to their general energy levels.

With travel favourably aspected, the Wood Dragon should also aim to take a holiday or break over the year. By choosing his destination well, he will enjoy the chance to relax and visit areas he is interested in.

As far as the Wood Dragon's domestic life is concerned, this will be a full and interesting year. During it he will do a lot to assist others and his thoughtfulness will mean a great deal. A younger relation could face a key decision in 2009 and the support the Wood Dragon is able to give should not be under-estimated. His abilities to empathize and gauge what is right will be greatly appreciated. Also, while he will often have many commitments, if he makes sure there is good communication and co-operation between everyone in his household, his domestic life can go well.

The Ox year can also bring some fine social opportunities. The Wood Dragon will often impress others and may well find his social circle widening over the year. For the unattached and the lonely, the Ox year can bring a real improvement in their situation, with the prospect of significant romance for some. February, April, August, December and early January could see the most social activity. However, while the Wood Dragon's relations with others will be positive this year, should he have doubts over anything he hears, it would be worth him clarifying the position himself. Without extra care, he could find himself being misled or making incorrect assumptions. Wood Dragons, do take note.

Generally, this is an encouraging year for the Wood Dragon but, as with all Dragons, he does need to be wary of rumour or acting too hastily. This is a year for proceeding steadily and methodically. However, by following 'proper procedures' and remaining true to what he knows, the Wood Dragon will fare well, with what he does now often proving of considerable value in the longer term.

TIP FOR THE YEAR
Avoid undue haste. It is better to proceed steadily and surely than risk making mistakes or misjudgements. Also, make the most of the chances you have to build on your skills and meet others. What you do this year can open up important doors in the near future.

The Fire Dragon

This will be a busy year for the Fire Dragon, with various calls on his time and attention. Though his actual progress may be modest and not always in line with expectations, what he does achieve will greatly add to his experience as well as provide some useful personal insights, and he will be able to build on these in subsequent years.

The Fire Dragon's domestic life will be especially active and some Fire Dragons will be celebrating an addition to their family. Home life will often be conducted at a fast pace. With so much to think about and plan, it is important that there is good communication and co-operation between all family members and that not too much falls on the shoulders of one person. Also, amid all the activity, the Fire Dragon does need to preserve time simply to share and enjoy with others. In this busy year it is important that there is a good balance between home, work and other commitments.

The Fire Dragon will also do a lot to assist those close to him, and whether supporting and helping his partner, tending to the needs of babies, encouraging children or assisting more senior relations, he will find his help and understanding will mean a great deal. Family life may be busy – sometimes demanding – but this can be a happy and often special year.

The Fire Dragon should also aim to take a holiday with his loved ones over the year. Even if it is not possible to travel too far, the rest and break from routine can do everyone a great deal of good.

Throughout the year the Fire Dragon will also value his close circle of friends. Not only will he enjoy meeting up with them, but some may be facing similar pressures to his own and he may be helped by talking over his concerns. The Fire Dragon's work and interests can also bring him into contact with others and new friendships may be made during the year. For any Fire Dragon who is feeling lonely, has had recent difficulties in his personal life or would welcome a more fulfilling social life, this is a year offering much brighter prospects and for some a chance meeting can quickly become significant. February, April to mid-May, August and December could see the most social activity.

However, while the Fire Dragon's relations with others will mainly be positive, two words of warning do need to be sounded. During the year the Fire Dragon does need to be wary of rumour and if he is in any doubt over anything, he should check the situation himself. Also, he does need to be careful about being drawn into any awkward situation that could have repercussions. This is a year to tread carefully and remain aware.

The Fire Dragon is by nature determined and ambitious, and in his work he will be keen to make the most of himself. Opportunities for progress may be limited this year, but he will be given an excellent chance to gain additional experience, add to his knowledge and prepare for the advances he will make in following years. There may be some scope for taking on new duties in 2009, but it will be next year when the real progress will be made. For many Fire Dragons the Ox year can be considered an important and necessary stage in their career and one which will prepare the way for future success.

To help with this, the Fire Dragon should make the most of any training opportunities that may be offered. Any Fire Dragon who feels it would be useful to acquire a further skill or qualification should look at ways in which he can obtain this. Experience, skills and qualifications gained in the Ox year can often be important in the longer term.

For Fire Dragons who are keen to widen their experience by moving to a different employer or are seeking work, the Ox year can be significant. Obtaining a new position will take a lot of time and effort, but with determination and self-belief, many Fire Dragons will be successful in securing a new job. It may not always be exactly what they wanted, but it can give them the chance to develop their skills in new ways and be an excellent platform on which they can build in the future. March, May, July and September could see the best opportunities.

The Fire Dragon's efforts at work over the year can lead to a rise in income, and financially the Ox year can see an improvement. However, with his many plans and outgoings, the Fire Dragon does need to manage his spending well and should be wary of making purchases or entering into agreements too hurriedly. Haste could lead to regrets or less satisfactory outcomes. Fire Dragons, do take note, budget well and if in doubt over a financial matter, do check your position carefully.

Generally, the Ox year can be a satisfying one for the Fire Dragon and the experience and skills he can gain at work can be to his benefit. However, it is his relations with others that can make the year special. Some Fire Dragons will become parents or see an addition to their family, while for many the love and support they are given and some of the friendships they enjoy will be of great value. Domestically and socially, this can be a busy and often very happy year.

TIP FOR THE YEAR
There will be a great many demands on your time and you do need to keep your lifestyle in balance. Too much attention to one area could cause problems in another. Also, with this being an important year as far as relations with others are concerned, do take any opportunities to meet others. On a personal level you can impress this year.

The Earth Dragon

The element of Earth has a steadying influence on a sign and can help the Dragon to be more methodical and realistic in his approach. This outlook will serve the Earth Dragon well this year.

One of the benefits of the Ox year will be the opportunity it will give the Earth Dragon to add to his skills and qualifications. Whether in work or education, this is a year for him to add to his knowledge and prepare himself for his future.

For those Earth Dragons currently studying for qualifications, this can be a rewarding year. However, it is not one for taking results for granted. The Ox year does require effort. By working consistently and methodically, however – and here again the Earth Dragon's organized approach will help – many Earth Dragons will do well, with their progress opening up possibilities for the future. The Ox year rewards effort and commitment.

For those Earth Dragons in work, including those who may be on an apprenticeship scheme, this is also an excellent year for adding to their skills. Even if some may feel their current position is routine and unfulfilling, by doing their best and demonstrating their commitment, they will find their efforts *will* be noticed. Some Earth Dragons could find senior colleagues particularly encouraging and this could lead to them being given more specialist training or the chance to add to or vary their role. Enthusiasm and commitment can make a great difference to how the Earth Dragon fares this year.

For any Earth Dragon who is unhappy in his present line of work, the Ox year can open up interesting possibilities. However, while the Earth Dragon may know what he wants to do, he would do well to seek advice and assistance. This could be through getting information from professional organizations or talking to employment or recruiting agencies. The more information and advice he can obtain, the more chance there will be of being alerted to new possibilities. For the keen and ambitious, this is not a year to go it alone as far as work prospects are concerned.

This also applies to Earth Dragons seeking work. Again, by obtaining advice, following suggestions and widening the scope of positions they are prepared to consider, many will be given an important opportunity. March, May, July and September could see some positive developments, but the key to doing well in the Ox year is to show commitment and make the most of the advice available.

The effort the Earth Dragon makes in his work can have a positive effect on his finances and many Earth Dragons will enjoy an increase in income as they take on greater responsibilities. For those in education, temporary or seasonal work can help their financial position. The Earth Dragon will, though, have many expenses over the year and with accommodation costs and an often lively social life, he will need to keep track of his spending. Also, if entering into a new agreement or undertaking a major purchase, he does need to check the terms and obligations involved. This is a year for thoroughness and care.

With his adventurous nature, the Earth Dragon will be tempted to travel over the year and some Earth Dragons will have the chance to visit some interesting and often fun destinations. To get the most out of his time away, the Earth Dragon would do well to save up in advance, as well as undertake some preparation for his travels. The better prepared and more knowledgeable he is, the more he will get to do and enjoy while away.

The Earth Dragon can also look forward to an active social life during the year. Earth Dragons who move to a new location will find that by going out and pursuing their interests, they will soon get to meet and befriend others. Socially, this can be a full and positive year.

Affairs of the heart are also well aspected, and whether the Earth Dragon has a partner, is enjoying romance or gets to meet someone new, this can be an interesting, exciting and often romantic year. February, April, August, December and early January will see the most social activity as well as bring good chances to meet others.

The aspects are certainly on the Earth Dragon's side this year but, as with any year, problems can loom. In 2009 the Earth Dragon does need to be wary of rumour or believing all he is told. When in doubt, it would be worth him checking the facts himself. He should also be wary of going against his better instincts. Sometimes problems can follow on from a mistake or misjudgement. In the Ox year, taking the time to think situations through will help. Similarly, the Earth Dragon should avoid rush and not expect things to happen all at once. Plans do need time to be set in motion. This is no year for hurry.

However, generally this is a constructive year for the Earth Dragon. In his work or education, the skills or qualifications he can gain can help his future prospects, and his personal life can also bring him a great deal of pleasure, with affairs of the heart often helping to make this a special time.

As a Dragon, you may cherish a certain independence and be keen to do a lot by yourself. However, in 2009 you do need to draw on the support, advice and assistance others can give. Your independent spirit may be commendable, but to make the most of your situation, you do need to involve others *and* listen to them. The more support you have behind you, the more favourable your year.

FAMOUS DRAGONS

Maya Angelou, Jeffrey Archer, Joan Armatrading, Joan Baez, Count Basie, Maeve Binchy, Sandra Bullock, James Coburn, Courteney Cox, Bing Crosby, Russell Crowe, Roald Dahl, Salvador Dali, Charles Darwin, Neil Diamond, Bo Diddley, Matt Dillon, Christian Dior, Placido Domingo, Fats Domino, Kirk Douglas, Faye Dunaway, Lee Evans, Dan Fogler, Bruce Forsyth, Sigmund Freud, Graham Greene, Che Guevara, James Herriot, Paul Hogan, Joan of Arc, Boris Johnson, Tom Jones, Immanuel Kant, Martin Luther King, John Lennon, Abraham Lincoln, Elle MacPherson, Queen Margrethe II of Denmark, Andrew Motion, Hosni Mubarak, Florence Nightingale, Nick Nolte, Sharon Osbourne, Al Pacino, Gregory Peck, Pelé, Edgar Allan Poe, Vladimir Putin, Keanu Reeves, Sir Cliff Richard, George Bernard Shaw, Martin Sheen, Alicia Silverstone, Ringo Starr, Princess Stephanie of Monaco, Dave Stewart, Karlheinz Stockausen, Shirley Temple, Maria von Trapp, Andy Warhol, Raquel Welch, the Earl of Wessex, Mae West.

23 JANUARY 1917 ⁓ 10 FEBRUARY 1918	*Fire Snake*
10 FEBRUARY 1929 ⁓ 29 JANUARY 1930	*Earth Snake*
27 JANUARY 1941 ⁓ 14 FEBRUARY 1942	*Metal Snake*
14 FEBRUARY 1953 ⁓ 2 FEBRUARY 1954	*Water Snake*
2 FEBRUARY 1965 ⁓ 20 JANUARY 1966	*Wood Snake*
18 FEBRUARY 1977 ⁓ 6 FEBRUARY 1978	*Fire Snake*
6 FEBRUARY 1989 ⁓ 26 JANUARY 1990	*Earth Snake*
24 JANUARY 2001 ⁓ 11 FEBRUARY 2002	*Metal Snake*

THE
SNAKE

THE PERSONALITY OF THE SNAKE

I think
And think some more.
About what is,
About what can be,
About what may be.
And when I am ready,
Then I act.

The Snake is born under the sign of wisdom. He is highly intelligent and his mind is forever active. He is always planning and always looking for ways in which he can use his considerable skills. He is a deep thinker and likes to meditate and reflect.

Many times during his life he will shed one of his famous Snake skins and take up new interests or start a completely different job. The Snake enjoys a challenge and he rarely makes mistakes. He is a skilful organizer, has considerable business acumen and is usually lucky in money matters. Most Snakes are financially secure in their later years, provided they do not gamble – the Snake has the distinction of being the worst gambler in the whole of the Chinese zodiac!

The Snake generally has a calm and placid nature and prefers the quieter things in life. He does not like to be in a frenzied atmosphere and hates being hurried into making a quick decision. He also does not like interference in his affairs and tends to rely on his own judgement rather than listen to advice.

At times the Snake can appear solitary. He is quiet, reserved and sometimes has difficulty in communicating with others. He has little time for idle gossip and will certainly not suffer fools gladly. He does, however, have a good sense of humour and this is particularly appreciated in times of crisis.

The Snake is certainly not afraid of hard work and is thorough in all that he does. He is very determined and can occasionally be ruthless in order to achieve his aims. His confidence, willpower and quick thinking usually ensure his success, but should he fail it will often take a long time for him to recover. He cannot bear failure and is a very bad loser.

The Snake can also be evasive and does not willingly let people into his confidence. This secrecy and distrust can sometimes work against him and it is a trait that all Snakes should try to overcome.

Another characteristic of the Snake is his tendency to rest after any sudden or prolonged bout of activity. He burns up so much nervous energy that he can, if he is not careful, be susceptible to high blood pressure and nervous disorders.

It has sometimes been said that the Snake is a late starter in life and this is mainly because it often takes him a while to find a job in which he is genuinely happy. However, he will usually do well in any position that involves research and writing and where he is given sufficient freedom to develop his own ideas and plans. He makes a good teacher, politician, personnel manager and social adviser.

The Snake chooses his friends carefully and while he keeps a tight control over his finances, he can be particularly generous to those he likes. He will think nothing of buying expensive gifts or treating his friends or loved ones to the best theatre seats in town. In return he demands loyalty. The Snake is very possessive and can become extremely jealous and hurt if he finds his trust has been abused.

The Snake is also renowned for his good looks and is never short of admirers. The female Snake in particular is most alluring. She has style, grace and excellent (and usually expensive) taste in clothes. A keen socializer, she is likely to have a wide range of friends and the happy knack of impressing those who matter. She has numerous interests and her opinions are often highly valued. She is generally a calm-natured person and while she involves herself in many activities, she likes to retain a certain amount of privacy in her undertakings.

Affairs of the heart are very important to the Snake and he will often have many romances before he finally settles down. He will find that he is particularly well suited to those born under the signs of the Ox, Dragon, Rabbit and Rooster. Provided he is allowed sufficient freedom to pursue his own interests, he can also build up a very satisfactory relationship with the Rat, Horse, Goat, Monkey and Dog, but he should try to steer clear of another Snake as they could very easily become jealous of each other. The Snake will also have difficulty in getting on with the honest and down-to-earth Pig, and will find the Tiger far too much of a disruptive influence on his quiet and peaceloving ways.

The Snake certainly appreciates the finer things in life. He enjoys good food and often takes a keen interest in the arts. He also enjoys reading and is invariably drawn to subjects such as philosophy, political thought, religion or the occult. He is fascinated by the unknown and his enquiring mind is always looking for answers. Some of the world's most original thinkers have been Snakes, and although he may not readily admit it, the Snake is often psychic and relies a lot on intuition.

The Snake is certainly not the most energetic member of the Chinese zodiac. He prefers to proceed at his own pace and to do what he wants. He is very much his own master and throughout his life he will try his hand at many things. He is something of a dabbler, but at some time – usually when he least expects it – his hard work and efforts will be recognized and he will invariably meet with the success and the financial security he so desires.

THE FIVE DIFFERENT TYPES OF SNAKE

In addition to the 12 signs of the Chinese zodiac there are five elements and these have a strengthening or moderating influence on the signs. The effects of the five elements on the Snake are described below, together with the years in which the elements were exercising their influence. Therefore those Snakes born in 1941 and 2001 are Metal Snakes, those born in 1953 are Water Snakes, and so on.

Metal Snake: 1941, 2001

This Snake is quiet, confident and fiercely independent. He often prefers to work on his own and will only let a privileged few into his confidence. He is quick to spot opportunities and will set about achieving his objectives with an awesome determination. He is astute in financial matters and will often invest his money well. He also has a liking for the finer things in life and a good appreciation of the arts, literature, music and good food. He usually has a small group of extremely good friends and can be generous to his loved ones.

Water Snake: 1953

This Snake has a wide variety of interests. He enjoys studying all manner of subjects and is capable of undertaking quite detailed research and becoming a specialist in his chosen area. He is highly intelligent, has a good memory and is particularly astute when dealing with business and financial matters. He tends to be quietly spoken and a little reserved, but he does have sufficient strength of character to make his views known and attain his ambitions. He is very loyal to his family and friends.

Wood Snake: 1965

The Wood Snake has a friendly temperament and a good understanding of human nature. He is able to communicate well and often has many friends and admirers. He is witty, intelligent and ambitious. He has numerous interests and prefers to live in a quiet, stable environment where he can work without too much interference. He enjoys the arts and usually derives much pleasure from collecting paintings and antiques. His advice is often highly valued, particularly on social and domestic matters.

Fire Snake: 1917, 1977

The Fire Snake tends to be more forceful, outgoing and energetic than some of the other types of Snake. He is ambitious, confident and never slow in voicing his opinions – and he can be very abrasive to those he does not like. He does, however, have many leadership qualities and can win the respect and support of many with his firm and resolute manner. He usually has a good sense of humour, a wide circle of friends and a very active social life. He is also a keen traveller.

Earth Snake 1929, 1989

The Earth Snake is charming, amusing and has a very amiable manner. He is conscientious and reliable in his work and approaches everything he does in a level-headed and sensible way. He can, however, tend to err on the cautious side and never likes to be hassled into making a decision. He is adept in dealing with financial matters and is a shrewd investor. He has many friends and is very supportive towards the members of his family.

PROSPECTS FOR THE SNAKE IN 2009

The Snake may not always feel at ease with the fast pace of the Rat year (7 February 2008 to 25 January 2009) and the remaining months will be busy and sometimes demanding. However, despite the pressures, this can be an important time. The Rat year welcomes innovation and with his deep-thinking ways, the Snake can often benefit. This is very much a time for acting on his ideas.

In his work the Snake will need to keep his wits about him, especially as he may well face increased pressures and an often growing workload. To cope, the Snake will need to remain organized and concentrate on priorities. However, amid the activity there will be good chances to make progress and if the Snake detects the possibility of furthering his career in some way, he should follow it up. His initiative can be well rewarded, but this is very much a time for effort and follow-through.

One of the aspects of the Snake's character is his independent and slightly reserved nature. He does tend to keep his thoughts to himself and set about his activities in his own way. In the remaining Rat months he would do well to open up more. By talking about his situation and hopes, he will enable his family, friends and other associates to assist and advise him. In addition, by making the most of his social opportunities he will not only enjoy himself but also be able to meet and impress others. The closing months of the Rat year can see a lot of social activity.

Overall, the Rat year can bring some good opportunities for the Snake, but to benefit he does need to be active, put himself forward and be prepared to involve others in his activities.

The Year of the Ox begins on 26 January and will be a reasonable one for the Snake. It will certainly contain some good times, but can also bring challenges. This is no year for the Snake to slacken off or be less than thorough. As so many signs will discover, the Ox year can be an exacting one.

In his work the Snake can make steady progress, but he does need to remain disciplined and focused. This is a time for effort and realism, and should the Snake absorb himself too much in his own thoughts and theories, he could find himself at odds with other people. This is very much a year for concentrating on what he has to do and making the most of his current situation. More creative Snakes may sometimes feel stifled by the rigid nature of the Ox year, but they can take heart, for the following Tiger year is much more conducive to innovation and imagination.

However, while the Ox year can be demanding, the Snake can still gain a lot from it. By tackling the challenges before him, he will not only have the chance to further his skills but also to gain important new experience.

Throughout the year the Snake should aim to make the most of his opportunities, whether these involve undertaking training, assisting colleagues, varying his role in some way or applying for another position. This may not be a year for major advances, but it can bring steady progress and enable the Snake to build on his skills and talents.

For Snakes who are eager to change their present job or seeking work, the Ox year may not be easy. Openings could be limited and the Snake could face a lot of competition.

However, the Snake is tenacious and once he has set himself an objective he is not one to rest until he has achieved it. To secure a new position he will, however, need to widen the scope of what he is prepared to consider as well as show initiative when making applications and at interview. Giving some thought to what he could bring to the position or obtaining additional information about the company could also be helpful. In view of his resolve, opportunities could present themselves at almost any time of the year, although April to mid-July and October could see some particularly promising developments.

One particular benefit of the Ox year will be the chance it will give the Snake to undertake some self-development. This is an excellent time for personal study and if there is a subject that intrigues him or a skill or course that he considers would be useful to him, he should follow it up. It could not only be fulfilling now but also of value in the near future.

The Snake would also do well to set himself a personal objective for the year. Whether this is connected with his well-being and level of exercise or a resolution he wants to keep, by giving some thought to ways in which he can better himself or correct certain habits, he can certainly benefit from what he does. This may require discipline and self-control, but by keeping in mind the potential benefits and drawing on the support of others, he can find it becoming another valuable aspect of the year.

In financial matters, however, the Snake will need to be his vigilant and thorough self. This is not a year for entering into transactions or making major purchases without careful thought. Where paperwork is concerned, the Snake does need to check the small print as without increased care, problems could arise and mistakes be made. Financially, this is a year for caution.

This need for awareness also applies to the Snake's domestic life. In his relations with others he does need to listen closely to his loved ones as well as show flexibility when making arrangements. Remaining too rigid could lead to disagreements. In the Ox year, communication and co-operation are both important and necessary.

However, while the Snake's home life will often be busy and require co-operation, it will contain many rewarding times. Whenever the Snake has ideas for activities that can be shared, he should put them forward.

The Snake usually tends to be selective in his social-izing, but he should not let the general activity of the year prevent him from going to events that appeal to him or keeping in regular contact with his friends. His social life can give him the chance to relax and unwind and bring an important balance to his lifestyle. Quite a few Snakes will also find certain interests they have bringing them into contact with others and some good friendships will be made as the year progresses. For Snakes who are unat-tached, a meeting of minds could turn into a significant romance. April, May, August and September could see a lot of social activity.

Generally, the Snake can fare well in the Ox year, but it does require effort. The Snake prefers to proceed in his own way and at his own pace, and he will sometimes find the pressures and demands of the year considerable. However, with focus and discipline and good co-operation with others, he can not only make useful progress but also add considerably to his skills and experience. And as far as his personal development is concerned, this can be a satisfying and often rewarding year.

The Metal Snake

The Metal Snake takes his responsibilities seriously and the element of Metal reinforces his self-willed nature. However, in 2009 he does need to watch his independent tendencies. Although he will have plans for the year, for these to be realized he does need to liaise readily with others and draw on their help and advice. This need to consult others applies to most areas of his life. Throughout the year, if he has any concerns or finds himself in a dilemma, it is important he is forthcoming.

In view of the prevailing aspects of the year, the Metal Snake will need to be especially thorough when dealing with paperwork and financial matters. He should read forms and documents carefully and question anything that is unclear. To delay or miss details could be to his detriment as well as involve him in extra correspondence. Also, he does need to make sure that important documents, including policies and guarantees, are kept safely and are up to date. The Ox year is not a time to be lax with paperwork and if at any time the Metal Snake has problems, it would be worth him contacting a helpline or someone with the expertise to advise him.

This need for care also applies to any major purchases he may be considering. The Ox year is not one for rush and by taking the time to look at the options available, the Metal Snake will make far better decisions.

A more positive aspect of the year will be the way the Metal Snake is able to enjoy his personal interests and with his keen mind, if he sees a subject or course that appeals to him, he should follow it up. The Ox year very much favours personal development.

The Metal Snake will also appreciate the support he receives from those close to him, but at all times he does need to be mindful of their advice and suggestions. They do speak with his interests at heart and although the Metal Snake may have his own opinion, they may suggest other possibilities worth considering. In the Ox year the Metal Snake does need to listen as well as show some flexibility.

Also, where practical undertakings are concerned, possibly tasks in the home or garden, if ideas and talents are pooled, the results can be far more satisfying. This is not a year for the Metal Snake to adopt a too much of a go-it-alone approach. He will, however, delight in some of the family activities that take place as well as in following the progress of those close to him. The year can also give rise to a particularly special moment as a loved one realizes an ambition.

The Metal Snake will also often find his interests bringing him into contact with others and if he is a member of a society or group, or decides to join one, he will often find himself sharing his knowledge and insights as well as enjoying the social opportunities that arise. Again, this is not a year for adopting too solitary an approach and any Metal Snake who would welcome greater company would do well to consider joining a local group or enrolling on a course. Mid-March to May, August and September could be especially good times for meeting others.

The Metal Snake will also enjoy the travel opportunities that arise during the year and whether he is visiting friends or relations or going away for a holiday, a break will do him a lot of good. However, it would be worth checking his itinerary carefully and reading up about his destination in advance. This way he will not only go better prepared but appreciate his time away all the more.

Generally, the Ox year can be a constructive one for the Metal Snake. However, throughout the year he will need to watch his independent tendencies and take the views of others into account. Metal Snakes, take note. This can be a positive year, but it is one to be aware and accommodating in attitude.

TIP FOR THE YEAR
Take your time. Think ahead and discuss your ideas with others rather than proceeding hurriedly and independently. Also, be your vigilant self when dealing with paperwork and finance. Thoroughness is the order of the day.

The Water Snake

The Water Snake is generally careful and cautious and likes to think ahead. He is not one for hasty action or embarking on change lightly and in the Ox year he will often be giving a lot of thought to his future. This year may not be one for dramatic change, but it may set significant wheels in motion.

At work many Water Snakes will have built up considerable experience and reached positions of responsibility. Although they will often be able to use their expertise well, some may still feel unfulfilled and yearn to put their skills to better use. Over the year, if an opportunity arises in their place of work or they see an opening elsewhere, they should act quickly. Opportunities for change may be limited in 2009 and they do need to be grasped as soon as possible.

Also, while the Water Snake may be experienced in his area of work, he should take full advantage of any training that may be offered. Not only will this allow him to keep his skills up to date and be informed of new developments, but it could also suggest possibilities for the future. What happens in the Ox year can sometimes have far-reaching significance.

Most Water Snakes, while giving thought to their future, will remain in their present line of work, but for those intent on change or seeking work, the Ox year can bring some interesting developments. Although there could be disappointments in their quest and some positions they thought they were ideal candidates for may not be offered them, the Ox year can work in unexpected ways. For some a chance they thought was unlikely to materialize could open up for them, or they could obtain a position that will give them the opportunity to develop their knowledge in new ways. What happens can have an important bearing on the next few years. April to mid-July and October could see some particularly interesting developments, but generally this is a year for the Water Snake to make the most of his situation and to look ahead.

The Water Snake's thoughts may also concern his interests. Some Water Snakes will feel the time is right for fresh challenges and if there is a subject or recreational pursuit that appeals to them, they should aim to find out more.

Some may decide to give greater attention to their physical as well as mental well-being and be attracted to disciplines such as yoga, tai chi or meditation. Whatever they choose to do, by taking action and doing something purposeful, these Water Snakes will not only feel inspired and energized but often benefit physically as well. Any Water Snake who decides to start any keep-fit discipline or exercise regime should obtain medical advice about its suitability and the best way for him to proceed. But certainly what many Water Snakes choose to pursue this year can have value both now and in following years.

The Water Snake will need to remain his careful self, however, when dealing with financial matters. As well as existing obligations, many Water Snakes will have additional family expenses and would do well to make early provision for them if possible. Also, if considering a major purchase for his home, the Water Snake should take the time to check his options. Although he does not usually rush into things, this is a year to avoid haste and impulse buys. And if he has any concerns over a financial matter, he should seek advice. Financial matters do require considerable care this year.

In the Water Snake's home life this can be a busy and eventful year, with the Water Snake often feeling excited about the progress of a loved one. During the year he will do a lot to help and advise those who are special to him and his support and time will be valued. However, while he will gladly assist others, the Water Snake is not always forthcoming when it comes to his own concerns and he does need to watch this. Not only will greater openness on his part give others more chance to encourage and advise him, but it will also allow him to benefit from their opinions and knowledge.

The Water Snake will also appreciate some of the planned activities of the year and whether completing a domestic project, spending time with his loved ones or travelling, he will find the Ox year can bring some particularly pleasurable times. The key, though, is good communication and greater openness.

The Water Snake tends to have a close social circle and during the year he will enjoy meeting his friends as well as going to events that appeal to him. Those Water Snakes who are members of a society or interest-related group, or who decide to join one, will not only find this a good way to meet others but could also find themselves playing an active role. The Ox year does tend to draw out the Water Snake's talents. Some Water Snakes may like to keep themselves to themselves, but this is a year when they could find themselves in the spotlight. April, May and August to early October could see the most social activity.

Generally, the Ox year will be an interesting one for the Water Snake and the progress he makes and ideas he has will often have a bearing on his prospects over the next few years. His domestic life and close circle of friends will mean a lot to him and he does need to be receptive to the advice of others. Overall, however, a satisfying year and one that can have long-term value.

TIP FOR THE YEAR

As a Water Snake you have a keen mind and over the year you could derive much satisfaction from setting yourself a personal challenge or taking up a new interest. The long-term implications of what you start in the Ox year should not be underestimated.

The Wood Snake

There is a Chinese proverb that declares, *he who comprehends the times is great*, and by remaining aware and adapting to the Ox year the Wood Snake can gain a great deal from it.

In his work this can be a demanding year, with increased pressures and a heavy workload. The Wood Snake may also be affected by delays, bureaucracy or the attitude of others. The Ox year may in parts be testing, but it is at such times that the Wood Snake can display his finer qualities. By foreseeing possible difficulties, dealing with situations as they arise and doing what he can, he can not only accomplish a great deal but also do his reputation a lot of good.

Another important factor over the year will be the Wood Snake's relations with his colleagues. This is a year to liaise closely with others as well as remain aware of their views. The Wood Snake's perceptive nature will help, but the more consultation and co-operation there is, the better it will be for everyone concerned. Should any difference of opinion arise, the Wood Snake must be careful he does not allow this to overshadow what he does. His ability to handle sometimes challenging situations will help. Over the year he should also make the most of any chances he has to network. The contacts, connections and sometimes friendships he makes can be helpful both in his present situation and the near future.

Most Wood Snakes will remain with their present employer during the year and can often benefit from internal opportunities, including chances for promotion, but for those who are keen to move elsewhere or are seeking work, this can be a significant year. Obtaining a new position may not be easy, but by seeking expert guidance and considering different ways in which they can use their skills, these Wood Snakes may find interesting possibilities opening up. Mid-April to mid-July and October could see some intriguing developments, but central to how the Wood Snake fares will be his instinct, his drive and the way he is able to put himself across to others. The Ox year can be challenging, but it is at such times that the Wood Snake so often shows his best.

Although many Wood Snakes can look forward to a rise in income, this is a year signalling care. In particular, if the Wood Snake is considering any large purchase or transaction or takes on any new agreements, he does need to look closely at the implications and any obligations involved. In view of the plans and hopes he has for the year, possibly including travel, he does need to budget well.

The Wood Snake will, however, derive particular pleasure from his interests and recreational pursuits and should make sure he sets time aside for them. Whether they are practical or creative in nature, he will benefit from them. In addition, if he sees a course that appeals to him or has an idea he is keen to pursue, he should follow it up. For many Wood Snakes, their interests can develop well this year and be personally rewarding.

The Wood Snake will also see a great deal of activity in his domestic life and will do a lot to assist those close to him. A younger relation in particular could have some important decisions to make and the support and advice the Wood Snake gives and his ability to empathize will be of great value. More senior relations could also be grateful for the assistance the Wood Snake is able to give. In this already busy year, he will often find himself in demand. In view of this, should he wish to carry out any practical projects, he does need to allow plenty of time for them *and* be flexible in his planning. In the Ox year practical activities often take longer than anticipated. Wood Snakes, do take note. As busy and occasionally demanding as home life may be, it will, however, contain some very special moments and the Wood Snake will play a central and valued part.

As with all Snakes, the Wood Snake does take his time building friendships and prefers to have a few close friends. However, over the Ox year he will get to meet some people with whom he will get on especially well and could well find himself adding to his social circle. Some of his new acquaintances could prove particularly helpful and for the unattached, romance could beckon. Mid-March to May, August and September could see the most social activity, but throughout the Ox year the Wood Snake's perceptive and straightforward nature will be appreciated by many.

Overall, the Ox year will be a busy one for the Wood Snake and there will be considerable demands on his time. However, by concentrating on what needs to be done and liaising closely with others, he will accomplish a great deal and this can prove important over the next few years.

Be aware of what is going on around you, including the views of others. This way you will be better able to handle any challenging situations as well as benefit from some of the developments of the year. Also, do spend quality time with your loved ones and allow some time for your own interests. In this busy year you do need to keep your lifestyle in balance.

The Fire Snake

This will be an interesting year for the Fire Snake, although how he fares will depend a lot on his attitude. Over the year he will need to show flexibility rather than stick rigidly to certain plans or objectives. This way he will not only have more chance to benefit from the opportunities of the year but also will get to do far more.

This need for flexibility particularly applies to his work. Although many Fire Snakes will have built up considerable experience, over the year there will often be chances for them to vary their role. By making the most of such opportunities, the Fire Snake will not only be broadening his experience but also helping his prospects. This is a year to adapt to change. Also, while the Fire Snake does have his long-term ambitions, he is still in the relatively early stages of his career and the experience he can gain now can be to his future benefit.

For Fire Snakes who feel restricted in their present position, as well as those seeking work, the Ox year can bring some significant opportunities. However, rather than pursue just one type of work, these Fire Snakes should be flexible and widen the scope of what they are prepared to consider. This way there will not only be more possibilities open to them, but many will be able to secure a position that will allow them to use their skills in new ways and have the potential for future development. To progress in the Ox year the Fire Snake should not be too narrow in his approach but make the most of opportunities *as they arise*. Mid-April to mid-July and October could see important developments and with the Fire Snake's prospects looking promising in the following Tiger year, what is accomplished now can often be a useful platform to build on.

Another key feature of the Ox year will be the positive way in which the Fire Snake is able to develop his interests. Some Fire Snakes could be tempted to try something completely new or become absorbed in a different pastime. Those who do take up a new pursuit this year will often feel energized by the opportunity this gives them to develop their talents. Again, this is a year for flexibility. Also, Fire Snakes who have particularly busy schedules should make sure they allow time for their recreational pursuits rather than being continually active. To keep himself on good form this year the Fire Snake does need to give some thought to his general lifestyle.

In financial matters he should be disciplined. With his current obligations and the purchases he will want to make, as well as any additions he may be considering for his home, he will need to manage his spending and give careful thought to more major purchases. He also needs to deal with financial paperwork carefully and query anything that may be unclear, as well as return documents on time. This is a year to be vigilant and thorough.

The Fire Snake's domestic life will be busy but rewarding. Over the year he will do a lot to encourage and support his loved ones and his efforts can make a considerable difference. This may already be a busy year, but the energy the Fire Snake puts into his home life will truly reward everyone involved. Sharing plans, including home projects, and spending quality time together will not only strengthen relationships but also lead to some pleasing and proud moments.

The Fire Snake will also be grateful for the support of his close friends during the year and their advice and often specialist knowledge can be of great help to him, particularly in view of some of the work possibilities that may arise and the interests he may be considering taking up. He will also appreciate some of the social opportunities of the year. April, May and August to early October could see the most social opportunities and those Fire Snakes who would welcome new friendships, especially if they are alone or have moved to a new area, can often see an improvement in their situation.

Overall, the Fire Snake can fare well in the Ox year, but to benefit he will need to be adaptable in his approach and make the most of his chances *as they arise*. With flexibility, willingness to put himself forward and the support of others, this can be an interesting time for him.

TIP FOR THE YEAR

As a Fire Snake you have a great many talents and this year will give you the chance to use them as well as take some of them in new directions. Make the most of what happens. Also, do keep your lifestyle in balance and give time to loved ones and personal interests.

The Earth Snake

This will be a significant year for the Earth Snake, not only marking the start of a new decade in his life but also bringing some important choices. While progress may sometimes be slow, the Earth Snake can fare well.

In his personal life this can be an eventful year. In addition to enjoying the company of his current friends there will be plenty of opportunities for him to meet other people and over the year many Earth Snakes will find their social circle widening. Earth Snakes who move over the year will also find this will give them the opportunity to make new friends. Late March to May and August to early October could see the most social activity. For some the Ox year can bring romance, and although this may sometimes be meaningful, many Earth Snakes will prefer to enjoy the present rather than seek longer-term commitments.

The Earth Snake will also value his domestic life over the year and those close to him will help with decisions he may have to take as well as offer general assistance. Although the Earth Snake may at times keep his thoughts to himself (like all Snakes, he does have a private and independent side to his nature), by being forthcoming, he will benefit from the advice and encouragement he is given. There may be a considerable gap of years between him and more senior relations, but if he is open and communicative he can draw on their experience and be reassured by their support and affection for him.

Another rewarding aspect of the year will concern the Earth Snake's personal interests. Not only will he enjoy the satisfaction and sometimes good social element these can bring but may wish to build on what he knows and promote his talents. When putting an idea forward, he would do well to listen closely to any feedback he may be given. The Ox year can be instructive.

There will be travel opportunities for many Earth Snakes over the year and while they will often be excited at the prospect of going away, they would do well to save up in advance and check that all their documentation is in order. That way, mistakes or delays are less likely to occur and the Earth Snake will get far more from his travels.

For Earth Snakes in education this can be an important year, with their results often having a bearing on their future. Although their workload will sometimes be daunting and they may feel uncertain about some aspects of their course, by focusing on what needs to be done and remaining disciplined, many will be delighted with what they achieve. This is a year for perseverance and dedication. If at any time the Earth Snake has doubts or problems, it is important that he talks to others, whether tutors, relations or close friends. Support *is* there for him and this is no time to withdraw into himself or keep concerns to himself. Generally, though, for Earth Snakes in education the Ox year can be significant and give them the skills and qualifications they need to progress, either now or in following years.

For Earth Snakes in work, the Ox year can give them a good chance to build on their experience. Although some may feel they are not making the most of their potential, they will find the year bringing some interesting developments. Sometimes openings could arise in their existing place of work as colleagues move on or changes create new positions. Whenever a suitable opportunity arises, if the

Earth Snake puts himself forward and shows his desire to learn and progress, he will often be given the chance and encouragement he needs. In the Ox year, effort and willingness will be noticed and rewarded.

This also applies to Earth Snakes seeking work or who decide to change the nature of what they do. Their quest will require determination and initiative, but by being prepared to persevere and having faith in themselves, they will find openings *will* arise. In some cases the Earth Snake would do well to find out more about the duties involved in a particular job and so be better informed at interview. The Ox year is not one for swift developments and progress will need to be worked for, but what is achieved can often be significant in the longer term. April to mid-July and October could see some good opportunities.

Throughout the Ox year, however, the Earth Snake will need to manage his finances with considerable care. With an active social life, possible travel, the items he may want to buy and the interests he may pursue, there will often be a great temptation to spend, but the Earth Snake does need to be wary about too much impulse buying or too many unnecessary risks. If he is to do all he wants, he needs to exercise care and discipline.

Overall, the Earth Snake will be satisfied with how the Ox year develops, and the progress he makes and experience and qualifications he gains can have an important bearing on following years. The Ox year may sometimes be slow moving, but its significance can be considerable. And with a widening social circle and the satisfaction that personal interests can bring, there will be a lot for the Earth Snake to enjoy.

Be patient. You may be keen to race ahead, but this is a year for taking one step at a time. Results will need to be worked for, but by building up your experience and concentrating on what you have to do, you can prepare for the more substantial success you are soon to enjoy.

FAMOUS SNAKES

Muhammad Ali, Tim Allen, Ann-Margret, Lord Baden-Powell, Kim Basinger, Ben Bernanke, Björk, Tony Blair, Michael Bloomberg, Michael Bolton, Johannes Brahms, Pierce Brosnan, Casanova, Chubby Checker, Jackie Collins, Tom Conti, Alistair Darling, Cecil B. de Mille, Bob Dylan, Sir Edward Elgar, Sir Alex Ferguson, Sir Alexander Fleming, Mahatma Gandhi, Greta Garbo, Art Garfunkel, J. Paul Getty, Dizzy Gillespie, W. E. Gladstone, Johann Wolfgang von Goethe, Princess Grace of Monaco, Stephen Hawking, Audrey Hepburn, Jack Higgins, Liz Hurley, James Joyce, Stacy Keach, Ronan Keating, J. F. Kennedy, Carole King, Cyndi Lauper, Courtney Love, Mao Tse Tung, Chris Martin, Henri Matisse, Dmitri Medvedev, David Miliband, Robert Mitchum, Piers Morgan, Alfred Nobel, Mike Oldfield, Jacqueline Onassis, Pablo Picasso, Mary Pickford, Brad Pitt, Daniel Radcliffe, Franklin D. Roosevelt, Mickey Rourke, J. K. Rowling, Jean Paul Sartre, Franz Schubert, Shakira, Charlie Sheen, Brooke Shields, Paul Simon, Delia Smith, Ben Stiller, Madame Tussaud, Shania Twain, Dionne Warwick, Charlie Watts, Ruby Wax, Kanye West, Oprah Winfrey, Victoria Wood, Virginia Woolf.

11 FEBRUARY 1918 ～ 31 JANUARY 1919   *Earth Horse*

30 JANUARY 1930 ～ 16 FEBRUARY 1931   *Metal Horse*

15 FEBRUARY 1942 ～ 4 FEBRUARY 1943   *Water Horse*

3 FEBRUARY 1954 ～ 23 JANUARY 1955   *Wood Horse*

21 JANUARY 1966 ～ 8 FEBRUARY 1967   *Fire Horse*

7 FEBRUARY 1978 ～ 27 JANUARY 1979   *Earth Horse*

27 JANUARY 1990 ～ 14 FEBRUARY 1991   *Metal Horse*

12 FEBRUARY 2002 ～ 31 JANUARY 2003   *Water Horse*

THE

HORSE

THE PERSONALITY OF THE HORSE

There are many worn paths,
but the most rewarding
is the one you decide on
and forge yourself.

The Horse is born under the signs of elegance and ardour. He has a most engaging and charming manner and is usually very popular. He loves meeting people and likes attending parties and other large social gatherings.

The Horse is a lively character and enjoys being the centre of attention. He has many leadership qualities and is much admired for his honest and straightforward manner. He is an eloquent and persuasive speaker and has a great love of discussion and debate. He also has a particularly agile mind and can assimilate facts remarkably quickly.

He does, however, have a fiery temper and although his outbursts are usually short lived, he can often say things that he will later regret. He is also not particularly good at keeping secrets.

The Horse has many interests and involves himself in a wide variety of activities. He can, however, get involved in so much that he can often waste his energies on projects that he never has time to complete. He also has a tendency to change his interests rather frequently and will often get caught up in the latest craze or 'in thing' until something more exciting turns up.

The Horse also likes to have a certain amount of freedom and independence. He hates being bound by petty rules and regulations and as far as possible likes to feel that he is answerable to no one but himself. But despite this spirit of freedom, he still likes to have the support and encouragement of others in his various enterprises.

Due to his many talents and likeable nature, the Horse will often go far in life. He enjoys challenges and is a methodical and tireless worker. However, should things go against him and he fail in any of his enterprises, it will take a long time for him to recover and pick up the pieces again. Success to the Horse means everything. To fail is a disaster and a humiliation.

The Horse likes to have variety in his life and he will try his hand at many different things before he settles down to one particular job. Even then, he will probably remain alert to see whether there are any better opportunities for him to take up. He has a restless nature and can easily get bored. He does, however, excel in any position that allows him sufficient freedom to act on his own initiative or brings him into contact with a lot of people.

Although the Horse is not particularly bothered about accumulating great wealth, he handles his finances with care and will rarely experience any serious financial problems.

The Horse also enjoys travel and loves visiting new and faraway places. At some stage during his life he will be tempted to live abroad for a short period of time and due to his adaptable nature he will find that he will fit in well wherever he goes.

The Horse pays a great deal of attention to his appearance and usually likes to wear smart, colourful and rather distinctive clothes. He is very attractive to others and will often have many romances before he settles down. He is loyal and protective to his partner, but despite his family commitments he still likes to retain a certain measure of independence and have the freedom to carry on with his own interests and hobbies. He will find that he is especially well suited to those born under the signs of the Tiger, Goat, Rooster and Dog. He can also get on well with the Rabbit, Dragon, Snake, Pig and another Horse, but he will find the Ox too serious and intolerant for his liking. The Horse will also have difficulty in getting on with the Monkey and the Rat – the Monkey is very inquisitive and the Rat seeks security, and both will resent the Horse's rather independent ways.

The female Horse is usually most attractive and has a friendly, outgoing personality. She is highly intelligent, has many interests and is alert to everything that is going on around her. She particularly enjoys outdoor pursuits and often likes to take part in sport and keep-fit activities. She also enjoys travel, literature and the arts, and is a very good conversationalist.

Although the Horse can be stubborn and rather self centred, he does have a considerate nature and is often willing to help others. He has a good sense of humour and will usually make a favourable impression wherever he goes. Provided he can curb his slightly restless nature and keep tight control over his temper, he will go through life making friends, taking part in a multitude of different activities and generally achieving many of his objectives. His life will rarely be dull.

THE FIVE DIFFERENT TYPES
OF HORSE

In addition to the 12 signs of the Chinese zodiac there are five elements and these have a strengthening or moderating influence on the signs. The effects of the five elements on the Horse are described below, together with the years in which the elements were exercising their influence. Therefore those Horses born in 1930 and 1990 are Metal Horses, those born in 1942 and 2002 are Water Horses, and so on.

Metal Horse: 1930, 1990
This Horse is bold, confident and forthright. He is ambitious and a great innovator. He loves challenges and takes great delight in sorting out complicated problems. He likes to have a certain amount of independence and resents any outside interference in his affairs. He has charm and a certain charisma, but he can also be very stubborn and rather impulsive. He usually has many friends and enjoys an active social life.

Water Horse: 1942, 2002
The Water Horse has a friendly nature and a good sense of humour and is able to talk intelligently on a wide range of topics. He is astute in business matters and quick to take advantage of any opportunities that arise. He does,

however, have a tendency to get easily distracted and can change his interests – and indeed his mind – rather frequently, and this can often work to his detriment. He is nevertheless very talented and can often go far in life. He pays a great deal of attention to his appearance and is usually smart and well turned out. He loves to travel and also enjoys sport and other outdoor activities.

Wood Horse: 1954

The Wood Horse has a most agreeable and amiable nature. He communicates well with others and is able to talk intelligently on many different subjects. He is a hard and conscientious worker and is held in high esteem by his friends and colleagues. His opinions are often sought and, given his imaginative nature, he can often come up with some very original and practical ideas. He is usually widely read and likes to lead a busy social life. He can also be most generous and often holds high moral views.

Fire Horse: 1966

The element of Fire combined with the temperament of the Horse creates one of the most powerful forces in the Chinese zodiac. The Fire Horse is destined to lead an exciting and eventful life and to make his mark in his chosen profession. He has a forceful personality and his intelligence and resolute manner bring him the support and admiration of many. He loves action and excitement and his life will rarely be quiet. He can, however, be rather blunt and forthright in his views and does not take kindly to interference in his own affairs or to obeying orders. He is a flamboyant character, has a good sense of humour and will lead a very active social life.

Earth Horse: 1918, 1978

This Horse is considerate and caring. He is more cautious than some of the other types of Horse, but is wise, perceptive and extremely capable. Although he can be rather indecisive at times, he has considerable business acumen and is very astute in financial matters. He has a quiet, friendly nature and is well thought of by his family and friends.

PROSPECTS FOR THE HORSE IN 2009

The Year of the Rat (7 February 2008 to 25 January 2009) is not an easy one for the Horse and in the remaining months he will need to take careful note of what is going on around him. This is not a time when he can afford to be too independent in approach.

In his work the Horse should concentrate on his duties and the tasks that need to be done. He should also aim to work closely with colleagues and be an active part of any team. With combined effort, far more can be accomplished, and the Horse can also enhance his own reputation. Opportunities for progress may be limited in Rat years, but September and October could see some possibilities for those Horses wanting change or seeking work.

In financial matters the Horse needs to be alert and vigilant at this time. He would also do well to watch his spending and make early provision for some of the more substantial purchases he may have in mind.

In view of the mixed aspects of the Rat year, the Horse will often be grateful for the support of his family and friends, and whenever he has concerns or is under pressure, he will find it well worth talking to others. As the year draws to a close there will, though, be some fine social occasions for him to enjoy, with October and December being active months. The Horse's domestic life will also see an increase in activity at this time and by being fully involved, he will often derive a lot of pleasure from it and will particularly delight in the opportunity to meet up with some people he does not often see.

Parts of the Rat year will have been trying for the Horse, but during it he will have learned a great deal and he will be able to build on this in 2009.

The Year of the Ox begins on 26 January and is a much improved one for the Horse. This is a year that favours effort and hard work, two qualities very central to the Horse personality, and he can look forward to encouraging developments.

As the Ox year starts the Horse should try to draw a line under any disappointments of the last 12 months. This year offers far brighter prospects and is not a time for the Horse to feel fettered by plans which may not have gone his way. He should look forward rather than back and set about his activities with renewed determination. For the keen and active, this can be a *very* rewarding year.

The aspects are especially favourable in the Horse's work, with many Horses being able to make significant progress. In some cases, they will find themselves excellently placed when senior colleagues move on and promotion possibilities open up or there are chances to use their skills in other ways. Although many Horses may be nursing disappointments from the Rat year, it will have given them excellent experience which can now be to their benefit. The Ox year is one for progress and by putting themselves forward when they see suitable openings, many Horses will make great headway. Late January, February, May and September could see some especially good opportunities.

Another interesting feature of the year will be the chance the Horse will have to adapt and use his skills and if he is offered any form of training or has the chance to vary his role in some way, he should take full advantage of it. Positive action and a willingness to broaden his skills can result in him doing more in his current situation as well as strengthening his prospects for the future.

This also applies to those Horses seeking work. While some may have become disheartened recently, the Ox year holds greater opportunity. If these Horses are eligible for training or refresher courses, they should take these up, as well as draw on the advice and information that is available to them. With perseverance, many will get the opportunity they have been wanting for some time. Work-wise, the Ox year is an encouraging one for the Horse and will give him the chance to make more of his talents.

The Horse's progress at work will also lead to an increase in income. Financially, this can be an improved year. To benefit, though, the Horse does need to manage his situation well and set sums aside for specific plans and requirements as well as consider reducing any borrowings. With care and control, however, many Horses can improve their financial situation over the year as well as appreciate the ways in which they use their money.

One of these may well be travel, as the Ox year will contain some interesting travel opportunities. If there is a particular destination the Horse would like to visit, he sees an offer that appeals to him or receives an invitation to stay with others, he should follow it up. Some Horses will also spend some time visiting places of interest in their area. Both travelling further afield and going out locally will give many Horses considerable pleasure over the year.

As always, the Horse will also value his social life and this can lead to some interesting times over the year. February, June, August and December could see the most social activity. However, when in company the Horse does need to be attentive and aware of the views and feelings of others. Although he is usually a good conversationalist, a *faux pas* or ill-judged comment could cause problems and he does need to be on his mettle. Similarly, for Horses enjoying romance or who find romance in 2009, this is a year for care and attentiveness to the feelings of others.

This also applies to the Horse's domestic life. With good communication and regular consultation over arrangements, domestic life can go well, but should the Horse decide to go his own way too often, disagreements could arise. This is a year when he does need to pay close attention to the views of others.

With the Horse's practical nature, he may well have plans that he is keen to carry out on his home or garden over the year. Here again, though, he does need to liaise with others. With combined effort, far more can be accomplished. Also, the Horse should make the most of the free time he has. Whether he is sharing interests with his loved ones or going out and visiting local attractions, he can find the Ox year bringing some very special times.

Overall, the Year of the Ox holds better prospects for the Horse and his efforts and commitment will be recognized and rewarded. He could enjoy the travel opportunities that arise as well as all the activity his domestic and social life can bring. Throughout the year he does need to listen to others and be aware of their views. Overall, though, he will have the chance to make more of himself.

The Metal Horse

This is a year of exciting potential for the Metal Horse, but also one for proceeding at a steady pace. While, in true Horse style, the Metal Horse may be eager for his hopes and plans to be realized as quickly as possible, the Ox year favours patience and persistence. A lot can be achieved in 2009, but results *do* need to be worked for.

For many Metal Horses, the Ox year will bring change. This could include starting a new academic course or job as well as, for some, a move to a new area. This will be an eventful year and will give the Metal Horse the chance to learn a lot about himself as well as find new strengths. Also, while he has an independent side to his nature, during the year he will have the chance to meet others who are in a similar position to his own and will find this reassuring. Whenever he has any concerns or anxieties, he should remember that he is not alone.

For Metal Horses who are in education, this can be an interesting year. As they get to study particular subjects in greater detail as well as learn new skills, they will often feel they are making real progress and will enjoy the challenge before them. The Ox year will also give many Metal Horses the chance to discover new talents which they will be keen to develop. This is a year of opportunity for them, although it is still a time to put in the effort and concentrate on what needs to be done.

For Metal Horses in work or seeking it, the Ox year will be important. For those already in a job there will often be the chance to move on to new duties as well as learn about different aspects of their work. Although the Metal Horse may find some of his work routine, by showing commitment and making the most of his situation, he will find his efforts will be recognized and he may be given the chance to extend his role. Late January to early March, May and September could see some interesting work developments, but whenever the Metal Horse sees a chance to learn more, he should put himself forward. His effort and commitment will bring results.

For those Metal Horses seeking work the Ox year can also see some important developments. However, rather than being too restrictive about the type of positions they are considering, these Metal Horses should look further afield. This way there will not only be more possibilities but also more chance to obtain a base to start from. Even if this is not ideal, it will provide them with some experience that they can build on later. In their quest, these Metal Horses should make full use of the advice that is available to them. Consulting employment agencies or obtaining information from organizations could alert them to possibilities worth considering. Work-wise, the Ox year is an encouraging one and if he makes the effort, the Metal Horse can be well rewarded.

He will fare reasonably well as far as finance is concerned this year, though he does need manage his money well and set sufficient aside to cover his obligations as well as any more ambitious plans he may have. With an often lively social life and the purchases he will be keen to make, he does need to be wary of too much extravagance or impulse buying. This is a year for sensible control over his purse-strings.

Another feature of the year is that there could be some good travel opportunities. If the Metal Horse does go away, however, he should make early and ample provision for it in his budget as well as ensure that he has all he may require. Although he is usually thorough, any extra attention he can give to his preparation can prevent problems or delays later on as well as allow him to do more while away.

The Metal Horse can also look forward to a full and active social life, and in view of the changes the Ox year can bring, there will be plenty of opportunities to meet new people and some important new friendships can be made. For some Metal Horses there could also be the possibility of romance, but the path of true love does not always run smoothly and rather than build up high expectations in the early stages of any relationship, these Metal Horses would do well to let a romance develop in its own time. February, June, August to mid-September and December could see the most social activity, but the Metal Horse will nearly always have something to look forward to.

He will also be grateful for the support and assistance he is given by his family, and whenever he has important decisions to make or has any concerns or worries, he does need to be forthcoming. His relations may be able to assist in ways he had not anticipated and sometimes just talking can clarify his best course of action in his own mind.

With the aspects concerning the Metal Horse's own development being so positive this year, he would also do well to spend time on his interests and look at ways in which he can develop certain skills. Whether he continues with his existing interests or is tempted to take up something new, he can often derive considerable pleasure from his activities. For some Metal Horses, their interests could also open up other possibilities. The emphasis of the Ox year is very much on personal discovery and development.

Overall, the aspects are promising for the Metal Horse, but to benefit he does need to make the most of the opportunities that come his way. With commitment, this can be a rewarding, enjoyable and constructive year.

TIP FOR THE YEAR
Do consult others. You can gain so much from their advice and support. Also, while you may like to see quick results, remember this can be a slow-moving year and your plans may take some time to be realized. Do bear this in mind and be prepared to show some patience.

The Water Horse
With his wide interests, keen nature and ability to use his time and opportunities well, the Water Horse will have a

lot in his favour this year. And a lot will go well for him. He will also benefit from the support of those around him and by involving others in his plans, he will often be able to do a lot more than anticipated. This is a year when communication, co-operation and a pooling of ideas will be far more effective than going it alone.

During the year many Water Horses will take considerable pleasure in making improvements to their home. Whether they are buying new equipment or furnishings or adding new comforts, by taking their time and considering the choices available, they will often appreciate what they accomplish. However, if any practical undertakings involve strenuous activity, the Water Horse does need to take care and call in a professional if necessary. He may be keen, but this is no year to take risks.

In addition to any enhancements the Water Horse may make to his home, he can look forward to some pleasing occasions with his loved ones. Interests and activities that can be shared can mean a great deal to him and many Water Horses will also delight in the success enjoyed by a close relation. The Water Horse's home and family life does mean a lot to him and some parts of 2009 will turn out to be very special.

However, while the year will see many good times, no year is ever free of problems and this one will be no exception. Should any difference of opinion arise, the Water Horse would do well to deal with it before it has a chance to escalate. Here a willingness to discuss matters and a more accommodating approach may help.

The Ox year will bring some good travel opportunities and many Water Horses could be tempted by offers they see and take full advantage of their chances to go away, including arranging some trips on the spur of the moment. In addition local attractions will appeal to many Water Horses and some will particularly enjoy visits to nearby places as well as to events and exhibitions in their vicinity.

The Ox year will also bring some interesting social opportunities. Often the Water Horse's travels will have a pleasing social element and his interests will frequently bring him into contact with others. Any Water Horse who would welcome company or a more meaningful social life will find that joining others at a social group or perhaps enrolling on an interest-related course would be worth considering. February, June, August to mid-September and December could see the most social activity.

The Water Horse's financial prospects are also encouraging and he may benefit from a gift, bonus or maturing policy. However, to make the most of his resources, he should give careful thought to the purchases he wants to make as well as take his time when making decisions. This way his choices will not only be more suitable but often made on more favourable terms. The key to so much in the Ox year is to proceed steadily and carefully. The Water Horse also needs to be thorough when dealing with financial correspondence and to make sure important documents and policies are maintained and kept carefully. Where bureaucracy is concerned, this is a year for vigilance.

On a positive note, the Ox year could have some pleasant surprises in store and if the Water Horse sees a competition that interests him, especially if it is related to a skill or some specialist knowledge he has, he would do well to enter it. For some, the Ox year can be very lucky.

Generally, this can be a satisfying year for the Water Horse and by involving others in his plans, he can accomplish a great deal. He should also seize the opportunities that come his way. By making the most of them, he will be pleased with how the year develops.

TIP FOR THE YEAR
Do talk to others and listen to what they have to say. With their support, you can do so much more. Also, consider visiting places of local interest and making the most of local amenities. This could lead to finding places and activities that you enjoy and that are not too far away!

The Wood Horse
This is a year of considerable promise for the Wood Horse and in view of the sometimes muted progress he may have experienced in the Rat year, he will be more determined than ever to make more of the next 12 months. And as a result, far more can open up for him.

The aspects are particularly encouraging as far as the Wood Horse's work prospects are concerned and with the considerable experience and reputation he has built up, he will often be in a good position to take advantage of the opportunities the year will bring. Often these will arise in his present place of work, with the Wood Horse being well placed to secure promotion or to take on greater responsibilities. Although this can involve a considerable step up and there will be a lot for the Wood Horse to learn, he will welcome the opportunity to use his skills in other ways and will feel more motivated than he has for some time.

One of the key features of the Ox year is that it is a time for personal *and* career development.

For those Wood Horses who feel they have achieved all they can in their present position and perhaps feel staid, as well as those seeking work, the Ox year can again bring important developments. By actively looking for new positions and widening the scope of what they are prepared to consider, they could see some interesting possibilities opening up. Sometimes these could arise in an almost fortuitous way, perhaps from a chance comment, something they may read or a suggestion made following a rejection, but by being aware and determined, many of these Wood Horses can secure a position that can give their career the boost they have been wanting for some time. Late January to early March, May and September could contain some interesting opportunities.

With the progressive aspects of the Ox year many Wood Horses will also be keen to develop certain interests they have. Whether this involves additional practice, learning new skills or undertaking some studying, by moving forward these Wood Horses will derive a lot of satisfaction from what they do. Any Wood Horses who have let their interests slip would do well to rectify this over the year, either by making time for activities they enjoy or taking up something new. They will find that personal interests and recreational activities can bring an importance balance to their lifestyle.

The Ox year can also bring some interesting travel opportunities and all Wood Horses should try to go away at some time during the year. A break and change of scene can be beneficial, and by choosing his destination well, and perhaps combining it with a personal interest, the Wood Horse will often delight in his travels. Local outings could also go well and be appreciated by everyone involved.

The year is also positively aspected as far as financial matters are concerned and in addition to an increase in income, many Wood Horses could benefit from an additional sum. To make the most of any upturn, the Wood Horse would do well to plan more expensive purchases in advance, as well as keep track of his spending. By managing his situation carefully he will not only make better decisions but also be able to do more with his money. However, while the financial aspects may be favourable, the Wood Horse should not be dilatory in dealing with paperwork. To delay returning financially related forms or to give scant attention to them could be to his detriment. Wood Horses, take careful note and do be thorough.

The Wood Horse also needs be attentive as far as his relations with others are concerned. With a sometimes heavy workload and possibly a new working routine to adapt to, there will be times when he becomes preoccupied with his own affairs. Also, when under pressure, his patience could sometimes wear thin. In the Ox year he does need to remain aware of this and when he is tired or tense he should be open about it so that others can understand and perhaps assist in some way. Similarly, if he has concerns over any domestic matter or the activities of another person, by being forthcoming he can help to ease problems or tensions and find solutions. Good communication can make an important difference over the year.

Home projects and shared interests can also mean a great deal and with the progress the Wood Horse or a loved one makes over the year, there could be some good reasons to celebrate. Home life can go well for the Wood Horse, but it *is* a case of balancing out commitments and remaining aware of the feelings of those around him.

The Ox year will also give the Wood Horse some excellent opportunities to meet others. In some cases he will have the chance to make new contacts through changes in his work or the interests he pursues, and with his eloquent and genial manner, he will impress many. While, due to other pressures, he may be selective in the social occasions he attends this year, by taking up invitations and going to events that appeal to him, he will benefit from the chance to relax and unwind. February, June, August and December could see the most social activity.

Generally, this is an encouraging year for the Wood Horse. Whether advancing his career or enjoying existing or new interests, he will find this an excellent time for personal development. His domestic and social life can also bring him much pleasure, but to truly benefit from the support others can give he does need be forthcoming, receptive and aware. Overall, a year of interesting developments.

TIP FOR THE YEAR
Although keen to make the most of yourself and the good opportunities the Ox year can bring, you must make sure you keep your lifestyle in balance. Too much attention in one area can start to bring problems in another. Do remain aware of this. Quality time with loved ones as well as a greater openness about your thoughts and concerns will help.

The Fire Horse

Well begun is half done runs the Chinese proverb, and this will hold good for Fire Horse this year. With careful thought and preparation, a lot can go in his favour, but should he rush or be inattentive, problems could arise. This is a year that rewards good planning and focus.

The aspects are especially encouraging as far as the Fire Horse's work prospects are concerned. Sometimes, as more senior personnel move on, the Fire Horse will be well positioned for promotion or will have the chance to take on a more specialist role or further his duties in some way. The Ox year does favour progress and many Fire Horses will be able to make more of their skills and knowledge during it.

For Fire Horses who feel openings are limited with their current employer and would welcome a change, as well as those seeking work, again the Ox year can be a pivotal time. By giving careful thought to what they would now like to do and seeking guidance from those with the information and expertise to advise, many could be alerted to new possibilities to consider. The Ox year can open some interesting doors. However, whether the Fire Horse takes on a position elsewhere or moves forward where he is, the proverb *well begun is half done* is very applicable. When taking on new duties, the Fire Horse does need to allow time to familiarize himself with the various aspects of his work and concentrate on what he has to do. Getting his new role off to a solid start will help him in the weeks and months ahead. And such is the nature of the year that one step forward can be the prelude to others, either later this year or next. This is very much a time when effort and commitment will be recognized and rewarded.

Another positive aspect of the year will be the good working relations the Fire Horse is likely to enjoy. Not only should he make the most of his chances to network and get himself better known, particularly when taking on a new role, but by working as part of a team he will get to accomplish more. He could also benefit from the support his colleagues are willing to give. Sometimes he may not always be aware of this, as they may put in private recommendations on his behalf, but with his skills, determination and reputation, he is likely to have a lot in his favour over the year.

His financial prospects are also encouraging. Many Fire Horses will enjoy a rise in income and some will also be able to supplement their earnings through an interest or skill they have. However, while this can be an improved year financially, the Fire Horse does need to remain disciplined in his spending and make allowance for his more substantial outgoings. It would also be worth considering using any financial upturn to reduce his borrowings or add to his savings. With care and control, many Fire Horses can see an improvement in their financial situation over the year as well as appreciate what they are able to do with their money. However, as with all Horses in the Ox year, financial paperwork does need careful attention and should the Fire Horse delay or be dilatory in dealing with it, problems or extra expense could result. Fire Horses, take note.

With the Fire Horse's enquiring and adventurous nature he usually enjoys travel and the Ox year will bring some excellent chances to go away as well as visit new areas locally. A holiday this year could be one of the best he has had for a long time.

Although the Fire Horse often leads an active lifestyle, it is also important that he gives some consideration to his well-being over the year. This includes making sure he has sufficient exercise and a healthy and well-balanced diet. If he feels some modifications could help, he should seek medical guidance.

Despite the busy nature of the year, it is also important that he allows time to spend on activities he enjoys and that help him relax. Also, if he receives invitations to go out or hears of events that he would like to attend, he should see what can be arranged. His social life can do him a lot of good. February, June, August and mid-November to December could see the most social activity.

The Fire Horse's domestic life will also be fairly active over the year and he will do a lot to help and advise both younger and more senior relations. Although sometimes his words may not be what others want to hear, his desire to help will be recognized and valued. In addition to the assistance he will give to others, he will be pleased with how certain plans and domestic activities move forward. Again, *well begun is half done*, and if joint activities and any more substantial purchases are carefully planned, everyone can benefit. Sharing domestic activities will also help to make home life all the more rewarding and the Ox year will bring some special times.

Overall, the Year of the Ox offers considerable scope for the Fire Horse and by looking to make progress, he can do well. Throughout the year he does need to be receptive to what others suggest, but with a willingness to act and to make the most of his opportunities, he can make this a fine year.

TIP FOR THE YEAR

This is a favourable time and if you are willing to put yourself forward, a lot can open up for you. Do be thorough, determined *and* prepared. This is a year for action.

The Earth Horse

This will be an important year for the Earth Horse, allowing him to make good progress as well as enjoy some pleasing developments in his personal life. This is very much a year for moving forward and the Earth Horse will feel more in control of his destiny than he has for some time.

In his domestic life the Ox year can bring some key developments, including a possible addition to the family. The Earth Horse will also be in demand. Whether assisting his partner, tending to the needs of babies or children or helping more senior relations, there will be many calls on his time and attention over the year. If he does what he can and remains aware of the views of others, his assistance will often be of more value than he may realize.

However, while the year will see a lot of activity, this can be a special time and the Earth Horse will enjoy tackling projects with his loved ones. He does, though, need to allow ample time for practical undertakings as well as avoid starting too much at once. Any Earth Horses who decide to move this year need to allow time to find suitable accommodation as well as to complete the moving process. Although the Earth Horse may be keen to move on, the Ox year is one that favours a steady and careful approach.

The Earth Horse will value the good friends he has over the year and will not only be glad to meet up and talk but also to share interests. If he receives any invitations, particularly if they are connected with his work or interests, he should make the most of them. Some of the people he meets now could be helpful to him in this and following years. February, June, August and December could see the most social activity. However, while the Earth Horse's social life can bring much pleasure and benefit, as with all Horses this year he does need to remain attentive when in company. A *faux pas* could cause problems and care is required.

In view of the busy nature of the year it is also important that the Earth Horse gives some consideration to his well-being. Being constantly busy in the day as well as possibly coping with disturbed nights could take its toll. To help, the Earth Horse should not only make sure he takes the time to rest and enjoy his personal interests but also has a well-balanced diet. Extra attention to his lifestyle can make an important difference. Earth Horses, do take note.

The aspects are encouraging as far as the Earth Horse's work prospects are concerned and there will be some excellent opportunities to make progress. For Earth Horses who are frustrated with their present situation and would like to use their skills in other ways, this is a year to seize the initiative. With determination and a willingness to seek out possibilities, they can find significant doors opening for them. They can be helped by the support of colleagues and other contacts, and keeping themselves informed of developments can be another contributing factor in their progress.

For Earth Horses who are seeking work or want to make a more major change, the Ox year can also bring significant opportunities. To benefit, though, these Earth Horses do need to keep alert, make enquiries and act smartly when opportunities arise. They also need to allow time for their applications to be considered and processed. The emphasis this year is on patience and persistence. Late January, February, May and September could see some encouraging developments.

The progress the Earth Horse makes in his work can also lead to a rise in income and financially this can be an improved year. By budgeting carefully and making allowances for their commitments and plans, many Earth Horses will be pleased with how they fare. The Earth Horse does need to deal with financial paperwork carefully, however, and if taking on any new agreement, check the obligations and question anything that may be unclear. This is a year for thoroughness and control.

Overall, the Earth Horse can fare well in the Ox year and enjoy some special moments in his family and social life. Although this may be a busy and sometimes demanding time, there will be a lot to appreciate. Work aspects are also encouraging and many Earth Horses will be given the chance to make important advances in their career. This is an active year which will bring some exciting possibilities.

TIP FOR THE YEAR

With so many demands on your time, keep well organized and draw on the assistance of others. Also, try to keep your lifestyle in balance. Allow some time for yourself and your own interests and to appreciate all you have around you.

FAMOUS HORSES

Roman Abramovich, Neil Armstrong, Rowan Atkinson, José Manuel Barroso, Samuel Beckett, Ingmar Bergman, Leonard Bernstein, Helena Bonham Carter, James Blunt, David Cameron, James Cameron, Jackie Chan, Ray Charles, Chopin, Sir Sean Connery, Billy Connolly, Catherine Cookson, Elvis Costello, Kevin Costner, Cindy Crawford, Michael Crichton, James Dean, Clint Eastwood, Thomas Alva Edison, Harrison Ford, Aretha Franklin, Bob Geldof, Samuel Goldwyn, Billy Graham, Gene Hackman, Rolf Harris, Rita Hayworth, Jimi Hendrix, Janet Jackson, Calvin Klein, Lemar, Lenin, Annie Lennox, Desmond Lynam, Sir Paul McCartney, Nelson Mandela, Angela Merkel, Michael Moore, Ben Murphy, Sir Isaac Newton, Louis Pasteur, Katie Price (Jordan), Lou Reed, Rembrandt, Ruth Rendell, Jean Renoir, Condoleezza Rice, Theodore Roosevelt, Helena Rubenstein, David Schwimmer, Alexander Solzhenitsyn, Barbra Streisand, Kiefer Sutherland, Patrick Swayze, John Travolta, Kathleen Turner, Vivaldi, Robert Wagner, Denzil Washington, Billy Wilder, Andy Williams, Brian Wilson, the Duke of Windsor.

13 FEBRUARY 1907 ⌇ 1 FEBRUARY 1908		*Fire Goat*
1 FEBRUARY 1919 ⌇ 19 FEBRUARY 1920		*Earth Goat*
17 FEBRUARY 1931 ⌇ 5 FEBRUARY 1932		*Metal Goat*
5 FEBRUARY 1943 ⌇ 24 JANUARY 1944		*Water Goat*
24 JANUARY 1955 ⌇ 11 FEBRUARY 1956		*Wood Goat*
9 FEBRUARY 1967 ⌇ 29 JANUARY 1968		*Fire Goat*
28 JANUARY 1979 ⌇ 15 FEBRUARY 1980		*Earth Goat*
15 FEBRUARY 1991 ⌇ 3 FEBRUARY 1992		*Metal Goat*
1 FEBRUARY 2003 ⌇ 21 JANUARY 2004		*Water Goat*

THE
GOAT

THE PERSONALITY OF THE GOAT

Amid the complexities of life,
it is the ability to appreciate that is so special.

The Goat is born under the sign of art. He is imaginative, creative and has a good appreciation of the finer things in life. He has an easy going nature and prefers to live in a relaxed and pressure free environment. He hates any sort of discord or unpleasantness and does not like to be bound by a strict routine or rigid timetable. He is not one to be hurried against his will, but despite his seemingly relaxed approach to life, he is something of a perfectionist and when he starts work on a project he is certain to give his best.

The Goat usually prefers to work in a team rather than on his own. He likes to have the support and encouragement of others and if left to deal with matters on his own he can get very worried and tend to view things rather pessimistically. Wherever possible he will leave major decision making to others while he concentrates on his own pursuits. If, however, he feels particularly strongly about a certain matter or has to defend his position in any way, he will act with great fortitude and precision.

The Goat has a very persuasive nature and often uses his considerable charm to get his own way. He can, however, be rather hesitant about letting his true feelings be known and if he were prepared to be more forthright he would do much better as a result.

The Goat tends to have a quiet, somewhat reserved nature, but when he is in company he likes he can often become the centre of attention. He can be highly amusing, a marvellous host at parties and a superb entertainer. Whenever the spotlight falls on him, his adrenaline starts to flow and he can be assured of giving a sparkling performance, particularly if he is allowed to use his creative skills in any way.

Of all the signs in the Chinese zodiac, the Goat is probably the most gifted artistically. Whether it is in the theatre, literature, music or art, he is certain to make a lasting impression. He is a born creator and is rarely happier than when occupied in some artistic pursuit. But even in this the Goat does well to work with others rather than on his own. He needs inspiration and a guiding influence, but when he has found his true *métier*, he can often receive widespread acclaim and recognition.

In addition to his liking for the arts, the Goat is usually quite religious and often has a deep interest in nature, animals and the countryside. He is also fairly athletic and there are many Goats who have excelled in some form of sporting activity or who have a great interest in sport.

Although the Goat is not particularly materialistic or concerned about finance, he will find that he will usually be lucky in financial matters and will rarely be short of the necessary funds to tide himself over. He is, however, rather self-indulgent and tends to spend his money as soon as he receives it rather than make provision for the future.

The Goat usually leaves home when he is young but he will always maintain strong links with his parents and the other members of his family. He is also rather nostalgic and is well known for keeping mementoes of his childhood and souvenirs of places that he has visited. His home will not be particularly tidy, but he knows where everything is and it will be scrupulously clean.

Affairs of the heart are particularly important to the Goat and he will often have many romances before he finally settles down. Although he is fairly adaptable, he prefers to live in a secure and stable environment and he will find that he is best suited to those born under the signs of the Tiger, Horse, Monkey, Pig and Rabbit. He can also establish a good relationship with the Dragon, Snake, Rooster and another Goat, but he may find the Ox and Dog a little too serious for his liking. Neither will he care particularly for the Rat's rather thrifty ways.

The female Goat devotes all her time and energy to the needs of her family. She has excellent taste in home furnishings and often uses her considerable artistic skills to make clothes for herself and her children. She takes great care over her appearance and can be most attractive to others. Although she is not the most organized of people, her engaging manner and delightful sense of humour create a favourable impression wherever she goes. She is also a good cook and usually derives much pleasure from gardening and outdoor pursuits.

The Goat can win friends easily and people generally feel relaxed in his company. He has a kind and understanding nature and although he can occasionally be stubborn, he can, with the right support and encouragement, live a happy and very satisfying life. And the more he can use his creative skills, the happier he will be.

THE FIVE DIFFERENT TYPES OF GOAT

In addition to the 12 signs of the Chinese zodiac there are five elements and these have a strengthening or moderating influence on the signs. The effects of the five elements on the Goat are described below, together with the years in which the elements were exercising their influence. Therefore those Goats born in 1931 and 1991 are Metal Goats, those born in 1943 and 2003 are Water Goats, and so on.

Metal Goat: 1931, 1991
This Goat is thorough and conscientious in all that he does and is capable of doing very well in his chosen profession. Despite his confident manner, he can be a great worrier and he would find it helpful to discuss his concerns with others rather than keep them to himself. He is loyal to his family and employers and will have a small group of particularly close friends. He has good taste and is usually highly skilled in some of aspect of the arts. He is often a collector of antiques and his home will be very tastefully furnished.

Water Goat: 1943, 2003
The Water Goat is very popular and makes friends with remarkable ease. He is good at spotting opportunities but does not always have the necessary confidence to follow

them through. He likes to have security both in his home life and work and does not take kindly to change. He is articulate, has a good sense of humour and is usually very good with children.

Wood Goat: 1955

This Goat is generous, kind hearted and always eager to please. He usually has a large circle of friends and involves himself in a wide variety of activities. He has a very trusting nature but he can sometimes give in to the demands of others a little too easily and it would be in his interests if he were to stand his ground more often. He is usually lucky in financial matters and, like the Water Goat, is very good with children.

Fire Goat: 1907, 1967

This Goat usually knows what he wants in life and often uses his considerable charm and persuasive personality to achieve his aims. He can sometimes let his imagination run away with him and has a tendency to ignore matters that are not to his liking. He is rather extravagant in his spending and would do well to exercise a little more care when dealing with financial matters. He has a lively personality, many friends, and loves attending parties and social occasions.

Earth Goat: 1919, 1979

This Goat has a considerate and caring nature. He is particularly loyal to his family and friends and invariably creates a favourable impression wherever he goes. He is reliable and conscientious in his work but sometimes finds it difficult to save and never likes to deprive himself of any little luxury he might fancy. He has numerous interests and is often very well read. He usually derives much pleasure from following the activities of the various members of his family.

PROSPECTS FOR THE GOAT IN 2009

The Year of the Rat (7 February 2008 to 25 January 2009) is an encouraging time for the Goat and by putting himself forward and seizing his opportunities, he will be able to make good headway. The closing months of the Rat year will bring some interesting developments.

One of the main features of the Rat year is that it favours creativity and this is a time for the Goat to promote himself. For those who are keen to make progress in their work or whose jobs involve communication, the closing months of the year can bring some good opportunities. November in particular may be an interesting and fortunate month, but for all Goats, whether content in their job, eager to move or seeking work, this is a time to be active and use their strengths to advantage. In view of the current trends, Goats who enjoy more imaginative and expressive pursuits should also make the most of their gifts and consider promoting what they do. They could be encouraged by the response.

The closing months of the Rat year will also bring an increase in social activity and many Goats will have the chances to go out and meet friends. December and early January could be especially busy. In his domestic life the Goat will also find himself in demand and with so much to fit in, the more arrangements that can be made in advance, the better. There could also be some interesting family news in the closing weeks of the year and both domestically and socially this can be a busy and generally pleasing time.

The Year of the Ox begins on 26 January and will be a mixed one for the Goat. While he has a generally easy-going nature and prefers to set about his activities in his own way, the Ox year favours practicality and the Goat may feel uneasy about certain developments. It is a time for keeping expectations modest and for being careful and aware. However, while the Goat may experience increased pressures during the year, he would do well to bear in mind the advice of the Chinese proverb *you won't get lost if you frequently ask for directions*. In 2009 the Goat should remember that there are many people he can turn to for advice and support and at more demanding or difficult times, he should do so.

One area that will require especial care is finance. Goats do like their pleasures and tend to spend their money easily. However, this is a year for keeping a tight control over the purse-strings and not succumbing to too much impulse buying. Without care, this could easily mount up and lead to forced economies or increased interest payments later on. Also, if the Goat takes on any new commitment or has important paperwork to deal with, he needs to check the details carefully.

In work matters the Goat will need to remain focused and concentrate on his objectives. Although his workload will sometimes be great and he may be uncomfortable with certain developments, by knuckling down he will not only accomplish a lot but also gain valuable experience. The Ox year may be challenging, but it can be to his benefit, as it will test and broaden his skills as well as give him the chance to become more established in his line of work. Also, while opportunities may be limited, for those Goats who are keen to progress in their career or change their job, there will certainly be chances to pursue. March, June, July and October could see some interesting possibilities, but in the Ox year it is a case of seizing opportunities as they arise.

This will also be a challenging year for Goats seeking work. Openings may be limited and there will be disappointments when certain applications do not go their way. However, despite the variable aspects, with effort, good advice and flexibility, the Goat's persistence can often lead to a new job. Results *will* need to be worked for, however, and these Goats should make every effort with their applications and at interview, including finding out more about the company and duties involved. Extra initiative on their part can make an important difference. Also, all Goats should make the most of any training opportunities. By keeping their skills up to date and learning new ones, they will not only be helping their present situation but also increasing the possibilities open to them.

Over the year the Goat's personal interests can be good ways for him to relax and unwind and do something different from his usual daily activities. Sometimes they could take him out of doors or give him the chance of additional exercise. Some Goats may set themselves a particular project or challenge for the year and so add extra purpose to what they do. The Goat should also take advantage of any travel opportunities and, if possible, aim to go away for a break or holiday. With the pressures and vexations of the Ox year, a change of scene can do him a lot of good.

With his genial nature the Goat gets on well with most people and both his domestic and social life will mean a great deal to him during the year. However, rather than assume that others know how he is feeling or the pressures he is under, it is important that he is prepared to talk over any anxieties or concerns. Not everyone is as perceptive as he is and he does need to be open and so give others more of a chance to understand and assist him.

The Goat's domestic life could be particularly busy this year and good co-operation will be needed. If there are any substantial household projects the Goat wants to undertake, he needs to allow ample time. The Ox year is not one for rush, and delays or snags will sometimes occur. However, busy though home life may be, it will contain many pleasures, and with good communication and rapport this can be a rewarding year.

The Goat will also appreciate his social life and this can give him a good chance to relax. Any Goat who is keen to build up his social contacts, especially if he has had some personal problems, will find that by going out more and perhaps joining groups or a course connected with one of his interests he can come into contact with others, including some who are like-minded. April and July to September could see the most social activity.

Overall, the Ox year will be a demanding one for the Goat and he could feel ill at ease with some of the pressures he has to face. However, by drawing on support of others, remaining organized and concentrating on what he has to do, he can still make headway as well as add to his skills and experience. This may be a year for keeping expectations modest, but it can be an instructive one, particularly as it will draw out certain qualities and strengths. And throughout the year, the Goat should remember there are many people who are willing to help him should he need it.

The Metal Goat

During the Ox year a lot will be asked of the Metal Goat and parts of the year could be challenging. However, this can be an important time and what the Metal Goat accomplishes can be very much to his future benefit.

For those Metal Goats in education this can be a significant year. Many will be nearing the end of certain courses and have work to complete and examinations to prepare for. With a lot resting on the results, these Metal Goats should plan what they have to do, remain focused and avoid leaving too much to the last moment. Their conscientious nature will help, but it is by working hard and staying disciplined that they will reap the rewards.

Also, if any problems or setbacks occur, for instance disappointing feedback or difficulty with a certain subject or piece of work, the Metal Goat should not let this weaken his resolve. The Ox year can sometimes be a stern test of his abilities, but rather than give up too easily or lose impetus, if he remains determined and keeps in mind what good results can lead to, in many cases he will not only overcome setbacks but also improve his performance. For some Metal Goats, initial disappointments could be a wake-up call and indicate the need for greater application.

In addition, if the Metal Goat does run into any particular difficulties, he will find it helpful to ask for advice rather than struggle on unaided. Often his tutors will be willing to advise him, but to benefit he does need to be forthcoming.

Many Metal Goats will also be giving some thought to their future. With important decisions to be made, the Metal Goat again needs to be open. If he is too reticent (and this can be a fault of some Goats), there is a risk that his own preferences may not always be apparent. In the Ox year the Metal Goat *does* need to be forthcoming.

For those Metal Goats entering work, the Ox year can again be challenging. Not only will there be new duties to learn and sometimes considerable adjustments made to their routine, but they might not always be satisfied with what they are asked to do. Some duties might be tedious and the Metal Goat might not be able to use certain skills and strengths as fully as he might like. However, while conditions may be frustrating, the Metal Goat *will* be getting experience that he can build on later. The Ox year may not be an easy one, but it can be instructive. Also, with the Metal Goat's prospects being much improved in the following Tiger year, the experience, training and quali-fications he can obtain now can stand him in excellent stead for later.

Whether seeking work or looking to move on from their present position, Metal Goats will find that March, mid-May to July and October will see the best opportunities. However, in the Ox year it is very much a case of making the most of chances as they arise.

The Metal Goat will, however, enjoy his socializing and in view of some of the changes that are taking place in his life, there will be good chances for him to meet others and make new friends. Any Metal Goat who is feeling lonely or anxious may well experience an improvement in his situation and meet someone he can really empathize with. April and late June to September could see the most social activity as well as bring the best chances to meet others.

As with so much this year, in his home life the Metal Goat does need to be forthcoming. More senior relations are keen to see him make the most of his potential, but for them to help and advise, the Metal Goat does need to be open. Also, while often busy, he should try to involve himself more readily in domestic activities. The greater his involvement in domestic life, the better the understanding and rapport he will enjoy.

In money matters the Metal Goat will need to remain disciplined and think carefully if tempted by spur of the moment purchases. He could save himself considerable expense by waiting for more favourable buying opportunities rather than proceeding too hastily. This is a year for sensible financial management.

The Ox year will bring its pressures and ask a lot of the Metal Goat, but it can be a significant one for him. By making the effort and meeting the challenges, he will learn a great deal and the qualifications and experience he is able to gain will be something he can build on in the years ahead. The impact of the Ox year can be far-reaching.

Two tips: In view of the pressures and decisions you may have to face, do seek advice. This is no year to keep concerns to yourself. Also, make the most of chances to enjoy your personal interests or meet others. This can often bring a pleasing element to your year.

The Water Goat

The element of Water helps to reinforce the Goat's awareness and abilities as a communicator. The Water Goat is highly perceptive, adept at picking up nuances. Little escapes him, but he can also be sensitive and worry a great deal, and in 2009 he could have a number of concerns as well as feel uncomfortable about certain developments. This may not be an easy year, but there is a lot the Water Goat can do to minimize or prevent some of the problems.

In his domestic life this will be a busy year, with the Water Goat taking great interest in the activities of family members. Because he is so caring, he will often find himself thinking about their situation, the pressures they may be under or decisions that need taking. As a result, there will be quite a few times when he will come to the assistance of his loved ones, and his timely and appropriate advice will be appreciated. However, while the Water Goat may be aware of the views of others, he should not let this stop him from expressing his own thoughts. It is better for him to be open rather than skirt round issues or keep particular concerns to himself when with discussion they could be addressed or helped in some way.

In addition to the assistance he gives to others, the Water Goat will often busy himself with household activities. Often his creative instincts will come to the fore and he will decide to change the arrangements of some rooms. However, such projects do need to be carefully costed and thought through and some may be more complicated than first imagined. Sometimes extra work, repairs or modifications may be needed, delays may occur or the Water Goat may find it difficult to find exactly what he wants. The Ox year can bring its vexations and the Water Goat will need to allow time and be patient in practical undertakings.

Although the aspects in the Ox year can be challenging, it will still have its pleasures and moments of success. Practical undertakings may take time and effort, but when they are completed they can bring the Water Goat considerable satisfaction. Also, joint activities, mutual interests and for some, gardening, can lead to many special occasions. In some cases it may be possible for the Water Goat to further a particular interest with a partner or family member, with each encouraging and supporting the other. Also, if he has particular ideas or would like to attend certain events, including some quite local ones, he should see what can be arranged. During the year some of his suggestions could work out particularly well.

The Water Goat will also enjoy the company of his close circle of friends and will appreciate meeting up with them. If he has concerns or is under pressure at any time, their support and advice could be of considerable value. In this sometimes variable year the Water Goat should remember that there are people he can talk to if he needs to. In addition, interests that bring him into contact with others can be of particular benefit to him. April and July to September could see the most social activity.

The Water Goat will, though, need to be careful in his financial dealings over the year. If planning more substantial purchases, he should take his time and check the suitability of what he is considering. The more thorough he is, the better. Similarly, when handling financial paperwork, he does need to be prompt and to check if he has any uncertainties. This is a year for vigilance and good control.

Despite this, the Water Goat should try to make provision for a holiday and if he plans this carefully, he will often benefit from his time away. Some Water Goats may be able to combine a holiday with pursuing one of their interests and this can make their break all the more enjoyable.

For Water Goats in work this can be a demanding year with some sometimes complex matters to deal with. However, with the experience he has behind him, the Water Goat will often be able to deal with these well and colleagues will be grateful for his knowledge and insights. For those Water Goats who retire, there could be surprises in store, with many receiving recognition and plaudits for all they have done.

Generally, though, the Ox year is one for care. Plans, activities and purchases do need to be thought through. And while the Water Goat will do much to support others, when under pressure himself, it is important that he is open and gives others the chance to help him in return. However, while the aspects may be mixed and certain activities may take longer than anticipated, the year will still have its pleasures, with family and social occasions and travel being particularly appreciated.

You are well meaning, but you can also be sensitive. Rather than shoulder too much on your own, do talk to others. Also encourage joint activities, as spending time with others can lead to some especially enjoyable moments.

The Wood Goat

This will be a demanding year for the Wood Goat, but by keeping his expectations modest and proceeding carefully, he can still make it a reasonable one.

At work many Wood Goats will have seen a lot of change in the previous Rat year and will be content to remain where they are and continue to learn about different aspects of their work. However, while a great many may not actively seek to change their job, they could be affected by new procedures. As a result, there could be some destabilizing times and the Wood Goat may have misgivings about what is taking place. In the Ox year, however, it is very much a case of making the best of his situation.

Nevertheless, there could be a positive element to what happens during the year. Some Wood Goats will have the chance to widen their skills or concentrate on more specialist tasks. Also, with the Wood Goat's prospects being more encouraging in the following Tiger year, what is achieved now can stand him in good stead for later on.

For Wood Goats seeking work, as well as those intent on change, the year can be difficult. Suitable openings could be limited and there could be a lot of competition. However, as the proverb reminds us, *every cloud has a silver lining*, and while there will be times in these Wood Goats' quest when they feel disheartened, by persisting, believing in themselves and not being too restrictive in their search, they can succeed. Sometimes an offer could come unexpectedly in the wake of a rejection. March, June, July and October could see the best opportunities, but with the aspects as they are, chances need to be taken as and when they arise.

In money matters the Ox year could bring times of increased expense and there could be many demands on the Wood Goat's resources, perhaps connected with family activities, certain plans or repair and maintenance costs. As a result the Wood Goat will need to remain disciplined in his spending and budget in advance for some of his more major plans and purchases. He should also be thorough when dealing with paperwork. A delay or oversight could have repercussions. Wood Goats, take note.

A more encouraging aspect of the year concerns the Wood Goat's personal interests and while he will often have many demands on his time, it is important he sets some aside for recreational pursuits. These can be a welcome contrast to his usual daily occupations and give him the chance to explore other talents as well as relax and unwind. In addition there could be some interesting travel opportunities, sometimes arising at short notice, and by taking advantage of them the Wood Goat can benefit from the break as well as enjoy the chance to visit new places.

The Wood Goat's social life in the Ox year may be quieter than some years, but he will appreciate the events he does attend all the more. Local events in particular could appeal to many Wood Goats and if they include family and friends, some particularly good times can be enjoyed. The Wood Goat will also value talking to his friends on any matters that may be causing him concern. Not only will this help release some of the strain he may be under, but it will also allow him to benefit from the advice and support that others can give. Wood Goats who are lonely or dispirited will find it worth getting involved in various activities. Some may, for instance, decide to help with charitable or community causes or join a group connected with an interest of theirs, but whatever they choose to do, positive action on their part can often bring an improvement in their situation. April and July to early October could see some interesting social opportunities.

The Wood Goat's domestic life will see considerable activity over the year and he may well do a lot to assist both younger and more senior relations. With his own commitments as well, there will be times when he will feel under pressure. However, the key to so much in the Ox year is to remain organized and, at busy times, to decide on priorities. Deferring certain household projects could be helpful to everyone concerned.

However, while the Wood Goat's domestic life will be busy it will also contain some memorable moments. Shared family activities could be particularly appreciated.

Overall, the Ox year will be challenging, with a lot being expected of the Wood Goat. Although there will be times when he will face difficulties, by concentrating on what needs to be done and drawing on the support available to him, he will actually accomplish a great deal and this will stand him in excellent stead for next year.

TIP FOR THE YEAR

Keep your expectations realistic and avoid risk. You will fare best by concentrating on what you know and setting priorities. Also, allow time to pursue your own interests and appreciate what you have around you.

The Fire Goat

There is a Chinese proverb that the Fire Goat would do well to bear in mind this year: *After a rough road comes the smooth path.* The road ahead may be challenging, but it will prepare the Fire Goat for the success that awaits in following years.

In his work the Fire Goat could find this a demanding time. In addition to an often increased workload, there could be additional pressures to cope with. These could include delays, bureaucracy, problems as new systems and procedures are introduced and the sometimes unhelpful attitude of certain colleagues. For one who is as conscientious and aware as the Fire Goat, parts of the year could be worrying. However, by doing his best and remaining focused, the Fire Goat will have the chance to develop his skills. It is often said that challenging times provide good learning opportunities and so it will be this year.

Although this may be a demanding year work-wise, many Fire Goats will decide to remain with their present employer and will often benefit from in-house opportunities to progress. For those who are intent on change or seeking work, their quest will not be easy. In addition to facing much competition, they may find openings limited or that they lack the experience some employers want. The job-seeking process will at times be frustrating, but by seeking advice and widening their options, many Fire Goats will succeed. What they are offered may be different from what they really want, but it could give them the chance to develop their skills in new ways and be something they will be able to take further, especially in the more progressive Tiger year that follows. March, June, July and October could see the best chances, but opportunities do need to be seized as soon as they arise.

Also, the Fire Goat does need to remain mindful and aware in his dealings with colleagues. Sometimes there could be a personality clash or difference of opinion and the Fire Goat should be careful he does not allow any problem to overshadow his work. With care and diplomacy (and the Fire Goat does have a tactful nature), problems can soon be resolved, but with the aspects as they are, this is something he does need to watch. More positively, his duties will often bring him into contact with others and in the process new contacts and acquaintances can be made.

Another important feature of the year is that it will give the Fire Goat a good chance to develop his personal interests and he will often take great pleasure in what he is able to do.

There will also be travel opportunities and whether he is going on holiday, visiting friends or taking advantage of a short break away, by making the most of such chances the Fire Goat can enjoy himself as well as benefit from the rest and change of routine. In view of some of the pressures of the year, it is important that he does have a respite from all the activity. His travels this year could be especially rewarding.

With his outgoing nature the Fire Goat enjoys company and over the year he can look forward to going to some interesting social events. Some could be connected with his work or interests and by making the most of such opportunities, the Fire Goat will often enjoy himself as well as add to his social circle. For Fire Goats who are alone and would welcome new friends, there will be excellent opportunities to meet others, with April and late June to September seeing the most social activity.

The Fire Goat's domestic life will be particularly busy this year and with his often considerable work schedule and others experiencing similar pressures, it is important there is good co-operation between all in his household. When the Fire Goat is tired or tense, the more support and understanding that can be shown, the better for all. However busy domestic life may be, if time is set aside for everyone to spend together, there will be some memorable moments. These may include some family successes, including headway made by younger family members, and some of the celebrations that are arranged. Some home improvements carried out over the year will also be appreciated, although these could take longer than anticipated.

In matters of finance, the Fire Goat does need to be careful. With his many outgoings and the plans and purchases he may be considering, he does need watch his spending and make allowance for more substantial expenses. This is a year for good management and prudence. The Fire Goat should also be prompt and thorough with any paperwork he may receive. Delay could cause problems and possible expense. Fire Goats, take note.

Overall, the Ox year can be a challenging one for the Fire Goat, but by doing his best and rising to the demands of the year, he will learn a great deal about himself and be able to develop his knowledge and skills. *After a rough road comes the smooth path*, and while some of the Ox year will be rough, the smooth path will eventually open up for the Fire Goat. And with his interests, friends and the support of his loved ones, there will be a lot for him to appreciate in the meantime.

TIP FOR THE YEAR
Deal with situations as they arise. As a Fire Goat you sometimes have a tendency to ignore matters not to your liking and this can sometimes exacerbate the problem. Be decisive, be open, rise to the challenges of the year and you will grow and ultimately gain a great deal.

The Earth Goat

This will be an important year for the Earth Goat. Not only will it mark a new decade in his life but it will be one in which he will be involved in some major decisions.

As the Earth Goat enters his thirties he may well find himself reflecting on his position and his achievements. There may also be a tinge of dissatisfaction, as he will know that he can do far more, and many Earth Goats will now decide to take some positive action. However, while they may be keen, the Ox year will not be an easy one. Progress can be slow and certain plans difficult to realize. But despite the variable aspects, the Earth Goat should remember the Chinese saying *a long journey will not deter one with high aspirations*. The journey the Earth Goat is on may be long and hard, but what he sets in motion in 2009 can be truly significant and even a pivotal moment in his life.

In the Earth Goat's work this is a year for building on his experience. As so many Goats will find, a lot will be asked of them in the Ox year and many will be facing an increased workload as well as contending with other pressures. Although parts of the year will be challenging, by concentrating on what needs to be done and remaining committed, the Earth Goat will not only be furthering his knowledge and skills but also doing his reputation a lot of good. Problems can bring out new strengths and so it will be for many Earth Goats this year. Also, with the Earth Goat's desire to move his career forward, he should make the most of any training that may be available to him or any chances to vary his role. By showing his desire to move ahead, he can prepare the way for the more significant advances he will make in the next few years. March, late May to July and October could see some interesting developments, but with the aspects as they are, it is case of keeping alert and making the most of opportunities as they arise.

The Earth Goat should also pay careful attention to his relations with colleagues and work in close co-operation with them as part of a team. If possible, he should make full use of networking opportunities and chances to meet other colleagues. Some could become good friends and be helpful as he looks to progress. However, with the aspects as they are, problems can occasionally arise and he could experience a difference of opinion or a clash of personalities. Although difficult, he should not let this direct his attention away from his duties, and dealing with the challenges of the year will help him to grow both in strength and stature. The Ox year may not be smooth, but it can be instructive *and* significant in the longer term.

For Earth Goats who are keen to change their job or looking for work, again this will not be a straightforward year. They could face many disappointments in the job-seeking process. However, with persistence and self-belief, they will find doors opening for them, sometimes unexpectedly, and their career could be set on an interesting new path. In the Ox year the Earth Goat does need to be open to possibility.

He will also need to be careful in money matters. Although many Earth Goats will enjoy a rise in income, with their current commitments and certain plans they may have, this is a time for discipline and control. In addition, when dealing with financial paperwork or entering into a new agreement, the Earth Goat does need to give this his full attention and obtain advice on anything that may be unclear. Similarly, if he is tempted to buy anything of a more speculative nature, he does need to be aware of the risks involved. This is a year for vigilance.

To mark this new decade in their life, many Earth Goats will consider travelling over the year and may decide to take a special break or holiday. By planning this carefully and discussing it with his loved ones, the Earth Goat will very much appreciate what is arranged. In addition to a holiday, there could also be opportunities to go away for a short break or to stay with others. Travel will be a pleasurable aspect of the Ox year.

The Earth Goat should also set time aside to develop his interests. Not only can these be a good way for him to relax, but they can also give him the chance to meet others, get out of doors or take more exercise. Although this may be a demanding year, his interests can do much to keep his lifestyle in balance.

In his domestic life this can be an eventful year, with some Earth Goats seeing an addition to their family. With the needs of babies or young children, as well as those of more senior relations, the Earth Goat will be very much in demand. However, while he will do a great deal to assist others, he himself will also be particularly grateful for the support he receives. Whenever he is under pressure or needs to make important decisions, he will find talking these over with his loved ones can be especially helpful. In some instances, they will be able to help him in ways he had not anticipated. Good communication will be very important over the year. Also, with the possible marking of his thirtieth birthday and other plans the Earth Goat may be keen to carry out in this busy year, the more that can be arranged in advance, the better.

The Earth Goat will also appreciate the support of close friends over the year and will enjoy many of the social opportunities that arise. His work and interests can also introduce him to new people and some new friends can be helpful to him. April and late June to September could see the most social activity.

Overall, the Ox year will be a demanding one for the Earth Goat, with problems and pressures to cope with. However, by remaining focused and concentrating on what needs to be done, he will be able to draw on his considerable personal qualities as well as add to his experience, and what he achieves can be significant later. Also, while the Ox year may be exacting, the love and support of others can help and encourage the Earth Goat. His thirtieth year may be challenging, but it can mark the start of an exciting and rewarding phase in his life.

TIP FOR THE YEAR
Persevere and have faith in yourself. The Ox year can be a test of your abilities, but by rising to its challenges, you can do yourself a lot of good. Learn from what happens. Your thirties can be a rewarding decade and your actions this year can prepare you for the opportunities that lie ahead.

FAMOUS GOATS

Pamela Anderson, Jane Austen, Daniel Bedingfield, Cilla Black, Carla Bruni-Sarkozy, Lord Byron, Coco Chanel, Mary Higgins Clark, Nat 'King' Cole, Jamie Cullum, Robert de Niro, Catherine Deneuve, Charles Dickens, Ken Dodd, Sir Arthur Conan Doyle, Umberto Eco, Douglas Fairbanks, Will Ferrell, Dame Margot Fonteyn, Jamie Foxx, Noel Gallagher, Bill Gates, Mel Gibson, Whoopi Goldberg, Mikhail Gorbachev, John Grisham, Oscar Hammerstein, George Harrison, Sir Edmund Hillary, Billy Idol, Julio Iglesias, Sir Mick Jagger, Norah Jones, Nicole Kidman, Sir Ben Kingsley, Matt le Blanc, John le Carré, Doris Lessing, Franz Liszt, Sir John Major, James McAvoy, Michelangelo, Joni Mitchell, Rupert Murdoch, Randy Newman, Des O'Connor, Sinead O'Connor, Michael Palin, Eva Peron, Marcel Proust, Keith Richards, Julia Roberts, Nicolas Sarkozy, William Shatner, Gary Sinise, Jerry Springer, Lana Turner, Mark Twain, Rudolph Valentino, Vangelis, Barbara Walters, John Wayne, Fay Weldon, Bruce Willis.

20 FEBRUARY 1920 ⁓ 7 FEBRUARY 1921   *Metal Monkey*

6 FEBRUARY 1932 ⁓ 25 JANUARY 1933   *Water Monkey*

25 JANUARY 1944 ⁓ 12 FEBRUARY 1945   *Wood Monkey*

12 FEBRUARY 1956 ⁓ 30 JANUARY 1957   *Fire Monkey*

30 JANUARY 1968 ⁓ 16 FEBRUARY 1969   *Earth Monkey*

16 FEBRUARY 1980 ⁓ 4 FEBRUARY 1981   *Metal Monkey*

4 FEBRUARY 1992 ⁓ 22 JANUARY 1993   *Water Monkey*

22 JANUARY 2004 ⁓ 8 FEBRUARY 2005   *Wood Monkey*

THE

MONKEY

THE PERSONALITY OF THE MONKEY

The more open to possibility,
the more possibilities open.

The Monkey is born under the sign of fantasy. He is imaginative, inquisitive and loves to keep an eye on everything that is going on around him. He is never backward in offering advice or trying to sort out the problems of others. He likes to be helpful and his advice is invariably sensible and reliable.

The Monkey is intelligent, well read and always eager to learn. He has an extremely good memory and there are many Monkeys who have made particularly good linguists. The Monkey is also a convincing talker and enjoys taking part in discussions and debates. His friendly, self assured manner can be very persuasive and he usually has little trouble in winning people round to his way of thinking. It is for this reason that the Monkey often excels in politics and public speaking. He is also particularly adept in PR work, teaching and any job that involves selling.

The Monkey can, however, be crafty, cunning and occasionally dishonest, and he will seize on any opportunity to make a quick gain or outsmart his opponents. He has so much charm and guile that people often don't realize what he is up to until it is too late. But despite his resourceful nature, the Monkey does run the risk of outsmarting even himself. He has so much confidence in his abilities that he rarely listens to advice or is prepared to accept help from anyone. He likes to help others but prefers to rely on his own judgement when dealing with his own affairs.

Another characteristic of the Monkey is that he is extremely good at solving problems and has a happy knack of extricating himself (and others) from the most hopeless of positions. He is the master of self preservation.

With so many diverse talents the Monkey is able to make considerable sums of money, but he does like to enjoy life and will think nothing of spending his money on some exotic holiday or luxury he has had his eye on. He can, however, become very envious if someone else has what he wants.

The Monkey is an original thinker and despite his love of company, he cherishes his independence. He has to have the freedom to act as he wants and any Monkey who feels hemmed in or bound by too many restrictions can soon become unhappy. Likewise, if anything becomes too boring or monotonous, the Monkey soon loses interest and turns his attention to something else. He lacks persistence and this can often hamper his progress. He is also easily distracted, a tendency that all Monkeys should try to over-come. By concentrating on one thing at a time, the Monkey will almost certainly achieve more in the long run.

The Monkey is a good organizer and even though he may behave slightly erratically at times, he will invariably have a plan at the back of his mind. On the odd occasion when his plans do not work out, he is usually quite happy to shrug his shoulders and put it down to experience. He will rarely make the same mistake twice and throughout his life he will try his hand at many different things.

The Monkey likes to impress and is rarely without followers or admirers. Many are attracted by his good looks, his sense of humour, or simply because he instils so much confidence.

Monkeys usually marry young and for it to be a success their partner must allow them time to pursue their many interests and indulge their love of travel. The Monkey has to have variety in his life and is especially well suited to those born under the sociable and outgoing signs of the Rat, Dragon, Pig and Goat. The Ox, Rabbit, Snake and Dog will also be enchanted by the Monkey's resourceful and outgoing nature, but he is likely to exasperate the Rooster and Horse, and the Tiger will have little patience with his tricks. A relationship between two Monkeys will work well – they will understand each other and be able to assist each other in their various enterprises.

The female Monkey is intelligent, extremely observant and a shrewd judge of character. Her opinions are often highly valued and, having such a persuasive nature, she invariably gets her own way. She has many interests and involves herself in a wide variety of activities. She pays great attention to her appearance, is an elegant dresser and likes to take particular care over her hair. She can be a doting parent and will have many good and loyal friends.

Provided the Monkey can curb his desire to take part in everything that is going on around him and concentrate on one thing at a time, he can usually achieve what he wants in life. Should he suffer any disappointment, he is bound to bounce back. He is a survivor and his life is usually both colourful and eventful.

THE FIVE DIFFERENT TYPES OF MONKEY

In addition to the 12 signs of the Chinese zodiac there are five elements and these have a strengthening or moderating influence on the signs. The effects of the five elements on the Monkey are described below, together with the years in which the elements were exercising their influence. Therefore those Monkeys born in 1920 and 1980 are Metal Monkeys, those born in 1932 and 1992 are Water Monkeys, and so on.

Metal Monkey: 1920, 1980

The Metal Monkey is very strong-willed. He sets about everything he does with dogged determination and often prefers to work independently rather than with others. He is ambitious, wise and confident, and is certainly not afraid of hard work. He is very astute in financial matters and usually chooses his investments well. Despite his somewhat independent nature, he enjoys attending parties and social occasions and is particularly warm and caring towards his loved ones.

Water Monkey: 1932, 1992

The Water Monkey is versatile, determined and perceptive. He also has more discipline than some of the other Monkeys and is prepared to work towards a certain goal rather than be distracted by something else. He is not always open about his true intentions and when questioned can be particularly evasive. He can be sensitive to criticism but also very persuasive and usually has little trouble in getting others to fall in with his plans. He has a very good understanding of human nature and relates well to others.

Wood Monkey: 1944, 2004

This Monkey is efficient, methodical and extremely conscientious. He is also highly imaginative and is always trying to capitalize on new ideas or learn new skills. Occasionally his enthusiasm can get the better of him and he can get very agitated when things do not quite work out as he had hoped. He does, however, have a very adventurous streak and is not afraid of taking risks. He also loves travel. He is usually held in great esteem by his friends and colleagues.

Fire Monkey: 1956

The Fire Monkey is intelligent, full of vitality and has no trouble in commanding the respect of others. He is imaginative and has wide interests, although sometimes these can distract him from more useful and profitable work. He is very competitive and always likes to be involved in everything that is going on. He can be stubborn if he does not get his own way and he sometimes tries to indoctrinate those who are less strong-willed than himself. He is a lively character, attractive to others and most loyal to his partner.

Earth Monkey: 1968

The Earth Monkey tends to be studious and well read, and can become quite distinguished in his chosen line of work. He is less outgoing than some of the other types of Monkey and prefers quieter and more solid pursuits. He has high principles, a very caring nature and can be most generous to those less fortunate than himself. He is usually successful in handling financial matters and can become very wealthy in old age. He has a calming influence on those around him and is respected and well liked. He is, however, especially careful about whom he lets into his confidence.

PROSPECTS FOR THE MONKEY IN 2009

The Year of the Rat (7 February 2008 to 25 January 2009) is a year favouring action and during it the Monkey can do well. There will be some excellent opportunities for him and by making the most of them he can look forward to some pleasing results. In addition, his outgoing nature will be a real asset and he will often impress others.

In his work the Monkey will often be able to use his skills to advantage and for those Monkeys who are keen to further their career, the closing months of the Rat year could bring some excellent possibilities, with November seeing encouraging developments.

Many Monkeys will also fare well in financial matters and in addition to a possible rise in income, some may benefit from a bonus or unexpected gift. The Monkey could also be fortunate in some purchases he makes at this time, either in acquiring specific items he has been wanting or in profiting from special purchasing opportunities that he sees.

The Monkey's domestic and social life is likely to become busier as the Rat year draws to an end and he should try to plan his activities well in advance. Here discussion with those around him would be an advantage. Also, there could be some special events for the Monkey to look forward to, including a possible family celebration. Late November to early January can be a particularly busy time and Monkeys who are enjoying romance or who meet someone new at this time can find this adding some excitement and sparkle to the latter part of the year.

The Monkey is resourceful and adaptable and able to read situations well and, as the Ox year begins, he will recognize that in order to do well and achieve his aims this year he *will* need to put in the effort. The Ox year, which starts on 26 January, is a time for application and the Monkey's results will be very dependent on his attitude.

Another important feature of the Ox year is that it is one for realism. In 2009 the Monkey cannot afford to spread his attention too widely or rely on fanciful or risky notions. He may possess a rich imagination and like to be involved in a lot of activity, but the best results this year will come from concentrating on specifics. Next year, the Year of the Tiger, will give him a freer rein, but 2009 is one for effort, discipline and focus.

However, while the Monkey's exuberance and style may be tempered during the Ox year, he can still gain a great deal from it. At work, rather than look to make a change, many Monkeys will decide to remain in their present place of work and to build on their skills. By concentrating on the areas they know, they will not only enjoy a more settled period but also become more established in their area of work. Quite a few could also benefit from internal changes in their workplace which allow them to focus on more specialist tasks.

Another positive aspect of the year will be the way in which the Monkey can add to his skills, and if he is offered training, can undertake some study, even if in his own time, or has the chance to vary or add to his role, he should make the most of it. Rather than regard this as a year for sweeping progress, he will find his more lasting gains coming from the experience he can obtain over the year.

For Monkeys who are intent on change or seeking work, the Ox year can be challenging. Although many may be keen to take their career in a new direction, this is not a year for going off on tangents or pursuing positions for which they do not have the necessary experience. These Monkeys could benefit from registering with the appropriate employment agencies and talking to people who are able to advise. With support and guidance, many can be successful in obtaining a new position this year and it will often be one they can build on in the future. April, May, September and November could see the best opportunities.

The Monkey will also need to be disciplined in money matters. If he is tempted by risks or overspending, problems could follow. In particular he should be wary about succumbing to too many spur of the moment whims or indulgences. He also needs to be thorough when dealing with financial forms and correspondence. As far as money matters are concerned, he does need to be on his mettle and avoid rush or risk.

One expense many Monkeys will have during the year will be travel. Whether the Monkey is going on holiday or for some short breaks, by budgeting in advance and planning ahead, he can look forward to visiting some particularly interesting destinations and having a good time while away.

This can also be a satisfying year as far as the Monkey's personal interests are concerned and by setting himself some specific aims and allowing time for these, he can benefit from what he decides to do. Some Monkeys who have been involved in a longer-term project could see it reach a successful conclusion this year. For personal interests, this can be a fulfilling time.

The Monkey will, though, need to give careful consideration to his well-being this year and should he feel below par, he should seek medical advice. This is not a year for ignoring ailments or concerns. Monkeys, do take note.

However, the Ox year can be a special one as far as the Monkey's domestic life is concerned. By spending quality time with his loved ones and supporting those around him, he will not only strengthen rapport and understanding but also enjoy himself. Shared interests and projects, including travel, will often mean a great deal to him. Also while, as with any year, there will be times of pressure and anxiety, by addressing these, talking matters through and ensuring good co-operation between everyone in his household, the Monkey will be helped through them. In the Ox year the Monkey's domestic life can be meaningful and helpful as well as bring him considerable pleasure.

With his outgoing nature the Monkey will also make the most of the opportunities he has to meet others. Any Monkey who has been feeling lonely or, because of work or education, moved to a new area will find the Ox year giving him the chance to establish a new social circle. February to early April, July and December could see the most social activity.

This can also be an interesting year as far as affairs of the heart are concerned. However, the Monkey should let any romance develop in its own time rather than make hurried commitments. Without haste, pressure or high expectations in the early stages, a relationship will have a better chance of being established on a firm basis.

The Monkey can do himself a lot of good during the Ox year and although his progress may not be easy or swift, by being realistic in his aims and doing his best, he will not only benefit from the experience he gains but also do a lot to help his future prospects. He needs to be disciplined in money matters, but with travel, social opportunities and a particularly rewarding domestic life, there will be a lot in the Ox year for him to appreciate.

The Metal Monkey

The Metal Monkey is ambitious and keen to make the most of himself. However, he also recognizes that some of his ambitions are for the longer term and to attain them he will need greater experience and the right opportunities. In 2009 he will have the chance to add to his skills and enhance his prospects. This is not a year for substantial progress, but what the Metal Monkey can learn can be significant. In addition his personal life can bring him a lot of pleasure and help make this a satisfying year.

Many Metal Monkeys will have seen considerable change in their work in recent years. They could not only have changed employer but also taken on new responsibilities. In 2009 these Metal Monkeys will have the chance to consolidate their position, become more proficient in what they do and master other aspects of their work. In addition, some of the pressures and problems that occur can be an excellent test of their abilities as well as reveal new strengths. For so many the Ox year can be instructive, with what they learn being of considerable value in the future.

Another positive feature of the year will be the opportunity the Metal Monkey will have to work with different colleagues. By being an active and co-operative team member, he will not only be enhancing his reputation but also gaining more support. Some Metal Monkeys could find more senior colleagues especially encouraging and their guidance will help their prospects.

Most Metal Monkeys will remain with their present employer over the year and use the time to build on their experience, but for those who feel unfulfilled and are keen to make a change, as well as those seeking work, the Ox year can be significant. Opportunities may be limited and obtaining a new position will not be easy. However, the Metal Monkey is blessed with a tenacious spirit and while he may face disappointments, by making every effort in the job-seeking process and stressing what he can offer to prospective employers, he may well be successful in securing a new position. Although this may sometimes be different from what he is used to and will often involve new working procedures, it will be something on which he can build in the future. Again, what is accomplished in 2009 should not be under-estimated. April, May, September and November could see the best opportunities.

Financial matters, however, will require care. Many Metal Monkeys will face considerable expense regarding their accommodation and in view of this and other commitments, the Metal Monkey does need to keep a tight rein over his spending. Whenever possible, he should also make advance provision for his plans. The more disciplined he is, the more he will be able to do. He should also be thorough when dealing with financial paperwork and if he has uncertainties he should seek clarification. This is not a year for taking risks.

Although the Metal Monkey will need to be careful in his spending this year, he may well decide to take a special holiday or go for some short breaks. With the pressures of the year, a change of scene can do him a lot of good.

Also, throughout the year the Metal Monkey should give some consideration to his well-being and should make sure he has a balanced and nutritious diet as well as takes regular exercise. To pay scant attention to his general lifestyle could leave him prone to ailments and not making the best of the year. Metal Monkeys, do take note and, if feeling off-colour or lethargic, do seek medical advice.

Although there will be many demands on his time, the Metal Monkey should also make sure he sets some aside for his personal interests and recreational pursuits. As well as bringing him pleasure, these can be good ways for him to unwind. In addition, with the encouraging aspects concerning his relations with others, he should make the most of his social opportunities over the year. With his genial manner, he will often impress. For the unattached, the Ox year can bring some interesting romantic possibilities, although the Metal Monkey should allow time for each person to get to know the other better rather than rush into a commitment. February to early April, July and December could see the most social activity.

The Metal Monkey's domestic life will also mean a great deal to him over the year and, although busy, by sharing decisions with his loved ones and setting about household activities with them, the Metal Monkey will appreciate a lot of what happens over the year. Quite a few Metal Monkeys will be moving to more suitable accommodation this year and home improvements can be especially satisfying.

Another important aspect of the year will be the support the Metal Monkey offers others, including both younger and more senior relations, as well as receives. For many Metal Monkeys, their domestic life in 2009 can be particularly special.

Overall, the Ox year can be a significant one for the Metal Monkey and although his actual progress may be modest, the experience he gains and contacts he builds up can be *very* beneficial in the longer term. Also, the care he puts into his relations with others, whether in his personal or working life, can be an important factor in how he fares as well as add a positive element to the year.

TIP FOR THE YEAR
To be at your best you do need to pay attention to your lifestyle. Also, value your relations with others. Your family, friends and colleagues can give you useful support.

The Water Monkey

This will be an important year for the Water Monkey, with a lot being expected of him. However, if he focuses on his priorities and remains disciplined, his achievements can be considerable and far-reaching.

For many Water Monkeys in education this is a year for effort and for concentrating on their work. With important examinations and sometimes course work to complete, they will need to remain well organized. It is better to work consistently throughout the year than leave too much to the last moment. The Water Monkey should also keep in mind what he is working towards and use this to spur himself on.

A positive feature of the year is that the Water Monkey will have greater chance to specialize in areas that particularly interest him. Some Water Monkeys will use this experience to decide on further education courses or the type of work they want to enter. The Ox year can have long-term significance.

The Water Monkey should also make the most of the opportunities available to him. This could involve trying out new subjects or taking part in recreational activities, including sport or music. If there is a skill the Water Monkey is keen to develop, he should look at ways in which he can do this and, if need be, obtain appropriate advice. Whatever he does, by being active, involved *and* willing to try, he can get a lot out of the year as well as open up possibilities for the future.

However, while the Ox year can see many positive developments, it does require application and discipline, and any who are tempted to rely on their wits (which some

Monkeys do) rather than put in the effort could face disappointments. Water Monkeys, do take note and do keep in mind the Chinese proverb *diligence leads to riches*.

For those Water Monkeys who decide to seek work, this can be a challenging year. Obtaining a position may not always be easy and many Water Monkeys will have to widen the scope of what they are prepared to consider. However, once they do secure an opening, it can give them the chance to gain useful experience. By demonstrating reliability and commitment and working well with others, these Water Monkeys can often open the way to something more fulfilling. Diligence and effort will be noticed and rewarded.

Some Water Monkeys may consider apprenticeship or work-release schemes where they can continue their education but also gain work experience. Although sometimes combining work and study may be difficult, by remaining disciplined and making the most of their opportunities, these Water Monkeys can work towards skills and qualifications that can be of considerable value in the longer term. Both educationally and as far as work experience is concerned, what is learned this year can be of future significance.

The Water Monkey will need to be careful in financial matters this year and although he may have some ambitious plans, he would do well to save towards these and remain disciplined in his general spending. He should also be wary of risks. This is a year for care and control.

With some of the pressures of the year, the Water Monkey also needs to pay attention to his well-being. Although he may keep himself active, to skimp on sufficient rest or neglect his diet could leave him prone to niggling ailments. In 2009 he does need to look after himself and to seek advice if he has any concerns.

He can, however, look forward to an often lively social life, with February to early April, July, mid-November and December seeing a lot of activity. Water Monkeys who are not as fully involved in the social scene as they would like will find that their interests can often bring them into contact with those who are like-minded and help them forge some significant friendships. Socially, this is a promising year.

The Water Monkey will also value the support he is given by those close to him. Although there may sometimes be a gap in years and differences in outlook, by being willing to talk and listen, the Water Monkey can gain a lot from the advice and assistance given him. Openness on his part can be to the benefit of all

The Year of the Ox is an important one for the Water Monkey, particularly in terms of what he learns during it. Although he may sometimes despair of all he has to do, if he rises to the challenge and has faith in himself, his achievements this year can be considerable.

TIP FOR THE YEAR

Make the most of opportunities to develop your skills. Your efforts in the Ox year can have considerable value and open up some intriguing possibilities.

The Wood Monkey

This will be a year of interesting opportunities for the Wood Monkey, although central to it will be planning, good organization and liaison with others.

As the year starts the Wood Monkey would do well to give some thought to what he wants to accomplish over the next 12 months. These ideas could be connected to his home, interests he wants to pursue or activities he has not had much time for over the last year. Whatever his aims, by making plans the Wood Monkey will not only get far more out of the year but also make more effective use of his time. He will also find those around him helpful and if he talks over his ideas, he will find this can give them some extra momentum.

However, while a lot can be achieved this year, the Wood Monkey does need be wary of too much haste. The Ox year is very much one that favours a more measured approach. The implications and costs of any plans also need to considered and sufficient time allowed for their completion. Wood Monkeys, do take note.

For many Wood Monkeys the Ox year can bring some especially good travel opportunities and if there is a particular destination the Wood Monkey would like to visit, he should discuss this with others and make enquiries as well as keep alert for special offers. Over the year a holiday or short break he arranges can bring him a great deal of pleasure. Some Wood Monkeys may even be able to combine a holiday with a personal interest or special occasion and so make their time away even more meaningful.

Another area which can bring the Wood Monkey a lot of pleasure is developing his interests. Setting himself some purposeful objectives would be well worth doing, particularly for Wood Monkeys who retire this year or have recently retired. Some may be tempted to take up interests that have intrigued them for a while. By following up his ideas, the Wood Monkey can gain a lot from the Ox year.

As with all Monkeys, though, the Wood Monkey does need to pay attention to his well-being. This includes making sure he has a balanced diet and regular exercise. If he has any concerns or is considering a new health or fitness discipline, it is important that he seeks medical advice.

The Wood Monkey will also need to be careful in financial matters and when considering any large purchase or expensive plan, especially if it is connected with his accommodation, he needs to keep a check on the costs and implications. Similarly, when dealing with financial forms, he needs to be careful and to check anything that might be unclear. If he delays his response or makes mistakes, he could be involved in some extra and often unwelcome correspondence. Wood Monkeys, do take note.

For Wood Monkeys in work this can be a demanding year and yet again they will need to remain focused and concentrate on what needs to be done. To become distracted or involved in other matters could lead to frustrations and delay. Work-wise, this may not be the smoothest of years. Those Wood Monkeys who retire or decide to lessen their working commitments will often be relieved to have the time to do other things.

However, the Wood Monkey will particularly value the social opportunities that arise this year and his personal interests will often give him the chance to meet others. Some Wood Monkeys will find their travels having a good social element. Certainly over the year there will be many occasions for the Wood Monkey to enjoy. The first quarter of the year and July and December could see the most social activity. For Wood Monkeys keen build up their social life, especially if they have recently changed location or now have more time available, it would be worth joining a local interest group or perhaps considering helping in the community in some way. By taking action and using his time purposefully, the Wood Monkey can derive a lot of satisfaction from what he does.

In his domestic life this can also be a rewarding year and by combining ideas and talents, the Wood Monkey and those around him will be pleased with what they are able to accomplish. The Ox year very much favours joint undertakings, with home or garden projects being particularly satisfying. The Wood Monkey will also do a lot to help others over the year and the time and advice he gives may be of more significance than he may realize. He does play a key role in the lives of many people and this will certainly be underlined during the course of the year.

The Ox year holds encouraging prospects for the Wood Monkey, but to benefit he does need to decide on what he wants to do and act on his ideas. With carefully thought through aims, this can be a constructive time and the Wood Monkey will be well supported by those around him.

TIP FOR THE YEAR

Do be forthcoming. Talk over your ideas and let others help. With combined effort, so much more can happen. Also, allow time for the results of your actions to filter through. The Ox year is not one for rush. Good planning is very much the order of the year.

The Fire Monkey

This will be a reasonable year for the Fire Monkey and while he may not achieve as much as he would like, by keeping his expectations modest he can make this a generally satisfying time.

The Fire Monkey's domestic life is particularly well aspected and by making sure he spends quality time with those close to him and plays a full part in domestic activities, he will find his home life going well and meaning a lot to him. There could be some moments during the year that could be a source of much personal pleasure, possibly including academic success, an engagement, marriage or the birth of a grandchild.

The Fire Monkey will also find others supportive and if at any time he has concerns, would welcome additional help or would value someone's opinion, he should ask. By being open he will not only benefit from what others say or do but also be able to build rapport and understanding. Even though with some of the pressures and commitments he has there will be moments when he will be tired or tense, he will get a lot of value from relaxing and enjoying the company of those who are special to him. With travel encouragingly aspected, he should also give some thought to taking a holiday during the year. Time spent with loved ones and the chance to have a rest from the usual routines can do him a lot of good.

With the aspects being so positive concerning the Fire Monkey's relations with others, his social life can also be a source of much pleasure. He will especially enjoy meeting up with close friends. There will also be opportunities to extend his social circle and with his amiable Fire Monkey nature, he will impress quite a few people. For Fire Monkeys who are alone, the Ox year can usher in an improvement in their situation. By going out more and making the most of their social life, they can make some important friendships. Mid-February to mid-April, July and December could see the most social activity.

Although the Fire Monkey will have many competing demands on his time, it is also important that he allows time for his interests and recreational pursuits. Not only can these be excellent ways for him to unwind and enjoy some of the rewards he works so hard for, but in some cases they can take him out of doors or provide him with the chance of additional exercise. In 2009 it is important that the Fire Monkey maintains a sensible work–lifestyle balance. Any Fire Monkey who has neglected his interests in recent times would do well to address this. He really can benefit as a result. In addition, he should pay attention to his well-being in the Ox year and give some consideration to his diet and general level of exercise. If he has any concerns, it would be worth seeking medical advice.

As far as money matters are concerned, this is a year for careful control. With home, family and possible travel expenses as well as the purchases he will be keen to make, the Fire Monkey does need to keep tabs on his outgoings and, where possible, make allowances for forthcoming expenses. By controlling his budget he will get to do a lot more.

At work this will be a demanding year, with many Fire Monkeys facing a heavier workload as well as some frustrations. The Ox year does call for increased effort and results will not always be easy to obtain. However, challenging though the year may be, any difficulties the Fire Monkey may face will be a good test of his abilities as well as add to his experience. As has so often been shown, difficulties can reveal strengths and bring out the best in people, and they will for many Fire Monkeys during the year. Also, in view of the prevailing aspects, the Fire Monkey would do well to be flexible in his approach and prepared to make the most of his present position, even if it is not always ideal. The lessons of 2009 can help both his reputation and his prospects.

For Fire Monkeys who are keen to advance their career, change their job or find work, this will not be an easy time. In addition to the sometimes limited openings, some applications that they had great hopes for might not go their way. However, one key feature of the Fire Monkey's personality is that he is tenacious and even though there may be disappointments along the way, by persevering, making every effort at interview and showing himself informed and willing, he may be given an opportunity to prove himself. Results *will* need to be worked for in 2009, but the challenges of the year can bring out some of the Fire Monkey's strengths. April, May, September and November could see the best opportunities, but with the aspects as they are, these do need to be seized as and when they occur.

Overall, there will be a lot in the Ox year that will bring the Fire Monkey pleasure and his relations with others will often mean a great deal to him. However, the Ox year is also one for effort and it will not always be easy or straightforward to make headway. The Fire Monkey does need to remain realistic in his expectations and aims.

TIP FOR THE YEAR

Do be open and draw on the support and advice of others. Also, despite your many commitments, keep your lifestyle in balance. By making sure you give time to others and maintain your social life and interests, you will benefit in a great many ways.

The Earth Monkey

In view of all that has happened in recent years, the Earth Monkey would do well to regard this as a good year to take stock, make the most of his present position and decide on his future plans. Although this may not be a year for major progress, what he accomplishes can be far-reaching.

One important feature of the Ox year is that it favours the Earth Monkey's relations with others and over the year he will often be grateful for the support and goodwill he is shown. Domestic life in particular can be a source of much pleasure and, while often busy, by making sure he spends time with those who are important to him, he will be well rewarded. This is also a good year for joint undertakings and whether deciding on home improvements or acquisitions, enjoying mutual interests or perhaps taking a holiday or break, the Earth Monkey and his loved ones will not only enjoy a better understanding but also have a more satisfying and productive year. In addition, the Earth Monkey will do a lot to help family members, with both younger and more senior relations often being grateful for his help and thoughtfulness.

The Earth Monkey's social life will also bring him a lot of pleasure during the year. Many Earth Monkeys will find their interests or work bringing them into contact with others and new friendships being made. For Earth Monkeys who are keen to build up their social life, particularly if they are alone, this can be an encouraging year and they can enjoy a considerable improvement in their situation. The first quarter of the Ox year and July and December could see the most social activity.

Travel can also feature prominently this year. If there is a particular destination the Earth Monkey is keen to visit or he sees an offer that appeals to him, he should follow it up. Some Earth Monkeys may be tempted to take advantage of short breaks, sometimes on the spur of the moment, and these can lead to some enjoyable times. Travel-wise, it is a case of making the most of opportunities as they arise.

The Earth Monkey usually involves himself in a lot of activities and in the Ox year to be on top form he does need be careful with his well-being. This includes making sure his diet is well balanced and that he takes regular exercise as well as has sufficient rest. If he should have any concerns or lack his usual zest, it would be worth seeking medical advice.

As far as his work prospects are concerned, this is a year for concentrating on what he knows and where his strengths lie. Many Earth Monkeys will choose to remain with their present employer over the year and build on their experience. Also, the Ox year can be an exacting one and whether meeting deadlines, overcoming problems or dealing with busy times, there will be good chances for the Earth Monkey to develop his skills. The experience he gains can stand him in excellent stead for when he next looks to move on.

With this being a positive year as far as his relations with others are concerned, the Earth Monkey should also work closely with his colleagues as well as take advantage of any chances to network. The contacts he makes can often be of use to him in the future. Again, while this may not be a year for major advances, positive action on the Earth Monkey's part can bear fruit later on.

For Earth Monkeys who are keen to move on from their present job or are seeking work, this can be a challenging time. Openings may be limited and competition fierce, and these Earth Monkeys will need to remain committed to their quest. However, extra effort can pay off. In particular finding out more about the duties involved in a certain position and the company itself can make the Earth Monkey a stronger candidate. Mid-March to May, September and November could see the best opportunities, but the Ox year very much calls for effort, determination and initiative.

The Earth Monkey also needs to be thorough when dealing with money matters. With all his commitments, family expenses and plans for the year, he will need to keep watch on his spending. In addition he should be wary of proceeding with major purchases too hurriedly. Time spent comparing prices and options, as well as waiting for favourable buying opportunities, can often save him some unnecessary expense. He should also be vigilant when dealing with financial paperwork and make sure that important policies are kept up to date. Inattention could lead to problems. Earth Monkeys, do take note.

Generally, the Ox year can be a reasonable one for the Earth Monkey. While progress may sometimes be difficult, it will give him the chance to build on his experience.

However, the most positive aspects of the year concern his relations with others, and his family and social life will often mean a great deal to him as well as be helpful in a lot of what he does.

TIP FOR THE YEAR

Be disciplined. As a Monkey you have wide interests and like to get involved in a lot of things. However, this year requires focus and you will get far more out of it by concentrating on your priorities.

FAMOUS MONKEYS

Gillian Anderson, Jennifer Aniston, Christina Aguilera, J. M. Barrie, Joe Cocker, Colette, John Constable, David Copperfield, Patricia Cornwell, Daniel Craig, Joan Crawford, Leonardo da Vinci, Timothy Dalton, Bette Davis, Danny De Vito, Celine Dion, Michael Douglas, Mia Farrow, Carrie Fisher, F Scott Fitzgerald, Ian Fleming, Dick Francis, Paul Gauguin, Jake Gyllenhaal, Jerry Hall, Tom Hanks, Harry Houdini, P. D. James, Katherine Jenkins, Julius Caesar, Buster Keaton, Edward Kennedy, Alicia Keys, Ban Ki-moon, Don King, Gladys Knight, Bob Marley, Kylie Minogue, V. S. Naipaul, Peter O'Toole, Anthony Perkins, Lisa Marie Presley, Debbie Reynolds, Little Richard, Anne Robinson, Mickey Rooney, Diana Ross, Michael Schumacher, Tom Selleck, Omar Sharif, Wilbur Smith, Rod Stewart, Jacques Tati, Elizabeth Taylor, Dame Kiri Te Kanawa, Justin Timberlake, Harry Truman, Venus Williams.

22 JANUARY 1909 ～ 9 FEBRUARY 1910   *Earth Rooster*

8 FEBRUARY 1921 ～ 27 JANUARY 1922   *Metal Rooster*

26 JANUARY 1933 ～ 13 FEBRUARY 1934   *Water Rooster*

13 FEBRUARY 1945 ～ 1 FEBRUARY 1946   *Wood Rooster*

31 JANUARY 1957 ～ 17 FEBRUARY 1958   *Fire Rooster*

17 FEBRUARY 1969 ～ 5 FEBRUARY 1970   *Earth Rooster*

5 FEBRUARY 1981 ～ 24 JANUARY 1982   *Metal Rooster*

23 JANUARY 1993 ～ 9 FEBRUARY 1994   *Water Rooster*

9 FEBRUARY 2005 ～ 28 JANUARY 2006   *Wood Rooster*

THE

ROOSTER

THE PERSONALITY OF THE ROOSTER

With a clear destination
and firm will,
I raise my sails
to the winds of fortune.

The Rooster is born under the sign of candour. He has a flamboyant and colourful personality and is meticulous in all that he does. He is an excellent organizer and wherever possible likes to plan his various activities well in advance.

The Rooster is highly intelligent and usually very well read. He has a good sense of humour and is an effective and persuasive speaker. He loves discussion and enjoys taking part in any sort of debate. He has no hesitation in speaking his mind and is forthright in his views. He does, however, lack tact and can easily damage his reputation or cause offence by some thoughtless remark or action. He has a very volatile nature and should always try to avoid acting on the spur of the moment.

The Rooster is usually very dignified in his manner and conducts himself with an air of confidence and authority. He is adept at handling financial matters and organizes his financial affairs with considerable skill. He chooses his investments well and is capable of achieving great wealth. Most Roosters save or use their money wisely, but there are a few who are the reverse and are notorious spendthrifts. Fortunately, the Rooster has great earning capacity and is rarely without sufficient funds to tide himself over.

Another characteristic of the Rooster is that he invariably carries a notebook or scraps of paper around with him. He is constantly writing himself reminders or noting down important facts lest he forgets – the Rooster cannot abide inefficiency and conducts all his activities in an orderly, precise and methodical manner.

The Rooster is usually very ambitious, but can be unrealistic in some of what he hopes to achieve. He occasionally lets his imagination run away with him and while he does not like any interference from others, it would be in his own interests to listen to their views a little more often. He also does not like criticism, and if he feels anybody is doubting his judgement or prying too closely into his affairs, he is certain to let his feelings be known. He can also be rather self centred and stubborn over relatively trivial matters, but to compensate for this he is reliable, honest and trustworthy, and this is appreciated by all who come into contact with him.

Roosters born between the hours of five and seven, both at dawn and sundown, tend to be the most extrovert of their sign, but all Roosters like to lead an active social life and enjoy attending parties and big functions. The Rooster usually has a wide circle of friends and is able to build up influential contacts with remarkable ease. He often belongs to several clubs and societies and involves himself in a variety of different activities. He is particularly interested in the environment, humanitarian affairs and anything affecting the welfare of others. He has a very caring nature and will do much to help those less fortunate than himself.

He also gets much pleasure from gardening and while he may not spend as much time in the garden as he would like, his garden is invariably well kept and productive.

The Rooster is generally very distinguished in his appearance and if his job permits he will wear an official uniform with great pride and dignity. He is not averse to publicity and takes great delight in being the centre of attention. He often does well at PR work or any job which brings him into contact with the media. He also makes a very good teacher.

The female Rooster leads a varied and interesting life. She involves herself in many different activities and there are some who wonder how she can achieve so much. She often holds very strong views and, like her male counterpart, has no hesitation in speaking her mind or telling others how she thinks things should be done. She is supremely efficient and well organized and her home is usually very neat and tidy. She has good taste in clothes and usually wears smart but very practical outfits.

The Rooster usually has a large family and takes a particularly active interest in the education of his children. He is very loyal to his partner and will find that he is especially well suited to those born under the signs of the Snake, Horse, Ox and Dragon. Provided they do not interfere too much in his various activities, the Rat, Tiger, Goat and Pig can also establish a good relationship with him, but two Roosters together are likely to squabble and irritate each other. The rather sensitive Rabbit will find the Rooster a bit too blunt for his liking, and the Rooster will quickly become exasperated by the ever inquisitive and artful Monkey. He will also find it difficult to get on with the anxious Dog.

If the Rooster can overcome his volatile nature and exercise tact, he will go far in life. He is capable and talented and will make a lasting – and usually favourable – impression almost everywhere he goes.

THE FIVE DIFFERENT TYPES OF ROOSTER

In addition to the 12 signs of the Chinese zodiac there are five elements and these have a strengthening or moderating influence on the signs. The effects of the five elements on the Rooster are described below, together with the years in which the elements were exercising their influence. Therefore those Roosters born in 1921 and 1981 are Metal Roosters, those born in 1933 and 1993 are Water Roosters, and so on.

Metal Rooster: 1921, 1981

The Metal Rooster is a hard and conscientious worker. He knows exactly what he wants in life and sets about everything in a positive and determined manner. He can at times appear abrasive and he would almost certainly do better if he were more willing to reach a compromise with others rather than hold so rigidly to his beliefs. He is very articulate and most astute when dealing with financial matters. He is loyal to his friends and often devotes much energy to working for the common good.

Water Rooster: 1933, 1993

This Rooster has a very persuasive manner and can easily gain the co-operation of others. He is intelligent, well read and enjoys taking part in discussions and debates. He has a seemingly inexhaustible amount of energy and is prepared to work long hours in order to secure what he wants. He can, however, waste a lot of valuable time worrying over minor and inconsequential details. He is approachable, has a good sense of humour and is highly regarded by others.

Wood Rooster: 1945, 2005

The Wood Rooster is honest, reliable and often sets himself high standards. He is ambitious, but he is also more prepared to work in a team than some of the other types of Rooster. He usually succeeds in life but does have a tendency to get caught up in bureaucratic matters and attempt too many things at the same time. He has wide interests, likes to travel and is very caring and considerate towards his family and friends.

Fire Rooster: 1957

This Rooster is extremely strong willed. He has many leadership qualities, is an excellent organizer and is most efficient in his work. Through sheer force of character he often secures his objectives, but he does have a tendency to be very forthright and not always consider the feelings of others. If he can learn to be more tactful he can often succeed beyond his wildest dreams.

Earth Rooster: 1909, 1969

This Rooster has a deep and penetrating mind. He is efficient, perceptive and particularly astute in business and financial matters. He is also persistent and once he has set himself an objective, he will rarely allow himself to be deflected from achieving his aim. He works hard and is held in great esteem by his friends and colleagues. He usually enjoys the arts and takes a keen interest in the activities of the various members of his family.

PROSPECTS FOR THE ROOSTER IN 2009

The Year of the Rat (7 February 2008 to 25 January 2009) is a tricky one for the Rooster and in the remaining months he will need to proceed carefully. Fortunately his methodical nature will help, but this is no time for risks or being too independent in his actions.

In his work the Rooster will need to concentrate on his duties. This is not a time for spreading his energies widely or becoming distracted by unhelpful matters. However, with his prospects about to enjoy a considerable upturn in 2009, anything he can do to gain experience in the closing Rat months can be to his benefit. Work-wise, August to November could see some interesting possibilities, but generally this is a time for care and looking to build up experience.

The Rooster will also need to remain disciplined in financial matters. With the end of the year often bringing increased spending, any provision he can make for this in advance could be helpful. Should he have concerns over any financial matter, he does need to check the situation and if need be get appropriate advice. This is no time for risks or being lax in what could be important matters.

The Rooster is born under the sign of candour and known for his open and forthright manner. However, in some situations if he is too blunt or candid he could upset people or undermine some good relationships. At the close of the Rat year he would do well to watch his words. However, while he will need to remain aware and discreet, both his domestic and social life can see considerable activity. October and December could be especially busy months, with the Rooster often enjoying the chance to go out as well as spend more time with others.

The Year of the Ox is a promising one for the Rooster. Not only will he feel more in control of his situation, but he will also benefit from some of its opportunities. The Ox year favours effort, method and order, and this suits the Rooster's personality.

The Chinese new year begins on 26 January and for any Rooster who is feeling disillusioned about his situation, this is very much a time to draw a line under what has happened and look to move on. As the Chinese proverb reminds us, *he who comprehends the times is great*, and this *is* a time for the Rooster to seize the moment.

The aspects are especially encouraging in his work and for Roosters who are keen to move their career forward or are seeking work, this is a year to keep alert, make enquiries and act quickly when opportunities arise. With determination and a strong belief in what they can offer, they can be given an important chance to prove themselves. These Roosters should not be discouraged if initial applications do not go their way. Sometimes a rejection could turn out to be a blessing as a more suitable position opens up or they are alerted to another possibility. With characteristic Rooster resolve, many will persevere in their quest and their efforts will be rewarded. Also, these Roosters should not be too restrictive in what they consider. The Ox year is an encouraging time and will allow the Rooster to use his skills in new ways.

For Roosters who are settled in their career, this is also a year of important developments. Often, as a result of their expertise and good work, there will be the chance to move on to an often more fulfilling role. The months from March to May and August and September could see some interesting developments.

In addition to the encouraging aspects as far as the Rooster's work prospects are concerned, he can benefit from developing his interests this year. If there are any skills he would like to learn, whether work-related or recreational, he should look at ways of acquiring them. By acting on his ideas, he can derive a lot of satisfaction from his activities. Also, with the aspects as they are, new interests or skills can sometimes have unexpected benefits as well as allow the Rooster to discover new strengths.

The progress the Rooster makes in his work can lead to a rise in income and some Roosters may also benefit from receiving a gift or sum from another source. Financially, this is a much improved year and this will persuade many Roosters to proceed with ideas they have been considering for some time. These could include replacing items in their home, carrying out modifications to their accommodation, pursuing their interests or travelling. However, while keen to carry out his ideas, the Rooster should take his time when making purchases. This way he will often make more suitable decisions. In addition, if he is able to use any financial upturn to reduce any borrowings or add to his savings, this could be helpful. With care, many Roosters can not only improve their financial situation during the year but also appreciate what they do with their money.

Travel is also favourably aspected and the Rooster would do well to consider going away for a holiday at some time in the year. By planning this carefully, he will often thoroughly enjoy his time away. Again, this is a year for making the most of ideas and opportunities.

With his ability to organize, the Rooster always plays a central role in his home life and over the year this can bring him a great deal of pleasure. By encouraging everyone to help one other and share household tasks, the Rooster will not only find home life going smoothly but also being very productive. Practical projects can go well and there will be some special times that everyone will appreciate, including the marking of some family successes as well as joint interests and travel. Roosters who have had recent strains in their home life can make a difference to their situation by talking, listening and giving more time to others. Domestically, this can be a rewarding year.

With his active and outgoing nature, the Rooster can also make the most of his social life this year and any Roosters who start 2009 at a low ebb will find the Ox year can usher in an improvement. Not only will there be increased opportunities to meet others, but the Rooster's personal interests or changes in his work can lead to new friendships being made. For the unattached, the Ox year has strong romantic possibilities, with February, June to August, December and January seeing the most social activity. However, while the Rooster will often revel in the social opportunities of the year, he does need to remain mindful of others. Sometimes his strong personality can mean that he dictates to people and he does need to watch this.

Overall, the Ox year has considerable potential for the Rooster. In his work there will be some excellent opportunities to put his skills to fuller use, while his home and social life can bring him a lot of pleasure. Another significant factor of the Ox year is that it is a time of hope and for any Rooster who has had recent problems, this is a year for moving on, for taking action and bringing about the improvement he wants. In the Ox year the Rooster's determination and sense of purpose can lead to a lot opening up for him.

The Metal Rooster

The Metal Rooster has many fine qualities. He is keen, hard working and also enjoys good relations with many people. In 2009 he will have a lot in his favour and will enjoy some progress and pleasing personal developments.

The Metal Rooster's relations with others will be especially important and for those with a partner there could be some good news to celebrate. This could include an engagement, a marriage, an addition to the family or a move to more suitable accommodation. Many Metal Roosters will also greatly benefit from the support given by family members and close friends, particularly during some of the busier parts of the year.

For Metal Roosters who are alone this can also be a significant time and, for some, mark the start of a significant new chapter in their life. If they have had recent personal difficulties or setbacks, this is a year to draw a firm line under what has happened and move forward. By concentrating on the present and involving themselves in a variety of activities, including possible new interests, they can help bring about the improvement they have been wanting for some time. A lot does rest with them, but over the year many could see quite a transformation in their situation. February to mid-March, June to August and the closing weeks of the Ox year could see the most social activity as well as being good months for meeting others. Many Metal Roosters who are unattached could even feel the effects of Cupid's arrow this year.

In addition to the positive aspects concerning the Metal Rooster's relations with others, another area that will bring him considerable benefit will be his personal interests. By setting time aside for activities he enjoys as well as looking to develop his skills, he can not only make this a personally satisfying time but also discover new strengths and open up new possibilities for the future. The emphasis in the Ox year is on action and while the Metal Rooster may have many competing demands on his time, pursuing his own interests can do him a lot of good.

At work this is a year of important developments. There will be excellent chances for those Metal Roosters who are established in a career to take on greater responsibilities and many will secure promotion. In some cases more senior colleagues could be especially encouraging and instrumental in helping their progress. With support, the experience he has gained and his own keen nature, the Metal Rooster will not only feel ready to move his career forward but will be able to reap the rewards of his recent endeavours. When openings arise, he should waste no time in putting himself forward.

For those Metal Roosters who would welcome a fresh challenge, the Ox year can again often bring the chance they want. This is no time to remain unfulfilled and by exploring possibilities and putting themselves forward, many will discover new types of work that not only interest them but also allow them to use their talents in other ways. The Ox year can bring important new possibilities. This also applies to Metal Roosters seeking work. Although some may have grown disillusioned recently, by looking to move on, their actions and resolve can help bring about the opportunities they want. March to May and mid-July to September could see some interesting developments, but the aspects are so encouraging that opportunities can arise at almost any time during the year.

The progress the Metal Rooster makes in his work can lead to a rise in his income and some Metal Roosters could also benefit from a gift or put an enterprising idea of theirs to good use. However, while the Metal Rooster's financial prospects are improving, with his existing commitments and some of the plans he may have, he does need to budget carefully. With good management, he will be able to take advantage of the prevailing conditions, but should he be tempted to spend more freely than he should or be lax in money matters, then he may not benefit quite as much from the year. Financially, this may be a fortunate time, but it is also one for discipline.

The Ox year will also bring travel opportunities for many Metal Roosters and the rest and change of scene can be highly beneficial.

Overall, the Metal Rooster will have a lot in his favour this year, but to benefit he does need to take the initiative. As Virgil wrote, 'Fortune favours the bold,' and in the Ox year fortune *will* favour the bold and active. For the Metal Rooster this is a year for making the most of his opportunities, and if he does so he can enjoy many pleasing developments in both in his work and his personal life.

TIP FOR THE YEAR
This is a promising time for you, but to benefit you do need to take action. Also, nurture your relations with others. The help you are given can be important in both your personal and professional life. This is a year to act *and* to enjoy yourself.

The Water Rooster

This will be a significant year for the Water Rooster and by making the most of his opportunities, he can do himself a lot of good. However, central to how he fares will be attitude. If he is committed and recognizes the value of what he is doing, his achievements can give him something solid to build on in the future.

In the Water Rooster's education there will often be considerable pressure, particularly as there will be different subjects to study, exams to prepare for and sometimes project work to complete. Although it may be daunting, by concentrating on what he has to do and putting in the effort, the Water Rooster's application and willingness can lead to encouraging progress being made. This is a year of opportunity and for those prepared to make the most of it, the rewards can be far-reaching.

In addition to academic work the Water Rooster can get a lot of pleasure from his interests and he should look to further his skills and knowledge over the year. Whether he enjoys more creative activities (the Water Rooster often excels in areas where he can express himself), sport or music, by practising and developing his skills, he will often derive a lot of satisfaction from what he does. Should there be ideas or interests he is keen to pursue, or should he have academic or more personal concerns at any time, he should talk to others about them. This way not only can he be better guided but in some cases his concerns can be eased or solved. Whether family, tutors or close friends, there are many people who believe in the Water Rooster and are keen to help, and in this important year he should draw on the assistance others are so willing to give.

The Water Rooster can also look forward to a pleasing social life and will particularly value some of the close friendships that he has. Not only can confidences be shared and support and encouragement given, but a great deal of fun can be had. Also, in view of the different activities the Water Rooster will become involved with over the year, there will be chances for him to get to know other people. Any Water Roosters who are hoping to make new friends, perhaps having changed school or location, can see an improvement in their situation as the year progresses. March, June to August, December and January 2010 will be the most active months socially.

As with so many of his sign, the Water Rooster enjoys shopping but rather than spend his money too readily, he would do well to consider his purchases carefully and save up for more expensive items. With greater discipline he will be able to put his money to better use as well as often get more pleasure and value from the things he buys.

The Ox year also favours travel and over the year there will be chances for many Water Roosters to go away, either on holiday, to visit other people or in some capacity connected with their education. By making the most of his invitations, the Water Rooster will often enjoy himself as well as have the chance to find out about new areas. The Ox year has an element of discovery about it and this can include travelling to some exciting new places.

For Water Roosters born in 1933 this can also be a satisfying year. Again travel can bring pleasure for many and whether going on holiday or visiting others, the Water Rooster will enjoy the opportunity to go away and possibly revisit some favourite places. In addition his personal interests can bring him a lot of pleasure and by using his knowledge to advantage, he can derive much satisfaction from his activities.

The Water Rooster will also find those around him supportive and by being open and discussing his ideas, as well as any concerns he may have, he will find others can do a lot to assist him. During the year he should remember that help is there should he need it.

The Water Rooster is usually meticulous, but over the year he does need to be careful when entering into any new transactions, especially if related to his accommodation, or attending to important paperwork. The details do need to be checked thoroughly and if the Water Rooster has any doubts, it would be worth obtaining further guidance.

For the Water Rooster, whether born in 1933 or 1993, this can be a satisfying year, particularly as it will enable him to enjoy his skills and interests, and he will often be encouraged by those around him. For the younger Water Rooster the year can mark an important stage in his education and the effort and commitment he puts in can often have far-reaching significance. This is a good year for the Water Rooster and one that he should use well.

TIP FOR THE YEAR
This is a year of great possibilities, but it does rest with you to make the most of your ideas and opportunities. With a willing attitude, backed by a belief in what you can do, you can accomplish a great deal.

The Wood Rooster

One of the key features of the Wood Rooster's personality is that he likes to plan ahead and this ability will be of great help to him this year. By giving careful thought to what he wants to do, he will not only get more out of the year but also benefit from some of its more favourable aspects.

Throughout the year the Wood Rooster will be helped by the support and goodwill of others, and whenever he has thoughts, plans or concerns, he should talk these over with those around him. Not only will this allow them to help and advise him, but it could also set some important wheels in motion. Indeed, just mentioning some hopes or ideas could give them the momentum they need to get started.

For those Wood Roosters in work there could be some important decisions to make. Some may take the opportunity to retire or reduce their working commitments, while others may have the chance to vary their role and take on a new challenge. However, in view of the changes this can involve, the Wood Rooster would do well to think through what is best for him as well as talk his situation over with those around him. Important decisions do need careful consideration. However, many Wood Roosters will be happy with the choices they make.

The Ox year will also give the Wood Rooster an excellent chance to make more of his personal interests and again he would do well to give some thought to this early on in the year. If there is a particular challenge or project he would like to take up or new interest that appeals to him, he should look into it. The Ox year is very much a year for action and Wood Roosters who retire and/or have some extra time available will benefit from putting this to purposeful use. For Wood Roosters who enjoy creative activities this is also very much a year for promoting their skills. They could be particularly encouraged by the response and new possibilities could open up for them as a result. Over the year the Wood Rooster's special talents can serve him well.

The Rooster often has a liking for the outdoors and for those Wood Roosters who have gardens, tending their land can bring them considerable pleasure. Also, with this being a year for following through ideas, some will be keen to make alterations or experiment with new stock and they will be interested to see how their plans take shape.

Travel, too, is favourably aspected and the Wood Rooster should aim to go away for a holiday during the year as well as take up any invitations he has to stay with others. Some Wood Roosters may also enjoy an occasional short break and many will appreciate the chance to visit some new and often interesting destinations.

The Wood Rooster's interests and travels can also have a good social element and over the year he will often appreciate spending time with others. March, June to August and last weeks of the Ox year could see the most social activity and for any Wood Rooster who is keen to lead a more active social life, particularly if he has seen recent changes in his life, this is very much a time for getting out more and becoming involved in different activities. In 2009 positive action can be well rewarded.

As far as financial matters are concerned, again this is a year for planning ahead. With all the Wood Rooster's plans for his accommodation, his interests and travel, he does need to manage his outgoings well and make early provision for more substantial outlays. Wood Roosters who retire this year and see a reduction in their earnings will be helped by considering the adjustments they may need to make. The key to so much in 2009 is careful consideration and in matters of finance this *will* make a difference.

The Wood Rooster's home life can be particularly special this year. There could well be some important family news to celebrate and the Wood Rooster will particularly value the support and assistance he is given. Encouraging a spirit of openness and making plans and decisions together will not only help general understanding but also lead to more going ahead and being enjoyed over the year.

In most respects this can be a good year for the Wood Rooster but, as with all years, problems will arise. Sometimes the Wood Rooster could find himself concerned about work-related or other decisions he has to take. At such times he should talk to others and, if need be, contact experts for advice. Similarly, if he has any personal concerns, again he should let others know, as they will often be able to help. Wood Roosters, *do* take note.

Overall, this can be a satisfying year for the Wood Rooster, but to get the most from it he does need to use his time well. With clear aims and the support of others, however, he can get to enjoy a lot over the year.

TIP FOR THE YEAR
This is a favourable year for you, but to benefit you do need to make the most of your ideas. A lot is possible and planning will be well rewarded.

The Fire Rooster

This is the sort of year that suits the Fire Rooster. It is a year when planning and effort can lead to some very positive results and in view of the mixed fortunes some Fire Roosters will have experienced of late, it can mark a welcome upturn in their situation.

At work the aspects are especially encouraging and many Fire Roosters will not only enjoy some heartening successes but also make important advances. For those who are well established in their career there will be the chance to make more of their strengths and their work is likely to go well. For those involved in creative or expressive endeavours in particular, the year can bring some personal successes, with work or ideas they put forward being well received.

Although many Fire Roosters will decide to remain with their present employer and will often benefit from promotion opportunities, for those who would welcome new challenges or the chance to take their career in a new direction, the Ox year can bring some interesting opportunities. By considering what they would now like to do and making enquiries (and here existing contacts could be helpful), these Fire Roosters could be alerted to possibilities worth pursuing. With their skills, reputation and commitment, many will be successful in their quest. Late February to May, August and September could see some interesting developments but opportunities could arise at almost any time during the year.

Fire Roosters seeking work, either at the start of the Ox year or during it, will also find that by remaining alert, seeking advice and widening the range of their search, they can gain a position that will allow them to build on their skills.

The positive aspects also apply to the Fire Rooster's personal interests and those who are skilled in a certain area should, if appropriate, put their work forward. For the creative Fire Rooster this can be a particularly successful time. Also, if the Fire Rooster has projects he is keen to tackle or subjects he would like to learn more about, he should find out more. As the saying reminds us, *there is no time like the present.*

The Ox year is also favourably aspected for travel and if there is a destination the Fire Rooster would like to visit or he sees an attractive travel offer, he should follow it up.

Over the year many Fire Roosters will enjoy visiting places new to them and will benefit from the rest and change that travel can bring.

The success the Fire Rooster enjoys at work can lead to a rise in income and some Fire Roosters may be able to supplement this by doing something extra. Earnings-wise, this can be a much improved year. To benefit fully, though, the Fire Rooster does need to manage his situation well and if he can reduce any borrowings, add to savings or pensions plans and set funds aside for more substantial purchases, he will find this helpful. However, while this can be a positive year financially, the Fire Rooster does need to be wary of more spontaneous purchases or proceeding too much on an ad hoc basis. Without discipline, any extra money he makes could quickly be spent. Fire Roosters, take note and do manage your resources well.

Domestically, this will be a pleasing year and although the Fire Rooster will often be busy with work and other commitments, if he makes sure quality time is spent with his loved ones, he can make this a rewarding and often constructive year. During it some Fire Roosters will decide to go ahead with improvements to their home that they have been considering for some time and while these may involve considerable effort, the Fire Rooster is likely to feel satisfied with what is achieved. He will also often assist and advise those close to him and his thoughtfulness and perceptive nature will be appreciated.

In view of the active nature of the year, the Fire Rooster may be rather selective in his socializing. However, by keeping in contact with friends and going to events that appeal to him, especially ones related to his interests, he will often greatly enjoy himself. In such a busy year it is important that he keeps his lifestyle in balance. February to mid-March, June to August and the closing weeks of the Ox year could see the most social activity and for the unattached, a chance meeting or someone they are already acquainted with could suddenly become more significant. The Ox year is a time of opportunity for the Fire Rooster both personally and professionally.

Overall, the Year of the Ox is certainly an encouraging one for the Fire Rooster and by making the most of his ideas, skills and opportunities, he can look forward to making good progress. This is a year for action, for believing in himself and putting himself forward.

TIP FOR THE YEAR
Do not let hopes, ideas and possibilities come to nothing – take action! It is better to make the most of your chances than remain frustrated or be left wondering what might have been. Over the year you will have a lot in your favour and now is a good time to act.

The Earth Rooster

This will be a special year for the Earth Rooster. Not only will it mark the start of a new decade in his life but he will be determined to get his forties off to a positive start. And the effect of his efforts this year can be far-reaching.

At work many Earth Roosters will feel they have reached an important juncture in their career. Some will consider they have done all they can in their present role and will be ready for change while others will be keen to take on increased responsibilities where they are. Either way, the Ox year can give these Earth Roosters the opportunities they want and by making enquiries and putting themselves forward, many will secure promotion or succeed in taking their career in a new direction. The Ox year is very much one for progress and will give the Earth Rooster the chance to make more of his particular strengths. The months from March to May and August and September could see interesting possibilities, but such are the encouraging aspects that opportunities could arise at almost any time of the year.

The Earth Rooster will also be helped by the support of his colleagues. Not only could he be encouraged by more senior colleagues who are keen for him to make more of his potential but some of his contacts could alert him to possibilities worth considering or give him useful moral support. In addition, all Earth Roosters should make the most of any chances they have to network and get themselves better known. With their ability to empathize, connect and communicate, they can do their situation a lot of good. This is very much a year when the Earth Rooster can make his talents count.

Another important feature of the year will be the way the Earth Rooster is able to build on his experience, and whether he changes to a new role or adds to his present responsibilities, there will be some excellent chances to develop his skills. To help with this, if the Earth Rooster has the chance to do any training or could do some studying by himself, he will not only find this helping his current position but also opening up possible avenues for the future. With the ambitions he has for the years ahead, what is started now can have significance in the future.

This also applies to Earth Roosters seeking work. Events can often work in fortuitous ways for them and by widening the scope of what they are prepared to consider, many will secure what can be an interesting new position with the potential for future development. Work-wise, this is a year of opportunity and even if some applications do not go their way, with persistence and self-belief many of these Earth Roosters will succeed in their aims.

The success the Earth Rooster enjoys at work can also lead to a rise in income and financially this is an improved year. However, to benefit, the Earth Rooster does need to remain disciplined in his spending and to make provision for his commitments and some of the more expensive plans and purchases he has in mind. With good control, many Earth Roosters can benefit from their increased earnings, but spending does need to be watched. Also, if the Earth Rooster is able to start or add to a pension policy or take advantage of tax-efficient savings schemes, he could find this to his long-term advantage.

Travel is well aspected during the year and to mark their fortieth birthday some Earth Roosters may be tempted to take a special holiday. The Earth Rooster could also enjoy a short break during the year and if he sees an offer that appeals to him or receives an invitation to stay with people he knows, he should follow it up. The Ox year can present him with some good opportunities.

Although the Earth Rooster will have many demands on his time, it is also important that he keeps his lifestyle in balance. This includes allowing time for socializing as well as for enjoying his personal interests. With the aspects being so positive, if he decides to set himself a particular project for the year he will often find this giving extra purpose and meaning to what he does. And for the more creative, new ideas could be well received and open up interesting possibilities.

For many Earth Roosters their interests could also have a pleasing social element and lead to new friendships. For the unattached, new romance is possible and will often be made all the stronger by a meeting of minds. February, June to August and the closing weeks of the year could see the most social opportunities, but throughout the Ox year the Earth Rooster's personable nature and talents as a communicator will be appreciated by many.

This will also be a busy year domestically and for those Earth Roosters who are parents there could be increased demands on their time as their children grow and get to do more. Although home life will often be conducted at a fast pace, by making sure there is good co-operation and communication, the Earth Rooster will enjoy it. His organizational talents will be appreciated by his loved ones and busy though his home life can be, it can also be immensely rewarding.

The Year of the Ox can be a successful one for the Earth Rooster and by putting himself forward and taking action, he can do himself a lot of good and get this new decade in his life off to a promising and sometimes exciting start.

To benefit from the encouraging aspects of the year, you do need to take action. If not, chances could slip by and some hopes remain unfulfilled. This is no year for standing still. You can greatly benefit from the good relations you have with your family, friends and colleagues, and their support and goodwill can be another positive and helpful factor throughout the year.

FAMOUS ROOSTERS

Mohamed al Fayed, Fernando Alonso, Beyoncé, Cate Blanchett, Barbara Taylor Bradford, Sir Michael Caine, Enrico Caruso, Christopher Cazenove, Eric Clapton, Joan Collins, Rita Coolidge, Craig David, Daniel Day Lewis, Minnie Driver, the Duke of Edinburgh, Gloria Estefan, Roger Federer, Errol Flynn, Benjamin Franklin, Dawn French, Stephen Fry, Melanie Griffith, Deborah Harry, Goldie Hawn, Katherine Hepburn, Paris Hilton, Catherine Zeta Jones, Quincy Jones, Diane Keaton, Søren Kierkegaard, D. H. Lawrence, David Livingstone, Ken Livingstone, Jayne Mansfield, Steve Martin, James Mason, W. Somerset Maugham, Paul Merton, Kate Middleton, Bette Midler, Van Morrison, Willie Nelson, Kim Novak, Yoko Ono, Dolly Parton, Matthew Perry, Michelle Pfeiffer, Priscilla Presley, Mary Quant, Joan Rivers, Kelly Rowland, Kevin Rudd, Jenny Seagrove, George Segal, Carly Simon, Britney Spears, Johann Strauss, Verdi, Richard Wagner, Serena Williams, Neil Young, Renée Zellweger.

---

10 FEBRUARY 1910 ∼ 29 JANUARY 1911   *Metal Dog*

28 JANUARY 1922 ∼ 15 FEBRUARY 1923   *Water Dog*

14 FEBRUARY 1934 ∼ 3 FEBRUARY 1935   *Wood Dog*

2 FEBRUARY 1946 ∼ 21 JANUARY 1947   *Fire Dog*

18 FEBRUARY 1958 ∼ 7 FEBRUARY 1959   *Earth Dog*

6 FEBRUARY 1970 ∼ 26 JANUARY 1971   *Metal Dog*

25 JANUARY 1982 ∼ 12 FEBRUARY 1983   *Water Dog*

10 FEBRUARY 1994 ∼ 30 JANUARY 1995   *Wood Dog*

29 JANUARY 2006 ∼ 17 FEBRUARY 2007   *Fire Dog*

THE
DOG

THE PERSONALITY OF THE DOG

I have my values
and beliefs.
These are my beacon
in an ever-changing world.

The Dog is born under the signs of loyalty and anxiety. He usually holds very firm views and beliefs and is the champion of good causes. He hates any sort of injustice or unfair treatment and will do all in his power to help those less fortunate than himself. He has a strong sense of fair play and will be honourable and open in all his dealings.

The Dog is very direct and straightforward. He is never one to skirt round issues and speaks frankly and to the point. He can be stubborn, but he is prepared to listen to the views of others and will try to be as fair as possible in coming to his decisions. He will readily give advice where it is needed and will be the first to offer assistance when things go wrong.

The Dog instils confidence wherever he goes and there are many who admire him for his integrity and resolute manner. He is a very good judge of character and can often form an accurate impression of someone very shortly after meeting them. He is also very intuitive and can frequently sense how things are going to work out long in advance.

Despite his friendly and amiable manner, the Dog is not a big socializer. He dislikes having to attend large functions or parties and much prefers a quiet meal with friends or a chat by the fire. He is an excellent conversationalist and is often a marvellous raconteur of amusing stories and anec-dotes.

The Dog is also quick witted and his mind is always alert. He can keep calm in a crisis and although he does have a temper, his outbursts tend to be short lived. He is loyal and trustworthy, but if he ever feels badly let down or rejected by someone, he will rarely forgive or forget.

The Dog usually has very set interests. He prefers to specialize and become an expert in a chosen area rather than dabble in a variety of different activities. He usually does well in jobs where he feels that he is being of service to others and is often suited to careers in the social services, the medical and legal professions and teaching. He does, however, need to feel motivated in his work. He has to have a sense of purpose and if ever this is lacking he can quite often drift through life without ever achieving very much. Once he has the motivation, however, very little can prevent him from securing his objective.

Another characteristic of the Dog is his tendency to worry and to view things rather pessimistically. Quite often his worries are totally unnecessary and are of his own making. Although it may be difficult, worrying is a habit that all Dogs should try to overcome.

The Dog is not materialistic or particularly bothered about accumulating great wealth. As long as he has the money necessary to support his family and to spend on the occasional luxury, he is more than happy. However, when he does have any spare money he tends to be rather a spendthrift and does not always put his money to its best use. He is also not a very good speculator and would be advised to get professional advice before entering into any major long term investment.

The Dog will rarely be short of admirers, but he is not an easy person to live with. His moods are changeable and his standards high, but he will be loyal and protective to his partner and will do all in his power to provide a good and comfortable home. He can get on extremely well with those born under the signs of the Horse, Pig, Tiger and Monkey, and can also establish a sound and stable relationship with the Rat, Ox, Rabbit, Snake and another Dog, but will find the Dragon a bit too flamboyant for his liking. He will also find it difficult to understand the imaginative Goat and is likely to be highly irritated by the candid Rooster.

The female Dog is renowned for her beauty. She has a warm and caring nature, although until she knows someone well she can be both secretive and very guarded. She is highly intelligent and despite her calm and tranquil appearance she can be extremely ambitious. She enjoys sport and other outdoor activities and has a happy knack of finding bargains in the most unlikely of places. She can also get rather impatient when things do not work out as she would like.

The Dog usually has a very good way with children and can be a doting parent. He will rarely be happier than when he is helping someone or doing something that will benefit others. Providing he can cure himself of his tendency to worry, he will lead a very full and active life, and in that life he will make many friends and do a tremendous amount of good.

THE FIVE DIFFERENT TYPES OF DOG

In addition to the 12 signs of the Chinese zodiac there are five elements and these have a strengthening or moderating influence on the signs. The effects of the five elements on the Dog are described below, together with the years in which the elements were exercising their influence. Therefore those Dogs born in 1910 and 1970 are Metal Dogs, those born in 1922 and 1982 are Water Dogs, and so on.

Metal Dog: 1910, 1970

The Metal Dog is bold, confident and forthright and sets about everything he does in a resolute and determined manner. He has a great belief in his abilities and has no hesitation about speaking his mind or devoting himself to some just cause. He can be rather serious at times and can become anxious and irritable when things are not going according to plan. He tends to have very specific interests and it would certainly help him if he were to broaden his outlook and become more involved in group activities. He is extremely loyal and faithful to his friends.

Water Dog: 1922, 1982

The Water Dog has a very direct and outgoing personality. He is an excellent communicator and has little trouble in persuading others to fall in with his plans. He does, however, have a somewhat carefree nature and is not as disciplined or as thorough as he should be in certain matters. Neither does he keep as much control over his finances as he should, but he can be most generous to his family and friends and will make sure that they want for nothing. He is usually very good with children and has a wide circle of friends.

Wood Dog: 1934, 1994

This Dog is a hard and conscientious worker and will usually make a favourable impression wherever he goes. He is less independent than some of the other types of Dog and prefers to work in a group rather than on his own. He is popular, has a good sense of humour and takes a keen interest in the activities of the various members of his family. He is often attracted to the finer things in life and can obtain much pleasure from collecting stamps, coins, pictures or antiques. He prefers to live in the country rather than the town.

Fire Dog: 1946, 2006

This Dog has a lively, outgoing personality and is able to establish friendships with remarkable ease. He is an honest and conscientious worker and likes to take an active part in all that is going on around him. He also likes to explore new ideas and providing he can get the necessary support and advice, he can often succeed where others have failed. He does, however, have a tendency to be stubborn. Providing he can overcome this, he can often achieve considerable fame and fortune.

Earth Dog: 1958

The Earth Dog is very talented and astute. He is methodical and efficient and is capable of going far in his chosen profession. He tends to be rather quiet and reserved, but has a very persuasive manner and usually secures his objectives without too much opposition. He is generous and kind and always ready to lend a helping hand when it is needed. He is also held in very high esteem by his friends and colleagues and is usually most dignified in his appearance.

PROSPECTS FOR THE DOG IN 2009

The Year of the Rat (7 February 2008 to 25 January 2009) is a generally encouraging one for the Dog and the closing months will be a time of considerable activity. However, to make the most of the prevailing aspects, the Dog does need to decide on what he wants to accomplish. With some clear ideas and his determined nature, he can make a lot happen.

At work the Dog will have the chance to use his strengths and enhance his reputation. For those Dogs who are eager to make progress in their career there could be some interesting openings to pursue, with September being a key time. For those seeking work, some important chances could also arise. Work-wise, the Rat year will certainly encourage the Dog to make the most of his abilities.

Many Dogs can also look forward to an improvement in their finances at this time, although, with increased spending likely towards the year's end, the Dog would do well to spread out some of his seasonal purchases as well as remain alert for favourable buying opportunities. By doing so, he could be fortunate in acquiring some bargains.

The Dog will be in demand at this time and his domestic and social life will see a lot of activity. To fit in everything he wants to do, he would do well to make his arrangements in conjunction with others and show some flexibility. This will allow him to do more, including taking up some unexpected social invitations or travel offers. October could be a particularly interesting month socially and for the unattached or those Dogs enjoying romance, the closing Rat months could be special in some way.

The Year of the Ox starts on 26 January and will be a challenging one for the Dog. Some of his plans could be affected by delays or problems and progress could sometimes be slow. However, while the Ox year will bring its frustrations, there are still positive aspects to the year and in the closing months the Dog can look forward to a noticeable improvement in his situation. As the proverb reminds us, *every cloud has a silver lining,* and the lessons of the Ox year can help to usher in a much brighter period.

In view of the prevailing aspects, however, the Dog would do well to keep his expectations modest and avoid unnecessary risk. The Ox year favours tradition and if the Dog allows his more rebellious or stubborn nature to come to the fore then problems could loom. This is very much a year for treading carefully and steadily.

At work the Dog will often decide to remain in his present place of employment and to concentrate on the areas he knows best. However, many Dogs will find their workload steadily increasing during the year and they may also have to adjust to new personnel or changes in procedure. While the Dog may be concerned by the developments, he does need to be careful not to undermine his own position. To appear inflexible or obtuse could cause difficulty or lead to him being passed over for a greater role. Dogs, do take note and do not jeopardize your recent good work by being unwilling to adapt.

However, while this is very much a year for care, the Dog can still benefit from the changes that take place. Some of his duties will give him the chance to gain important new experience as well as further his skills. If he is offered training or has the chance to vary his role in some way, this can be to his present and future benefit. What happens now can prepare him for the opportunities that await in 2010 and beyond.

For Dogs who are particularly keen to change their line of work or are looking for a job, the Ox year can be challenging. Despite their experience and the effort they put into their applications, they could face disappointments. However, while the Ox year may contain some disheartening moments, the Dog is blessed with a determined nature and in the wake of a setback he could find himself unexpectedly being offered a different position. The Ox year can sometimes work in curious ways and for the tenacious, (modest) progress is possible. Also, as many will find, what is achieved now can prove to be an important platform that they can build on in the future. May to mid-June and October to December could see some interesting possibilities.

Throughout the year, however, the Dog needs to be thorough in financial matters. With accommodation and possible travel expenses, he does need to manage his resources well and, where possible, make early provision for some of his more expensive plans. He should also deal with financial paperwork promptly and if he has any concerns or questions, seek advice. To delay or make assumptions could cause problems and sometimes incur additional costs. This is a year for care.

Although the Dog will keep himself busy over the year it would also be worth him giving some thought to ways in which he can develop his personal interests. This could be by furthering his knowledge in some way or setting himself a new project, but by doing something purposeful he will often derive a lot of satisfaction from his activities. And new interests or skills can open up some interesting avenues for the future.

Loyal, caring and protective, the Dog always sets much store by his home life and this can again be important this year. In view of some of the pressures he will face, he will often regard his home as his own private sanctuary. If he is open and prepared to talk about ideas he may be considering, he will find that those close to him are supportive and encouraging. Also, by contributing fully to home life, the Dog will value many of the occasions that take place and the strong rapport he enjoys with those around him. In this mixed year, his relations with others can be valuable and very special.

The Dog's social life can also add a pleasing element to the year and when he receives invitations to go out or sees events that appeal to him, he would do well to take these up. This is not a year for keeping himself to himself and missing out on opportunities to meet others. His social life can be an excellent way to keep his lifestyle in balance and some events will even turn out to be a lot more enjoyable than expected. April, September, December and January will see the most social activity.

The key message for the Dog in the Ox year is to tread carefully. He needs to be wary and adaptable and do his best in his current situation. As far as possible, he should avoid being drawn into difficult situations that could jeopardize his position through either his attitude or comments. However, by playing a full part in his home life, spending time with those who are important to him and using any chances to add to his knowledge and skills, he can still get a lot of value from the year and, importantly, be able to build on this in the more favourable Tiger year that follows.

The Metal Dog

The Metal Dog will have seen a lot happen in recent years and 2009 will give him a chance to take stock. This is a time for consolidation, developing skills and enjoying some pleasing personal developments. While not an easy or progressive year, it can be a constructive one.

Many Metal Dogs will have experienced change in their work over the last 12 months, either securing promotion, changing their employer or taking on new responsibilities. Instead of looking to make further changes, many will decide to remain where they are, concentrate on their duties and learn about different aspects of their work and industry. During the year their workload could increase or pressures arise and these will give the Metal Dog the chance to use and add to his skills. Work-wise, the Ox year may be challenging but, as has so often been shown, challenges can be instructive and bring out the best in people and so it will be for many Metal Dogs this year.

Another valuable aspect of the Ox year will be the opportunity it will give the Metal Dog to get to know other colleagues. This could be through his everyday duties or meeting people on courses or at meetings, or through a professional organization. By being active and making the most of his networking opportunities, the Metal Dog can enhance his prospects.

For Metal Dogs who are frustrated in their current position and keen to move on, as well as those seeking work, this will be an important year. Their quest will not be easy and many will face disappointments. However, the Metal Dog is blessed with a determined nature and while openings may be limited and some applications may not go his way, by having faith in himself and obtaining professional advice, as well as considering new ways in which he can develop his skills, he may well succeed in being offered an opportunity. Even though this may be different from what he was originally envisaging, it can prove a significant base to build on. What is achieved in this sometimes difficult year can often have important long-term value.

One other point that all Metal Dogs need to be aware of is that if they do find themselves in a volatile work situation they need to remain careful, tactful and alert. If not, problems could escalate and become an unwelcome distraction. Metal Dogs, do take note and do be careful in potentially awkward situations.

With the aspects as they are, work opportunities need to be taken when they arise, but May to mid-June and

October to December could see some interesting developments. The Metal Dog will find his situation will gradually improve as the Ox year draws to a close and some of his hard work will then be acknowledged and rewarded.

In this sometimes tricky year, the Metal Dog will also need to be careful with his finances. With his current commitments and plans for the year he does need to keep watch on his spending and be wary of buying too much on impulse. In addition, he should ensure that financial documents are up to date and kept securely. To be inattentive or careless could lead to problems and sometimes unnecessary expense. In financial matters this is a year for vigilance.

Although the Metal Dog will often be kept busy this year, he should make sure he sets a regular time aside for his interests and recreational pursuits. These can benefit him in many ways, including possibly helping him to relax, giving him additional exercise, bringing him into contact with others or allowing him to develop ideas or skills. The time the Metal Dog allows for recreation and pleasure this year can often be satisfying as well as doing him good.

The Metal Dog's domestic life will see a lot of activity over the year and it is important that there is good co-operation and communication between everyone in his household. For those Metal Dogs who are parents there will be the needs of their children to tend to and there will often be considerable demands on their time. However, busy though the year may be, it can be a special one. The Ox year may bring its pressures and tribulations, but domestically it can be a meaningful and often happy one, with many a Metal Dog valuing the support and love of those who are special to him.

In view of all the activity of the year, many Metal Dogs will keep their social life relatively low key. However, they should still keep in regular contact with their friends as well as go to interest- or work-related social events, as they will benefit by keeping in contact with others. For any Metal Dog who is alone, a chance encounter could become important as the year develops. April, September, December and January could see the most social activity, but the Metal Dog's prospects will gradually brighten in the last quarter of the year.

Overall, the Year of the Ox can be a challenging one for the Metal Dog and a lot will be expected of him. However, by concentrating on his priorities, he can still achieve a lot and in the process gain valuable new experience. This is a year for proceeding carefully and being wary in difficult or volatile situations. However, mixed though the aspects may be, the Metal Dog will value the support of his loved ones and his interests will also bring him a great deal of pleasure.

TIP FOR THE YEAR
Think through your actions and avoid haste or risk. The more thorough and measured you are, the better. Also, do balance out your activities and give time to those who are special to you as well as to your recreational pursuits. These can be real treasures in this busy and demanding year.

The Water Dog
This year the Water Dog would do well to remember the Chinese proverb *you won't get lost if you frequently ask*

for directions. With the prevailing aspects, if at any time he is facing problems, is in a quandary or would welcome advice, he would do well to draw on the assistance of others. As a Water Dog he may have firm views and like to do things his own way, but in 2009 a willingness to ask for directions would often give him the advice he needs.

At work this can be a demanding year, with many Water Dogs having new responsibilities and initiatives to deal with as well as bureaucratic or other pressures. However, while this may not be an easy time, if the Water Dog does his best and remains focused, he will not only impress others and broaden his experience but also do his reputation a lot of good. The Ox year can be an important test and prepare the Water Dog for greater responsibilities later on.

In addition to the experience the Water Dog can gain through his everyday work, he should make the most of any training opportunities or other chances to add to his skills. Sometimes these can arise through assisting or covering for colleagues or adding to his own duties. By showing willingness, he can benefit later. Also, if he feels another qualification would help his prospects, he should see what he can arrange. One of the principal and lasting benefits of the Ox year will be the knowledge and experience the Water Dog can gain. Making the most of his networking opportunities will also be helpful to him.

Generally, the Water Dog will find his work situation improving during the last quarter of the Ox year. However, for those Water Dogs who are keen on change, seeking promotion or looking for work, late April to mid-June and October to December could see some possibilities opening up. Those who are looking for a job will find that the advice they can obtain from employment agencies and others with the relevant information can make a considerable difference to their prospects as well as advise them of possibilities they may not have previously considered. This is not a year for the Water Dog to act alone.

As far as financial matters are concerned, the Water Dog will need to be careful. In view of the accommodation expenses he has and the purchases he wants to make, he will need to remain disciplined and keep a close watch on his general spending. Whenever possible, he should make early provision for his more expensive purchases or any deposits he may be required to make. With good management he will be able to go ahead with a lot of his plans, but the Ox year is one for care, planning and prudence.

The Water Dog can, however, derive a lot of pleasure from his interests and recreational pursuits over the year. While there will be frequent demands on his time, it is important that he preserves some for the activities he enjoys, some of which could give him the chance of additional exercise or the opportunity to get out of doors. Any projects or interest-related skills he would like to tackle could be especially satisfying and sometimes of future benefit.

The Water Dog will also appreciate his social life this year and by keeping in regular contact with his friends and going to social events that appeal to him, he will often not only enjoy himself but also meet some like-minded people. April, September and mid-November to January could see the most social activity. However, while the Water Dog's social life can be mainly positive, he does need to be careful should he find himself in a difficult or volatile situation. The Ox year can bring its awkward moments and there will be occasions when the Water Dog will need to be tactful *and* on his guard. Water Dogs, do take note and watch your words in potentially awkward situations.

The Water Dog's domestic life will be busy this year, but often very special. With the pressures the Ox year can bring, the Water Dog will be grateful for support and love of those close to him and should be open about any concerns or frustrations as well as forthcoming in asking for advice. *A worry shared is a worry halved,* as the saying goes, and the Water Dog will find this very true this year.

In addition to the support he will receive from those around him, the Water Dog will derive a lot of satisfaction from the domestic plans that he is able to carry out. Whether these concern home improvements, shared interests or travel, the Ox year can bring some very enjoyable occasions and there could also be some personal or family news to celebrate.

Overall, the Year of the Ox will be a challenging one for the Water Dog and progress will not be easy. However, by making the most of his situation, he will gain what can be invaluable experience that will prepare him for future progress. He will also value his social and domestic life and the support of loved ones and close friends will mean a great deal to him as well as help him through some of the more pressured times of the year.

TIP FOR THE YEAR
Two tips. With your ambitions for the future, you should make the most of any chances to build on your experience.

What you learn this year can be to your long-term benefit. Also, pay attention to your relations with others. This includes networking in your work and valuing your close friends and loved ones. They are very keen for you to realize your potential and their support and guidance can be significant.

The Wood Dog

This will be a busy year for the Wood Dog and while parts of it will be demanding, what he learns can be considerable.

One of the key features of the Ox year is that it is a time for effort and in the Wood Dog's education it is one for discipline and focus. As the Wood Dog progresses to more detailed work, he needs to organize his time well and concentrate on what needs to be done. Although there may be times when he may struggle with certain subjects and feel he is not making the headway he would like, by doing his best he will be adding to his knowledge and helping his education move forward.

He should also not be discouraged if certain work he presents or exams he takes do not turn out as well as he would like. Although disappointing, these results can alert him to possible gaps in his knowledge and ways to improve his approach and presentation. Again, the Ox year can be instructive and with the Wood Dog's prospects showing great improvement in 2010, the effort he puts in now can often be rewarded later. In addition he could find it helpful to bear in mind the benefits that can follow on from his current work. These may not only include the skills he is acquiring but also the qualifications he is working towards.

Again, what is undertaken this year can have far-reaching value.

In addition to the attention the Wood Dog gives to academic work this year he should take advantage of any opportunities he has to further his talents in other areas. These could include sport, music, drama, art or other activities that appeal to him. Whatever he does, by adding to his knowledge or trying out new activities, he will not only enjoy himself but also have the chance to make new friends.

Throughout the year the Wood Dog should also be open and forthcoming. He will find that if he is prepared to talk, problems can often be eased, solutions found or greater assistance given. In this demanding year the Wood Dog should know that help is there should he need it. Neither should he ignore his better judgement. This is a year for care.

More positively, there will be travel opportunities for many Wood Dogs and whether a holiday, a break or an educational visit, his visits to places new or of particular interest will often be enjoyable.

For Wood Dogs born in 1934 this is a year to proceed steadily and carefully. As many Dogs will find, problems can all too easily arise and to counter the more negative aspects the more senior Wood Dog does need to be thorough as well as be prepared to seek advice should anything be concerning him. This particularly applies to any important correspondence or financial matters he may have to deal with. In order not to be disadvantaged, the Wood Dog does need to attend to paperwork promptly as well as seek guidance on any matters that may be unclear. The Ox year is not one for risk or haste.

More positively, the Wood Dog can derive considerable pleasure from his personal interests, especially any that allow him to draw on his creative talents. He will also appreciate the support of family members and close friends over the year. Not only can they be encouraging but should he have concerns or need greater help, they will be willing to assist. In addition he would do well to take up any travel opportunities that arise and if he has the opportunity to visit or stay with others, this can lead to some rewarding occasions.

Overall, the Ox year may require care, but with support and a willingness to seize opportunities, the Wood Dog can still make it a satisfying one. It will bring opportunities for all Wood Dogs, whether born in 1934 or 1994, and give them the chance to develop certain skills and enjoy their interests. Also, while there will be pressures and more difficult times, the Wood Dog will be well supported and by being open and forthcoming, he can be helped a great deal. And what the younger Wood Dog can learn can do a lot to help his progress in following years.

TIP FOR THE YEAR
This will be a busy and sometimes demanding year and throughout you should be careful not to be too independent. With the support and goodwill of others, you can achieve so much more, and if born in 1994, the effort you put in now can be well rewarded in the future.

The Fire Dog

This will be a variable year for the Fire Dog and is one for care, patience and prudence.

For those Fire Dogs in work this can be a challenging and sometimes frustrating year. Although the Fire Dog may be keen to set about his duties and carry out certain plans, he could be blighted by niggling problems, the attitude of other people or circumstances not being quite right. For one as conscientious and eager as the Fire Dog, this could be perturbing. However, while the conditions may not always be helpful, there can still be benefits from what happens over the year. In some cases the problems and delays that arise will give the Fire Dog chance to reconsider his plans and so lead to new ideas. In addition the challenges he faces can bring out his strengths and these will often be noticed and appreciated.

Although this may not be an easy year work-wise, many Fire Dogs will remain with their current employer and concentrate on the work they know so well. Some, however, will decide to make a change, possibly choosing to work closer to home, reduce their hours or just do something different. For these Fire Dogs, as well as those seeking work, their quest will involve a lot of effort. In some cases openings will be limited and competition fierce. However, the Fire Dog is tenacious and once set on a course he will not give up easily. With initiative and effort, many Fire Dogs will eventually secure a position. It may not be easy, but persistence will prevail. The last quarter of the year could be the most promising time for work opportunities, but May to mid-June could also see possibilities arising.

A more encouraging area will concern the Fire Dog's personal interests and over the year he will not only derive much pleasure from what he does but can also benefit by adding to his knowledge, setting himself new aims or perhaps trying something new. Some Fire Dogs could find outdoor activities especially appealing, and those who like gardening or photography or follow sport will find their activities can mean a lot to them this year. The Fire Dog could also find that some of his interests have a good social element, and whether joining a local group, meeting other enthusiasts at events or sharing his ideas with a loved one, he will find the support he receives can often spur him on. Fire Dogs who are alone may form an important new friendship through a specific interest they have.

The Fire Dog should also take up any social invitations he receives. Going out and spending time with others will give him the chance to relax and unwind as well as often enjoy himself. When he is under pressure or has concerns, talking to others or just doing something different can do him a lot of good. April, September, December and January could see the most social activity.

The Fire Dog's domestic life can also be special this year. By giving time to others and sharing household activities and interests, he will not only achieve more but also strengthen the rapport he enjoys with his loved ones. Many Fire Dogs could delight in some family news and activities, particularly involving a younger relation. Throughout the year the Fire Dog should also be forth-coming with any concerns he may have, as that way he will give others the chance to support and help. His domestic life has always been a pivotal part of his life and the Ox year, despite its mixed aspects, will reinforce its value.

The Fire Dog does, though, need to be careful in money matters. When considering any large purchase, he should check the terms and implications involved. He also needs to be thorough when dealing with financially related forms and check on anything that may be unclear. This is a year for care.

Overall, this may not be the easiest of years for the Fire Dog, but provided he is prepared to adapt, he can do a lot to negate some of its more difficult aspects. This is a time to avoid risks and to be thorough. However, despite the pressures and tribulations the Ox year may bring, the Fire Dog can get a lot of value from his personal interests and friendships, as well as the support and affection of his loved ones. And during the last quarter of the year many Fire Dogs can look forward to a general improvement in their situation, especially with the approach of the more encouraging Tiger year.

TIP FOR THE YEAR

In the Ox year it is a case of making the most of your situation. Being inflexible or unwilling to adapt can lead to problems or undermine what you are hoping for. With all the activity of the year it is also important you take some time for yourself. Also, listen to friends and loved ones. They will be supportive and keen to help.

The Earth Dog

The Earth Dog is very perceptive and able to gauge situations with considerable skill, and over the year this will serve him well. The Ox year will be a mixed one and opportunities will be limited, but by keeping alert, adapting as required and being his cautious self, the Earth Dog can do much to minimize the more awkward aspects.

At work many Earth Dogs will have seen considerable change over the last 12 months and quite a few will have altered the nature of their role or taken on other responsibilities. For these Earth Dogs this is an ideal year to become more established as well as familiarize themselves with the different aspects of their work. Rather than looking to make progress in their career, they would do well to regard this as a year for consolidation and learning. Also, many will find their workload increasing and new objectives being set. The Ox year can be demanding, but it will give the Earth Dog the chance to use and improve his skills and what he learns can do his prospects a lot of good.

Another talent the Earth Dog has is his ability to relate well to people. He may be quieter than some, but he understands others well and is able to establish rapport and respect with ease. Over the year he should continue to build on the good working relations he has as well as to network and meet new people wherever possible. He will not only find this useful in his current situation but it may also help him in the future.

Many Earth Dogs will decide to concentrate on their present position over the year, but for those who are keen to move on, as well as those seeking work, the Ox year can be an important one. Securing a new job will not be easy, but the Earth Dog is not easily thwarted and by showing initiative and finding out additional information about the positions he applies for, he will find his efforts will make a difference and may well lead to success. While there could be quite a steep learning curve involved in any new position he takes on, what he achieves now can open up the way for greater opportunities in following years. Again, the Ox year may be demanding, but its significance is far-reaching. May to mid-June and the last quarter of the year could see some interesting work developments.

In view of the prevailing aspects, however, the Earth Dog will need to remain his cautious self when dealing with finance. If considering any major purchase or entering into what could be a long-term agreement, he does need to allow sufficient time to check the suitability, terms and implications. This is a year to be thorough. This also applies to important paperwork. To be dilatory or make assumptions could prove unwise later on. Earth Dogs, do take note. This is no year for haste or risk.

The Earth Dog's domestic life will see considerable activity over the year and here his talents for keeping tabs on a great many things at once and relating effectively to others will be real assets. With good communication, co-operation and organization, home life will often go well and there could be some special family highlights to look forward to. These could include the academic or personal success of a younger relation as well as the pride the Earth Dog takes in certain family achievements. His thoughtfulness and input can make a real difference to his home life this year.

However, while the Earth Dog's domestic life will be generally positive, no year is ever without its problems.

Should disagreements occur or the Earth Dog have concerns about the ideas or attitude of another person, it is important that he speaks out. This way possible difficulties can be addressed rather than linger in the background. Again, the Earth Dog's skill, care and empathy will be especially appreciated.

The Earth Dog tends to keep a relatively small social circle, but when he does go out he will often enjoy himself very much and should he see an event that appeals to him this year, especially if it is related to an interest of his, he should follow it up. He may prefer to have a quieter year socially, but this is no time for him to be reclusive or deny himself the pleasure that his social life can bring. Earth Dogs, do take note and do take advantage of your invitations as well as keep in regular contact with your very good friends.

Similarly, it is important that the Earth Dog does not allow his personal interests to suffer due to other demands on his time. In this busy year he does need to keep his lifestyle in balance and allow time for activities he enjoys. Outdoor pursuits could be particularly beneficial, including gardening.

Overall, in 2009 the Earth Dog will need to be careful as well as keep his expectations modest. This is very much a time for concentrating on what he can do rather than making unrealistic plans. If he remains aware and makes the most of his situation, he can derive a lot of satisfaction from what he does and build on it in the more progressive Tiger year that follows. And mixed though the aspects may be, the Earth Dog's domestic life and the support of his loved ones will often be a very special and encouraging factor over the year.

This is a year to be careful and aware. That way you will be better able to adapt to situations and avert problems before they have chance to arise. This is a year for treading carefully. However, you can still emerge from it with a good deal to your credit and with experience that will be valuable in the future. Your relations with others will also be positive, with your domestic life and close friendships being of great value.

FAMOUS DOGS

King Albert II of Belgium, Brigitte Bardot, Candice Bergen, David Bowie, George W. Bush, Kate Bush, Laura Bush, Naomi Campbell, Mariah Carey, King Carl Gustaf XVI of Sweden, José Carreras, Paul Cézanne, Cher, Sir Winston Churchill, Bill Clinton, Leonard Cohen, Jamie Lee Curtis, Matt Damon, Charles Dance, Claude Debussy, Dame Judi Dench, Joseph Fiennes, Robert Frost, Ava Gardner, Judy Garland, George Gershwin, Lenny Henry, O. Henry, Victor Hugo, Barry Humphries, Holly Hunter, Michael Jackson, Al Jolson, Felicity Kendal, Jennifer Lopez, Sophia Loren, Joanna Lumley, Shirley MacLaine, Madonna, Norman Mailer, Barry Manilow, Freddie Mercury, Liza Minelli, David Niven, Simon Pegg, Billie Piper, Sydney Pollack, Elvis Presley, Tim Robbins, Paul Robeson, Andy Roddick, Susan Sarandon, Jennifer Saunders, Claudia Schiffer, Dr Albert Schweitzer, Sylvester Stallone, Robert Louis Stevenson, Sharon Stone, David Suchet, Donald Sutherland, Chris Tarrant, Mother Teresa, Uma Thurman, Donald Trump, Voltaire, Prince William, Shelley Winters.

30 JANUARY 1911 ～ 17 FEBRUARY 1912   *Metal Pig*

16 FEBRUARY 1923 ～ 4 FEBRUARY 1924   *Water Pig*

4 FEBRUARY 1935 ～ 23 JANUARY 1936   *Wood Pig*

22 JANUARY 1947 ～ 9 FEBRUARY 1948   *Fire Pig*

8 FEBRUARY 1959 ～ 27 JANUARY 1960   *Earth Pig*

27 JANUARY 1971 ～ 14 FEBRUARY 1972   *Metal Pig*

13 FEBRUARY 1983 ～ 1 FEBRUARY 1984   *Water Pig*

31 JANUARY 1995 ～ 18 FEBRUARY 1996   *Wood Pig*

18 FEBRUARY 2007 ～ 6 FEBRUARY 2008   *Fire Pig*

THE
PIG

THE PERSONALITY OF THE PIG

It's the doing,
the giving,
the playing the part,
that makes life what it is.
And what it can be.

The Pig is born under the sign of honesty. He has a kind and understanding nature and is well known for his abilities as a peacemaker. He hates any sort of discord or unpleasantness and will do everything in his power to sort out differences of opinion or bring opposing factions together.

He is also an excellent conversationalist and speaks truthfully and to the point. He dislikes any form of falsehood or hypocrisy and is a firm believer in justice and the maintenance of law and order. In spite of these beliefs, however, the Pig is reasonably tolerant and often prepared to forgive others for their wrongdoings. He rarely harbours grudges and is never vindictive.

The Pig is usually very popular. He enjoys other people's company and likes to be involved in joint or group activities. He will be a loyal member of any club or society and can be relied upon to lend a helping hand at functions. He is also an excellent fundraiser for charities and is often a great supporter of humanitarian causes.

The Pig is a hard and conscientious worker and is particularly respected for his reliability and integrity. In his early years he will try his hand at several different jobs, but he is usually happiest where he feels that he is being of service to others. He will unselfishly give up his time for the common good and is highly valued by his colleagues and employers.

The Pig has a good sense of humour and invariably has a smile, joke or some whimsical remark at the ready. He loves to entertain and to please others, and there are many Pigs who have been attracted to careers in show business or who enjoy following the careers of famous stars and personalities.

There are, unfortunately, some who take advantage of the Pig's good nature and impose upon his generosity. The Pig has great difficulty in saying 'no', and although he may dislike being firm, it would be in his own interests to say occasionally, 'Enough is enough.' The Pig can also be rather naïve and gullible; however, if at any stage in his life he feels that he has been badly let down, he will try to become self reliant. There are many Pigs who have become entrepreneurs or forged a successful career on their own after some early disappointment in life. Although the Pig tends to spend his money quite freely, he is usually very astute in financial matters and there are many Pigs who have become wealthy.

Another characteristic of the Pig is his ability to recover from setbacks reasonably quickly. His faith and his strength of character keep him going. If he thinks that there is a job he can do or he has something that he wants to achieve, he will pursue it with a dogged determination. He can also be stubborn and, no matter how many may plead with him, once he has made his mind up he will rarely change his views.

Although the Pig may work hard, he also knows how to enjoy himself. He is a great pleasure seeker and will quite happily spend his hard earned money on a lavish holiday or an expensive meal – for the Pig is a connoisseur of good food and wine – or a variety of recreational activities. He also enjoys small social gatherings and if he is in company he likes he can very easily become the life and soul of the party. He does, however, tend to become rather withdrawn at larger functions or when among strangers.

The Pig is a creature of comfort and his home will usually be fitted with all the latest in luxury appliances. Where possible, he will prefer to live in the country rather than the town and will opt to have a big garden, for the Pig is usually a keen and successful gardener.

The Pig is very popular with others and will often have numerous romances before he settles down. Once settled, however, he will be loyal to his partner and he will find that he is especially well suited to those born under the signs of the Goat, Rabbit, Dog and Tiger and also to another Pig. Due to his affable and easy-going nature he can also establish a satisfactory relationship with all the remaining signs of the Chinese zodiac, with the exception of the Snake. The Snake tends to be wily, secretive and very guarded, and this can be intensely irritating to the honest and open hearted Pig.

The female Pig will devote all her energies to the needs of her children and her partner. She tries to ensure that they want for nothing and their pleasure is very much her pleasure. She can be a caring and conscientious parent and has very good taste in clothes. Her home will either be very clean and orderly or hopelessly untidy. Strangely, there seems to be no in between with Pigs – they either love housework or detest it! The female Pig does, however, have considerable talents as an organizer and this, combined with her friendly and open manner, enables her to secure many of her objectives.

The Pig is usually lucky in life and will rarely want for anything. Provided he does not let others take advantage of his good nature and is not afraid of asserting himself, he will go through life making friends, helping others and winning the admiration of many.

THE FIVE DIFFERENT TYPES OF PIG

In addition to the 12 signs of the Chinese zodiac there are five elements and these have a strengthening or moderating influence on the signs. The effects of the five elements on the Pig are described below, together with the years in which the elements were exercising their influence. Therefore those Pigs born in 1911 and 1971 are Metal Pigs, those born in 1923 and 1983 are Water Pigs, and so on.

Metal Pig: 1911, 1971
The Metal Pig is more ambitious and determined than some of the other types of Pig. He is strong, energetic and likes to be involved in a wide variety of different activities. He is very open and forthright in his views, although he can be a little too trusting at times and has a tendency to accept things at face value. He has a good sense of humour

and loves to attend parties and other social gatherings. He has a warm, outgoing nature and usually has a large circle of friends.

Water Pig: 1923, 1983

The Water Pig has a heart of gold. He is generous and loyal and tries to remain on good terms with everyone. He will do his utmost to help others, but sadly there are some who will take advantage of his kind nature and he should, in his own interests, be a little more discriminating and be prepared to stand firm against anything that he does not like. Although he prefers the quieter things in life, he has a wide range of interests. He particularly enjoys outdoor pursuits and attending parties and social occasions. He is a hard and conscientious worker and invariably does well in his chosen profession. He is also gifted in the art of communication.

Wood Pig: 1935, 1995

This Pig has a friendly, persuasive manner and is easily able to gain the confidence of others. He likes to be involved in all that is going on around him but can sometimes take on more responsibility than he can properly handle. He is loyal to his family and friends and derives much pleasure from helping those less fortunate than himself. He is usually an optimist and leads a very full, enjoyable and satisfying life. He also has a good sense of humour.

Fire Pig: 1947

The Fire Pig is both energetic and adventurous and he sets about everything he does in a confident and resolute manner. He is very forthright in his views and does not mind taking risks in order to achieve his objectives. He can, however, get carried away by the excitement of the moment and ought to exercise more caution in some of the enterprises in which he gets involved. He is usually lucky in money matters and is well known for his generosity. He is also very caring towards the members of his family.

Earth Pig: 1959

This Pig has a kindly nature. He is sensible and realistic and will go to great lengths in order to please his employers and to secure his aims and ambitions. He is an excellent organizer and is particularly astute in business and financial matters. He has a good sense of humour and a wide circle of friends. He also likes to lead an active social life, although he does sometimes have a tendency to eat and drink more than is good for him.

PROSPECTS FOR THE PIG IN 2009

There is a Chinese proverb that reminds us, *if you cannot do what you want, do what you can*, and this is very apt for the Pig in the remaining months of the Rat year. The Rat year (7 February 2008 to 25 January 2009) is a variable one for the Pig and he needs to be adaptable in his approach.

At work many Pigs will have to deal with change and whether this involves the arrival of new personnel, fresh initiatives or alterations in duties and routine, the Pig will need to remain flexible. With his prospects showing an improvement in the forthcoming Ox year, what he can achieve now can stand him in good stead for later, but the last few Rat months are not a time to rock the boat. October could, however, see some interesting developments for those Pigs seeking work.

The Pig should keep watch on his spending at this time and, if possible, make early provision for more substantial purchases. By giving himself additional time for these he is not only likely to identify some favourable buying opportunities but also to make more appropriate decisions.

With his outgoing nature, the Pig will find himself in demand in the closing months of the Rat year. September and the last weeks in 2008 could be especially busy and for those Pigs enjoying romance, this can often be a meaningful time. In the Pig's home life there will also be a lot for him to do and here again he will benefit by planning ahead and fitting in with the arrangements and needs of others.

Overall, the Rat year does call for flexibility on the Pig's part. By showing this, however, he can ultimately benefit as well as enjoy himself in the meantime.

The Year of the Ox begins on 26 January and holds encouraging prospects for the Pig. It is also one that suits his pioneering style. When he has aims and objectives he is keen to reach, the Pig is tenacious and bold, and his resolve will certainly help him a lot this year. In addition he could also enjoy a certain measure of luck and benefit both from the opportunities that come his way and the goodwill of others.

This is a year of good prospects at work, but as the Ox year starts the Pig should give careful thought to what he wants to achieve over the next 12 months. Not only will this give him objectives to work towards but it will also make him more aware of the opportunities he needs to follow up. As so many have found, when you start to plan and take positive steps, chances do begin to open up for you, with serendipity often coming into play, and so it will be for many Pigs this year. If they make the effort to move forward, interesting opportunities can and *will* arise.

For Pigs who are well established in their career, the Ox year will bring the chance to move on to greater and often more fulfilling responsibilities. This could either be with their existing employer or elsewhere, but many will secure promotion over the year and take their work to a new level. Those who feel they have become staid in their present position or have been hampered by a lack of opportunity will find the Ox year can bring the changes they want. To benefit, though, these Pigs do need to keep alert and to take action. That way they can often set important wheels in motion.

For Pigs who are hoping to take their career in a different direction or seeking work, the Ox year is again one of important possibilities. By giving careful thought to the type of work they would now like to do and obtaining advice from relevant agencies, these Pigs can find their efforts and commitment noticed and rewarded. February, March, July, October and November could see some encouraging developments, but even if some applications do not come to anything, with determination and belief, many Pigs will prevail. Work-wise, the aspects are very much on the Pig's side this year.

The Pig is noted for his skill in handling financial matters and over the year many Pigs will be able to substantially improve their situation. The progress the Pig makes in his work can often lead to a noticeable rise in income and some may be able to supplement this by putting an interest or skill to profitable use. For the enterprising, this can be a year of considerable financial reward. However, to make the most of any upturn, the Pig should use his money well. This could include saving for the longer term, reducing borrowings and proceeding with certain plans for his accommodation. With careful decisions and good management, many Pigs can prosper this year as well as help their longer-term position.

With travel favourably aspected, if there is a certain destination the Pig would like to visit, he should keep alert for opportunities. Many Pigs will see their travel hopes realized over the year and, in true Pig style, enjoy their time away.

In addition, if the Pig has certain aims or aspirations, particularly involving his personal interests, he should act on them. What he sets in motion can reinforce the constructive nature of the year. On the other hand, if he should decide to take things easy and let opportunities slip by, he could come to regret it in the future. This is no year for back-pedalling.

This will be an eventful year in the Pig's home life and many Pigs will see some major developments. For some this could include an addition to the family, a marriage or some other important piece of family news. Domestically, the Ox year can be a memorable one. Those Pigs who have been considering moving, perhaps to somewhere more convenient to their work or more suitable to their requirements, may well decide to go ahead with their plans. By setting the process in motion, these Pigs will find events often developing a momentum of their own. As with so much this year, when the Pig takes action, possibilities soon begin to open up for him.

With his wide interests and many friends, the Pig will often have opportunities to go out and socialize, with March, April, August, December and January seeing the most activity. There will be many chances for him to meet new people, although Pigs enjoying the early stages of romance should proceed steadily. To build up high expectations in the early stages or possibly rush into a commitment could lead to disappointment. In the Ox year it is better to allow relationships to evolve in their own time. Pigs, do take careful note and avoid unnecessary haste.

Overall, the Year of the Ox is one of considerable opportunity, but to benefit the Pig does need to act. The Ox year does require effort and for those who are not prepared to give it, it could be a time of wasted opportunity. In 2009 a lot rests on the Pig's willingness to move forward. For those who do, the rewards can be substantial.

The Metal Pig
This is a year that will suit the Metal Pig and by making the most of it, he can look forward to accomplishing a great deal.

The Metal Pig has a keen and ambitious nature and in his work he is likely to feel that the time is now right to take his career forward. As a result, the Ox year can mark a significant stage in his overall career development.

Many Metal Pigs will already have established themselves in a particular type of work and will not only have a lot of experience behind them but will also have built up a solid reputation and some useful contacts. In 2009 they will often find themselves being singled out for a greater role or for promotion. The Ox year is very much one for progress.

The aspects are also encouraging for those Metal Pigs who wish to take their career in a new direction. For some this could involve becoming self-employed and with good advice and backing, these Metal Pigs will often revel in the opportunity now before them. February, March, July, October and November could see some interesting developments, but the accent throughout the year is very much on exploring possibilities.

With this emphasis on moving forward, many Metal Pigs will also be keen to add to their skills. This could include taking courses or doing some personal study related to their industry, but by doing something positive, the Metal Pig can gain a great deal of satisfaction from his activities. This also extends to his recreational pursuits. By allowing time for these and adding to his knowledge and skills, he can again benefit from what he does. As with so much this year, the more effort he puts into his various activities, the more he will take from them.

For the enterprising (and the Pig does have entrepreneurial skills), some interests and ideas could also generate some financial gain. The Ox year is one of considerable opportunity and financial matters are positively aspected. However, to get the most from any upturn, the Metal Pig should set some money aside for accommodation plans and purchases and, if he is able, take advantage of tax incentives to make longer-term savings. With good management, he can not only benefit in the present but also help his future.

With this being a year for action, some Metal Pigs will also move to accommodation that better suits their needs. While this will entail considerable disruption, these Metal Pigs will often delight in the advantages their new home offers. Those who remain where they are will also often have ambitious plans for their home and will appreciate any improvements they make.

The Metal Pig will also do a lot to help his loved ones over the year and in return he will often be buoyed up by the help he receives. In view of his ambitions for the year, this can be a useful spur to him. Many Metal Pigs will find their home life going well this year and being both busy and meaningful.

With the many demands on his time, the Metal Pig may decide to cut back on his socializing over the year. However, he should still keep in regular contact with his friends and try to set time aside for events that appeal to him. His social life can bring an important balance to his lifestyle. March, April, August, December and January could see the most activity. For the unattached Metal Pig, the Ox year can bring some good romantic possibilities, but new relationships should be allowed to develop in their own time rather than conducted in a rush.

Overall, the Year of the Ox is one of considerable opportunity for the Metal Pig. At work there will be chances for him to take his career to new levels and or to branch off in new directions. He can also derive a lot of satisfaction from developing his skills and interests. But throughout the year the love and support of those around him will be a major factor, helping him to make the most of his strengths, qualities and often special talents.

TIP FOR THE YEAR
Over the year you would do would do well to remember the words of Virgil: 'Fortune favours the bold.' This is a year of opportunity and by making the most of your talents, you can make important progress as well as take considerable satisfaction from what you do.

The Water Pig

There is a Chinese proverb that reminds us *those who accumulate good deeds will have many to celebrate*, and with his genial, generous and keen nature, the Water Pig will have the opportunity to celebrate this year. This is time for progress.

In his personal life this will be a busy and often significant year. For many Water Pigs accommodation will feature prominently and a move may well be on the cards. Although this will bring extra pressure, Water Pigs who do move will revel in the chance to get installed in a new home and make it their own. However, it is not just accommodation that can bring excitement this year. For some Water Pigs major personal decisions will be made and the year can see them possibly getting engaged, marrying or seeing an addition to the family. The Ox year can be memorable in several different and exciting ways.

For unattached Water Pigs, the Ox year can also bring a transformation in their situation. A chance encounter could become very special and while it is recommended that all Pigs in the Ox year allow time for new romances to develop, many of those Water Pigs who start the year alone could soon feel the effects of Cupid's arrow and find new happiness. For any who have experienced recent disappointments in a relationship, this is a year for drawing a line under what has gone before and looking to the future. The Ox year can mark the start of a new and more positive chapter in their lives.

Although the Water Pig will often be very busy and engrossed in all that he is doing, it is also important that he draws on the willingness of others to assist him. If he is involved in taking decisions about his accommodation, making major purchases or entering into long-term agreements, he would do well to seek the opinions of those with the experience to advise. He may be keen and eager, but he should not let haste lead him to overlook what could be important factors. Water Pigs, do take note.

Water Pigs who become parents this year should also draw on the help of family and close friends where necessary. Although they may want to do a lot by themselves, the assistance of others could be invaluable. It is important that the Water Pig remembers he can turn to others for advice and moral encouragement should he need to.

With his sincere and outgoing nature, the Water Pig is able to get on well with many people and over the year he will not only appreciate meeting up with his friends and going to parties and events but could also find his work and personal interests having a good social element to them. Water Pigs who move over the year can quickly form a new social circle. On both a personal and a social level this can be a pleasing and often significant year, with March, April, August, December and January seeing the most activity.

At work the Water Pig will have seen a lot happen in recent years. He will not only have gained a great deal of valuable experience but in some cases have learned from mistakes or setbacks. Now, with this experience, plus the wisdom and insights he has, he will feel the time is ripe for progress. And his efforts and sheer willpower will open some significant doors. If there are opportunities in his present place of work, the Water Pig will often find his reputation and in-house knowledge of tremendous value and will be well placed for promotion. However, if he feels he could do better elsewhere or is not using his strengths in the way he would like, he should keep alert for opportunities, make enquiries and register with the appropriate agencies. By taking positive action, many Water Pigs will be able to secure a better position over the course of the year and what is achieved now can often be instrumental in their later success.

The aspects are also encouraging for those Water Pigs seeking work. While some may have become disillusioned recently, if they persist in their quest, they may well be given the chance to re-establish their career. This is a year of opportunity for all Water Pigs, with February, March, July, October and November seeing some particularly interesting developments.

The progress the Water Pig makes in his work can also bring a welcome increase in income. However, with heavy spending likely over the year, the Water Pig does need to manage his money well and be wary of making too many impulse buys. This is a year for budgeting and control, and should the Water Pig have problems or uncertainties over a financial matter at any time, he should seek professional advice.

The Water Pig always likes to keep himself active and while his free time may be limited this year, he should still make sure he sets some aside for recreational pursuits he enjoys. These can not only bring him pleasure but also be good ways for him to relax and unwind. With travel favourably aspected, he should try to take a holiday or break at some time during the year. The rest and change of routine can do him a lot of good as well as reward him for the efforts he will make during the year.

Overall, the Year of the Ox is one of considerable opportunity for the Water Pig. With his talents, strengths and ambitions, he can make important headway. His personal life is also well aspected and the love, support and friendship he enjoys can make the Ox year a special and personally rewarding one.

TIP FOR THE YEAR

This is a year of great opportunity, but you do need to take the initiative and act. You should also draw on the willingness of family, friends and colleagues to support you. Their help can make a considerable difference to what you achieve.

The Wood Pig

This is a year of considerable scope for the Wood Pig and by setting about his aims and activities in his usual robust way, he will find a lot going in his favour.

For Wood Pigs born in 1995 this will be an important year in their education. As they advance in their studies they will find pressures increasing and may sometimes struggle with certain subjects or concepts. However, by being willing to learn *and putting in the effort,* not only will they be able to make good headway but they will also lay the foundation needed for future progress. Educationally, this will be an important year and it should not be wasted.

Also, while there will be times when the young Wood Pig is frustrated with certain subjects or feels he is not making the progress he would like, he should not let this weaken his resolve. It is by being stretched that he can learn, and with a willing attitude, his efforts this year *will* bring results. As the Chinese proverb states, *read and reap the rewards,* and in the Ox year both reading and studying can have far-reaching value.

During the year the Wood Pig will also have great fun spending time on his own interests. Whether these are sports related or allow the Wood Pig to develop talents in other areas, he will often be satisfied with his achievements. The Ox year can be an encouraging one, but to benefit the Wood Pig does need to make the most of his opportunities.

The Wood Pig will also value his close circle of friends during the year and not only will there be much mutual support and encouragement but shared interests will also bring a good deal of fun. Any Wood Pigs who are not as involved in the social scene as they would like will find that specific interests they have can enable them to meet others who are like-minded. These are constructive times for the Wood Pig.

Throughout the year he should also avail himself of the support and assistance those around can give, and whether at home or at school, if he has any concerns, he should let others know. If there is an activity he is keen to try out or a skill he would like to develop, again he should talk to others. This way his hopes will stand a greater chance of being realized.

For Wood Pigs born in 1935 this can also be a satisfying year, although to benefit from the encouraging aspects these Wood Pigs should again be forthcoming and share their ideas with others. With discussion and a pooling of ideas, talents and effort, far more will happen.

One interesting aspect of the year will be the range of ideas the Wood Pig will have and while some may not come to anything, others will take root and add something positive (and sometimes different) to the year. Quite a few Wood Pigs will be tempted to take up a new interest or vary an existing one and will delight in the challenge this gives. If they are able to join a local group, there could also be a valuable and supportive social element to what they do. Many a Wood Pig has a great appreciation of the outdoors and those with gardens will often spend many a happy hour tending their land.

There will also be good travel opportunities for the Wood Pig during the year and he may get the chance to visit areas he has long wanted to see. This is a time for making the most of his ideas.

Throughout the year the Wood Pig will be helped by the supportive attitude of those around him and his domestic life can be both active and rewarding. With the emphasis on joint effort, the more he can encourage others to share in his activities, the better. Similarly, talking about any concerns or difficulties he may have will give others more chance to help. With the positive aspects of the year, many Wood Pigs can also look forward to an important family event that will be a source of much personal pride. As far as domestic life is concerned, this can be a special year.

The Wood Pig is often careful and attentive in money matters and in keeping important paperwork and policies up to date. However, in the Ox year if any matter is giving him concern, it is important that he seeks guidance. While this is a positive year, it is not one for taking financial risks or jumping to conclusions. Wood Pigs, take note and do remain your usual thorough selves.

For all Wood Pigs, whether born in 1935 or 1995, this is an encouraging year. By drawing on the support of others and acting on their ideas, they will see many of their activities working out well.

TIP FOR THE YEAR
Be forthcoming and let others know of your hopes and ideas. With their help, a lot can be achieved. Also, enjoy pursuing your personal interests and consider ways in which you can take them further.

The Fire Pig

With his broad interests and keen nature, the Fire Pig likes to keep himself active and in the Ox year his prospects are most encouraging. This is a time for developing his ideas and enjoying the fruits of his labours, and he will have a great deal in his favour.

One important aspect of the year will be the level of support the Fire Pig receives. In view of some of his hopes for the year, by being forthcoming he can benefit from the assistance others can give and may even find that just mentioning ideas can get them underway. This *is* a progressive time.

In his domestic life the Fire Pig's practical nature is likely to come to the fore and accommodation matters may feature prominently. Some Fire Pigs may decide to move to a location they have long favoured and to accommodation that better suits their needs. For these Fire Pigs the Ox year can be a time of great upheaval, but with joint decisions and effort, they will delight in the new opportunities and changes in lifestyle that a move can bring. Even for those Fire Pigs who decide to remain where they are this can be a year of considerable practical activity as they make improvements to their home, including changing the décor, furnishings and equipment in certain rooms.

In addition to the practical activity of the year the Fire Pig will also appreciate many aspects of his home life. Whether sharing interests, visits and trips out or taking up chances to travel further afield, there will certainly be a lot for the Fire Pig to enjoy. Domestically, this can be a busy, sometimes surprising, but very rewarding year.

The aspects are also encouraging on a social level and the Fire Pig will often have the chance to go out and spend time with others. For Fire Pigs who move to a new area or who, perhaps because of previous commitments, have kept their social life relatively low key recently, this can be a promising year and they can get to know many new people. March, April, August and closing weeks of the Ox year could see the most social activity. Also, with their caring nature, some Fire Pigs will give time to a charitable cause or assist someone they know and they can see a lot following on from their actions.

For Fire Pigs in work this will be an interesting year. Those who are settled in a job will often be pleased with the way they are able to use their knowledge and skills. Also, due to their experience, some may take on a training or mentoring role. For many this can be a fulfilling year. However, some Fire Pigs will feel the time is right for change and will either aim to take up a new challenge or perhaps reduce the time spent commuting and find work more locally. For these Fire Pigs, as well as those seeking work, the Ox year can bring some interesting opportunities. To benefit, though, these Fire Pigs should remember that the emphasis in Ox years is very much on effort and it is by being resolute and persevering that they will find possibilities opening up for them. Some could find some contacts they have especially helpful. From the start of the Ox year to early April and then July, October and November could see some interesting work developments, but throughout 2009 the Fire Pig will be very much in the driving seat and determining the course his work takes through his own efforts.

As far as money matters are concerned, this can be an expensive year, particularly for those Fire Pigs who move or decide to make major improvements to their accommodation. In view of this, the Fire Pig does need to manage his money well and watch the costs of any major undertaking. With good control and planning, he will be pleased with how he fares, but this is a year requiring good self-discipline. If at any time he has doubts or concerns, he should obtain professional advice or contact a helpline.

A satisfying aspect to the year will be the pleasure the Fire Pig will derive from his personal interests. If there has been an activity or subject that has been intriguing him for some time, this would be an excellent year to find out more. Some Fire Pigs may decide to take up a fitness activity or modify their diet. By seeking medical advice on the best way to proceed, they can benefit from their actions and reinforce the positive nature of the year.

In so many ways this is a time of considerable opportunity for the Fire Pig and he can accomplish a great deal. However, the year does require effort and the Fire Pig needs to take the initiative and act on his ideas. Those who do can gain a lot this year, but those who are more reticent could lose out. In 2009 it is effort and action that will bring the rewards.

TIP FOR THE YEAR

You should make a special point of liaising with others this year. Their assistance can help you a lot. Also, it could be worth considering taking up a new interest or challenge. With this being a year of opportunity, you will often welcome the chance to try out something new.

The Earth Pig

This will be a significant year for the Earth Pig. Not only does it mark the start of a new decade in his life but it is one in which he can make good progress and see some of his hopes realized. It is a year for action and some well-deserved (and sometimes overdue) success. However, to benefit from prevailing aspects, the Earth Pig will need to decide on what he wants and remain focused. With clear-cut aims, he will not only use his time and energy more effectively but also be better able to benefit from some of the opportunities that will come his way.

An important feature of the year will be the level of support the Earth Pig enjoys. Those around him are likely to encourage and advise him well and whenever the Earth Pig is considering an idea or has a decision to take, he would do well to talk things over, particularly with those who have the relevant experience. Their good advice and support will spur him on.

In his domestic life this will be a full and interesting year. In addition to the possible marking of his fiftieth birthday, there will be several occasions during the year that will particularly please him. These will not only include celebrating some of his own achievements but also the success enjoyed by others in his household. For those Earth Pigs who are parents, this can be a significant year in the lives of their children, either as they make progress in their education or take major personal decisions. In the Ox year the Earth Pig will see a lot happening in the lives of his loved ones and will appreciate the activities that he is able to share with them.

The one aspect the Earth Pig will need to be careful of is that if he is ever under great pressure at work or anxious over some matter, he does need to be open rather than keep his concerns to himself or allow his frustrations to spill over into home life. He is usually most thoughtful in this respect, but a key feature for all Pigs in the Ox year is that support is there for them if they need it. Earth Pigs, do remember this and do be forthcoming.

The Earth Pig's social life is positively aspected this year and while he may be selective in his socializing, he will often enjoy meeting up with friends and going to events that appeal to him. His work and personal interests could also give rise to some excellent social opportunities and by making the most of these and using his networking skills, he will get to impress many people. Earth Pigs who are alone and would welcome new friendships or perhaps romance will find their fiftieth year can be a special one. A chance encounter could become significant and it could almost seem as if fate were playing its own special part. However, the Earth Pig should let any new relationship blossom in its own time rather than put pressure on it in the early stages. March, April, August and closing Ox months could see the most social activity as well as the best opportunities to meet others.

Although the Earth Pig will have many demands on his time, it is also important that he does not neglect his recreational pursuits, particularly those that take him out of doors or give him the chance of additional exercise. Some Earth Pigs could also bring extra meaning to what they do by setting themselves a challenge or aim for the year.

At work this is a year of major developments for the Earth Pig. With the experience he has built up, he may well be a prime candidate for promotion. Often this will occur in his present place of work as more senior colleagues move on or new initiatives are introduced, but if opportunities are limited or the Earth Pig is keen for a new challenge, by keeping alert and making enquiries, he will find doors opening for him. Here again, positive effort can lead to important developments.

This also applies to those Earth Pigs who are seeking work or wanting to take their career in a new direction. By being active, following through their ideas and exploring possibilities, they will find their initiative well rewarded. The Earth Pig has an enterprising nature and some will decide to become self-employed over the year and will revel in the opportunity now before them. Work-wise, this can be a significant year and while opportunities could arise at almost any time, February, March, July and October could see some particularly encouraging developments.

The success many Earth Pigs will enjoy during the year will often lead to a rise in income. However, to benefit, the Earth Pig does need to remain disciplined. With all the plans and hopes he has for the year, together with possible family activities and accommodation expenses, he would do well to budget carefully. Also, if he is able, he should use any financial improvement to reduce any borrowings as well as add to his longer-term savings. With care and good control, he will generally be pleased with what he is able to do.

Overall, the Ox year is one of great opportunity for the Earth Pig and by acting on his ideas, he can achieve a lot.

He will often derive a great deal of pleasure from his interests and his travels, but central to his activities will be the high level of support and goodwill he will be shown. For the Earth Pig, his fiftieth year can turn out a special and often significant one.

TIP FOR THE YEAR
In this favourable and important year you would do well to decide on your main aims and then concentrate on them. With focus and perseverance, this can be a time of considerable success. You should also draw on the support of others and the information and advice that is available to you. This is a year of good fortune. Use it well.

FAMOUS PIGS

Bryan Adams, Woody Allen, Julie Andrews, Marie Antoinette, Fred Astaire, Humphrey Bogart, James Cagney, Maria Callas, Hillary Rodham Clinton, Glenn Close, the Duchess of Cornwall, Noël Coward, Simon Cowell, Brian Cowen, Oliver Cromwell, Billy Crystal, the Dalai Lama, Ted Danson, Dido, Richard Dreyfuss, Ben Elton, Ralph Waldo Emerson, Rupert Everett, Henry Ford, Stephen Harper, Emmylou Harris, William Randolph Hearst, Ernest Hemingway, Henry VIII, Conrad Hilton, Alfred Hitchcock, Sir Elton John, Tommy Lee Jones, Carl Gustav Jung, Stephen King, Kevin Kline, Hugh Laurie, Nigella Lawson, David Letterman, Jerry Lee Lewis, Meat Loaf, Ewan McGregor, Ricky Martin, Johnny Mathis, Dannii Minogue, Wolfgang Amadeus Mozart, Michael Parkinson, James

Patterson, Luciano Pavarotti, Iggy Pop, Maurice Ravel, Ronald Reagan, Ginger Rogers, Françoise Sagan, Carlos Santana, Arnold Schwarzenegger, Kevin Spacey, Steven Spielberg, Sir Alan Sugar, David Tennant, Emma Thompson, Holly Valance, Jules Verne, David Walliams, Amy Winehouse, Michael Winner, the Duchess of York.

APPENDIX

The relationships between the 12 animal signs, both on a personal level and business level, are an important aspect of Chinese horoscopes and in this appendix the compatibility between the signs is shown in the two tables that follow.

Also included are the names of the signs ruling the hours of the day and from this it is possible to find your ascendant and discover yet another aspect of your personality.

Finally, to supplement the earlier chapters on the personality and horoscope of the signs, I have included a guide on how you can get the best out of your sign and the year.

RELATIONSHIPS BETWEEN THE SIGNS

Personal Relationships

KEY
1 Excellent. Great rapport.
2 A successful relationship. Many interests in common.
3 Mutual respect and understanding. A good relationship.
4 Fair. Needs care and some willingness to compromise in order for the relationship to work.
5 Awkward. Possible difficulties in communication with few interests in common.
6 A clash of personalities. Very difficult.

	Rat	Ox	Tiger	Rabbit	Dragon	Snake	Horse	Goat	Monkey	Rooster	Dog	Pig
Rat	1											
Ox	1	3										
Tiger	4	6	5									
Rabbit	5	2	3	2								
Dragon	1	5	4	3	2							
Snake	3	1	6	2	1	5						
Horse	6	5	1	5	3	4	2					
Goat	5	5	3	1	4	3	2	2				
Monkey	1	3	6	3	1	3	5	3	1			
Rooster	5	1	5	6	2	1	2	5	5	5		
Dog	3	4	1	2	6	3	1	5	3	5	2	
Pig	2	3	2	2	2	6	3	2	2	3	1	2

Business Relationships

KEY

1 Excellent. Marvellous understanding and rapport.
2 Very good. Complement each other well.
3 A good working relationship and understanding can be developed.
4 Fair, but compromise and a common objective are often needed to make this relationship work.
5 Awkward. Unlikely to work, either through lack of trust, understanding or the competitiveness of the signs.
6 Mistrust. Difficult. To be avoided.

	Rat	Ox	Tiger	Rabbit	Dragon	Snake	Horse	Goat	Monkey	Rooster	Dog	Pig
Rat	2											
Ox	1	3										
Tiger	3	6	5									
Rabbit	4	3	3	3								
Dragon	1	4	3	3	3							
Snake	3	2	6	4	1	5						
Horse	6	5	1	5	3	4	4					
Goat	5	5	3	1	4	3	3	2				
Monkey	2	3	4	5	1	5	4	4	3			
Rooster	5	1	5	5	2	1	2	5	5	6		
Dog	4	5	2	3	6	4	2	5	3	5	4	
Pig	3	3	3	2	3	5	4	2	3	4	3	1

YOUR ASCENDANT

The ascendant has a very strong influence on your personality and, together with the information already given about your sign and the effects of the element on your sign, it will help you gain an even greater insight into your true personality according to Chinese horoscopes.

The hours of the day are named after the 12 animal signs and the sign governing the time you were born is your ascendant. To find your ascendant, look up the time of your birth in the table below, bearing in mind any local time differences in the place you were born.

11 p.m.	to	1 a.m.	The hours of the Rat
1 a.m.	to	3 a.m.	The hours of the Ox
3 a.m.	to	5 a.m.	The hours of the Tiger
5 a.m.	to	7 a.m.	The hours of the Rabbit
7 a.m.	to	9 a.m.	The hours of the Dragon
9 a.m.	to	11 a.m.	The hours of the Snake
11 a.m.	to	1 p.m.	The hours of the Horse
1 p.m.	to	3 p.m.	The hours of the Goat
3 p.m.	to	5 p.m.	The hours of the Monkey
5 p.m.	to	7 p.m.	The hours of the Rooster
7 p.m.	to	9 p.m.	The hours of the Dog
9 p.m.	to	11 p.m.	The hours of the Pig

RAT

The Rat ascendant is likely to make the sign more outgoing, sociable and careful with money. A particularly beneficial influence for those born under the signs of the Rabbit, Horse, Monkey and Pig.

OX

The Ox ascendant has a restraining, cautionary and steadying influence that many signs will benefit from. This ascendant also promotes self confidence and willpower and is especially good for those born under the signs of the Tiger, Rabbit and Goat.

TIGER

The Tiger ascendant is a dynamic and stirring influence that makes the sign more outgoing, action-orientated and impulsive. A generally favourable ascendant for the Ox, Tiger, Snake and Horse.

RABBIT

The Rabbit ascendant has a moderating influence, making the sign more reflective, serene and discreet. A particularly beneficial influence for the Rat, Dragon, Monkey and Rooster.

DRAGON

The Dragon ascendant gives strength, determination and ambition to the sign. A favourable influence for those born under the signs of the Rabbit, Goat, Monkey and Dog.

SNAKE

The Snake ascendant can make the sign more reflective, intuitive and self reliant. A good influence for the Tiger, Goat and Pig.

HORSE

The Horse ascendant will make the sign more adventurous, daring and on some occasions fickle. Generally a beneficial influence for the Rabbit, Snake, Dog and Pig.

GOAT

The Goat ascendant will make the sign more tolerant, easy-going and receptive. It could also impart some creative and artistic qualities. An especially good influence for the Ox, Dragon, Snake and Rooster.

MONKEY

The Monkey ascendant is likely to impart a delicious sense of humour and fun to the sign. It will make the sign more enterprising and outgoing – a particularly good influence for the Rat, Ox, Snake and Goat.

ROOSTER

The Rooster ascendant helps to give the sign a lively, outgoing and very methodical manner. Its influence will increase efficiency and is good for the Ox, Tiger, Rabbit and Horse.

DOG

The Dog ascendant makes the sign more reasonable and fair-minded as well as giving an added sense of loyalty. A very good ascendant for the Tiger, Dragon and Goat.

PIG

The Pig ascendant can make the sign more sociable and self indulgent. It is also a caring influence and one that can make the sign want to help others. A good ascendant for the Dragon and Monkey.

HOW TO GET THE BEST FROM YOUR CHINESE SIGN AND THE YEAR

Each of the 12 Chinese signs possesses its own unique strengths and by identifying them you can use them to your advantage. Similarly, by becoming aware of possible weaknesses you can do much to rectify them and in this respect I hope the following sections will be useful. Also included are some tips on how you can get the best from the Year of the Ox.

The Rat
The Rat is blessed with many fine talents, but his undoubted strength lies in his ability to get on with others. He is sociable, charming and a good judge of character. He also possesses a shrewd mind and is good at spotting opportunities.

However, to make the most of his abilities, the Rat does need to impose some discipline upon himself. He should resist the (sometimes very great) temptation of getting involved in too many activities all at the same time and should decide upon his priorities and objectives. By concentrating his energies on specific matters he will fare much better as a result. Also, given his personable manner, he should seek out positions where he can use his personal relations skills to good effect. For a career, sales and marketing could prove ideal.

The Rat is astute in dealing with finance, but while often thrifty, he can sometimes give way to moments of indulgence. Although he deserves to enjoy the money he has so carefully earned, it would sometimes be in his interests to exercise restraint when tempted to satisfy too many expensive whims!

The Rat's family and friends are important to him and while he is loyal and protective towards them, he does tend to keep his worries and concerns to himself and would be helped if he were more willing to discuss his anxieties. Others think highly of him and are prepared to do a lot to help him, but for them to do so the Rat does need to be less secretive and guarded.

With his sharp mind, keen imagination and sociable manner, the Rat does, however, have much in his favour. When he has commitment, he can be irrepressible and, given his considerable charm, often irresistible as well! Provided he channels his energies wisely, he can make much of his life.

Advice for the Rat's Year Ahead

GENERAL PROSPECTS

The Rat is resourceful, quick-witted and keen, but this is a year for commitment and hard work and to benefit from it he will need to put in the effort. For those who are prepared to do so, however, the rewards can be substantial.

CAREER PROSPECTS

A year of steady progress. A lot may be expected of the Rat, but the skills he is able to acquire can prove to be important in the future.

FINANCE

A reasonable year, with the Rat often benefiting from an increase in income. However, this is a time for discipline and control over his spending.

RELATIONS WITH OTHERS

The Rat can gain a great deal from the support and goodwill of others this year. His interests can lead to him meeting new people and it is a favourable time for new friendships and romance.

The Ox

Strong willed, determined and resolute, the Ox certainly has a mind of his own! He is persistent and sets about achieving his objectives with dogged determination. In addition he is reliable and tenacious and is often a source of inspiration to others. He is an achiever, and he often achieves a great deal. However, to really excel, he would do well to try and correct some of his weaknesses.

Being so resolute and having such a strong sense of purpose, the Ox can be inflexible and narrow minded. He can be resistant to change and prefers to set about his activities in his own way rather than be dependent on others. His dislike of change can sometimes be to his detriment and if he were prepared to be more adaptable and adventurous he would find his progress easier.

The Ox would also be helped if he were to broaden his range of interests and become more relaxed in his approach. At times he can be so preoccupied with his own activities that he is not always as mindful of others as he should be, and his demeanour can sometimes be studious and serious. There are times when he would benefit from a lighter touch.

However, the Ox is true to his word and loyal to his family and friends. He is admired and respected by others and his tremendous willpower usually enables him to achieve a great deal in life.

Advice for the Ox's Year Ahead

GENERAL PROSPECTS

This is the Ox's own year and it will give him the chance to make more of himself. It will require effort, but if the Ox decides on his plans and takes action, a lot can go his way. One crucial factor in how he fares this year will be the level of support he is shown, and the more he can act in unison with others, the better.

CAREER PROSPECTS

This is a year for commitment and steady progress. Results may not necessarily be quick in coming, but with persistence the Ox can make satisfying headway and gain valuable experience.

FINANCE
The Ox's efforts can bring him financial rewards this year, but he needs to keep control of his spending.

RELATIONS WITH OTHERS
In 2009 the Ox should not underestimate the value of good relations with others. Colleagues and new contacts could be especially helpful in work situations, while in his personal life there will be possible celebrations in store and for those enjoying or seeking romance, their own year can be truly special.

The Tiger

Lively, innovative and enterprising, the Tiger enjoys an active lifestyle. He has a wide range of interests, an alert mind and a genuine liking of others. He loves to live life to the full. However, despite his enthusiastic and well-meaning ways, he does not always make the most of his considerable potential.

By being so versatile, the Tiger does have a tendency to jump from one activity to another or dissipate his energies by trying to do too much at the same time. To make the most of himself he should try to exercise a certain amount of self-discipline. Ideally, he should decide how best he can use his abilities, give himself some objectives and then stick to them. If he can overcome his restless tendencies, he will find he will accomplish far more as a result.

Also, in spite of his sociable manner, the Tiger likes to retain a certain independence in his actions, and while few begrudge him this, he would sometimes find life easier if he were more prepared to work in conjunction with others. His reliance upon his own judgement does sometimes mean that he excludes the views and advice of those around him, and this can be to his detriment. The Tiger may possess an independent spirit, but he must not let it go too far!

The Tiger does, however, have much in his favour. He is bold, original and quick-witted. If he can keep his restless nature in check, he can enjoy considerable success. In addition, with his engaging personality, he is well liked and much admired.

Advice for the Tiger's Year Ahead

GENERAL PROSPECTS

In the Ox year the Tiger would do well to watch his exuberant nature, proceed carefully and be prepared to adapt as required. However, the experience he gains will stand him in excellent stead for the future.

CAREER PROSPECTS

The Tiger will face new demands and pressures this year and may have misgivings about certain developments. However, it is a case of making the best of his situation. What happens this year can be a contributing factor in some of the successes he will enjoy in 2010.

FINANCE

The Tiger needs to be wary of rush or risk this year and this is especially true in money matters. This is a year for more care, less speed and good control and planning.

RELATIONS WITH OTHERS

The Tiger's relations with others can be fairly positive this year, but disagreements are apt to flare up and unguarded comments, indiscretions or inattention to the views of others could cause problems. However, some new friendships and contacts made over the year can have long-term value.

The Rabbit

The Rabbit is certainly one who appreciates the finer things in life. With his good taste, companionable nature and wide range of interests, he knows how to live well – and usually does!

However, for all his finesse and style, the Rabbit does possess traits he would do well to watch. His desire for a settled lifestyle makes him err on the side of caution. He dislikes change and as a consequence can miss out on opportunities. Also, there are many Rabbits who will go to great lengths to avoid difficult and fraught situations, and again, while few may relish these, sometimes in life it is necessary to take risks or stand your ground. At times it would certainly be in the Rabbit's interests to be bolder and more assertive in going after what he desires.

The Rabbit also attaches great importance to his relations with others and while he has a happy knack of getting on with most people, he can be sensitive to criticism. Difficult though it may be, he should really try to develop a thicker skin and recognize that criticism can provide valuable learning opportunities, as can some of the problems he strives so hard to avoid.

However, with his agreeable manner, keen intellect and shrewd judgement, the Rabbit does have a lot in his favour and invariably makes much of his life – and enjoys it too!

Advice for the Rabbit's Year Ahead

GENERAL PROSPECTS

A demanding year with increased pressures and sometimes frustrating situations. The Rabbit will have the chance to develop new strengths but this is a time for patience, persistence and adapting to the situations he is faced with.

CAREER PROSPECTS

A busy year with a lot being expected of the Rabbit. However, while he may sometimes be anxious about his situation, by remaining focused and rising to the challenge, he will not only have the chance to impress others but also to gain valuable new experience.

FINANCE

The Rabbit will need to be his careful and thorough self when dealing with money matters. This is no year for rush and the more time he allows for making purchases and carrying out plans, the better.

RELATIONS WITH OTHERS

In view of some of the pressures and frustrations he will face, the Rabbit's loved ones can do a lot to support him this year. However, to benefit the Rabbit does need to be forthcoming. There will also be some excellent chances for him to make some valuable new friendships.

The Dragon

Enthusiastic, enterprising and honourable, the Dragon possesses many admirable qualities and his life is often full and varied. He always gives his best and even though not all his endeavours may meet with success, he is nonetheless resilient and hardy, and is much admired and respected.

However, for all his qualities, the Dragon can be blunt and forthright and, through sheer strength of character, sometimes domineering. It would certainly be in his interests to listen more closely to others rather than be so self-reliant. Also, his enthusiasm can sometimes get the better of him and he can be impulsive. To make the most of his abilities, he should give himself priorities and set about his activities in a disciplined and systematic way. More tact and diplomacy might not come amiss either!

However, with his lively and outgoing manner, the Dragon is popular and well liked. With good fortune on his side (and the Dragon is often lucky), his life is almost certain to be eventful and fulfilling. He has many talents, and if he uses them wisely he will enjoy much success.

Advice for the Dragon's Year Ahead

GENERAL PROSPECTS

The Dragon has considerable energy and likes to involve himself in a great many activities. However, in 2009 he would do well to show greater patience. This can be a slow-moving year. Although this can be frustrating for the Dragon, by using his time well and seizing his opportunities, he can fare reasonably well.

CAREER PROSPECTS

This can be a satisfying year and by making the most of their chances, Dragons can do both their present situation and future prospects considerable good. They should aim to work closely with colleagues as well as make the most of opportunities to meet others as over the year they can impress many.

FINANCE

The Dragon's efforts this year can lead to an increase in income, but to benefit he will need to manage his resources well and be attentive when dealing with paperwork.

RELATIONS WITH OTHERS

The Dragon will enjoy positive relations with his family, friends and colleagues this year and can look forward to making some important new friendships and work contacts. For some Dragons, affairs of the heart can also make this a special time. The Dragon does need be wary of rumour or becoming involved in what could be an awkward situation, but generally this will be a pleasing year.

The Snake

The Snake is blessed with a keen intellect. He has wide interests, an enquiring mind and good judgement. He tends to be quiet and thoughtful and plans his activities with considerable care. With his fine abilities he often does well in life, but he does possess traits which can undermine his progress.

The Snake is often guarded in his actions and sometimes loses out to those who are more action-oriented and assertive. He also likes to retain a certain independence in his actions and this too can hamper his progress. It would be in his interests to be more forthcoming and involve others more readily in his plans. The Snake has many talents and possesses a warm and rich personality, but there is a danger that this can remain concealed behind his often quiet and reserved manner. He would fare better if he were more outgoing and showed others his true worth.

However, the Snake is very much his own master. He invariably knows what he wants in life and is often prepared to journey long and hard to achieve his objectives. He does, though, have it in his power to make that journey easier. Lose some of that reticence, Snake, be more open and assertive, and do not be afraid of the occasional risk!

Advice for the Snake's Year Ahead

GENERAL PROSPECTS

A reasonable year, but throughout the Snake will need to remain alert and be prepared to adapt to the situations that arise. A key benefit of the Ox year will be the way in which he is able to develop his skills.

CAREER PROSPECTS

The Ox year can provide some good opportunities for the Snake and allow him to make headway as well as widen his skills. However, throughout the year he will need to keep alert and make the most of chances *as they arise.*

FINANCE

The Snake will need to remain his usual cautious self when dealing with money matters this year. This is no time for risk or for hurrying purchases or plans. Also, paperwork needs close and thorough attention.

RELATIONS WITH OTHERS

There are many people who are keen for the Snake to do well and willing to give him support. However, to benefit he needs to be open and receptive. The more he is prepared to talk to others, the better. His domestic and social life can be particularly rewarding this year and new interests are also favourably aspected.

The Horse

Versatile, hard working and sociable, the Horse makes his mark wherever he goes. He has an eloquent and engaging manner and makes friends with ease. He is quick-witted, has an alert mind and is certainly not averse to taking risks or experimenting with new ideas.

The Horse possesses a strong and likeable personality, but he does also have his weaknesses. With his wide interests he does not always finish everything he starts and he would do well to be more persevering. He has it within him to achieve considerable success, but to make the most of his talents he does need to overcome his restless tendencies. When he has made plans, he should stick with them.

The Horse loves company and values both his family and friends. However, there will have been many a time when he will have lost his temper or spoken in haste and regretted his words. Throughout his life he needs to keep his temper in check and be diplomatic in tense situations. If not, he could risk jeopardizing the respect and good relations he so values.

However, the Horse has a multitude of talents and a lively and outgoing personality. If he can overcome his restless and volatile nature, he can lead a rich and highly fulfilling life.

Advice for the Horse's Year Ahead

GENERAL PROSPECTS
The Ox year will contain some fine opportunities for the Horse and by seizing them and developing his skills he can fare well. He should take up any travel possibilities that come his way, including using some of his free time to visit places nearby. Throughout the year he does, though, need to listen closely to others and be attentive in company.

CAREER PROSPECTS
The Horse is a hard and diligent worker and in 2009 he will often be able to make good progress. Colleagues, contacts and others who are able to advise or assist can be of great value to him this year.

FINANCE
The Horse's progress will often lead to a rise in income and some Horses could also benefit from receiving something extra. However, the Horse does need to manage his money well, planning his purchases as well as being thorough when dealing with paperwork.

RELATIONS WITH OTHERS

This will be a busy year with the Horse in demand. In his domestic life he can look forward to some good times. However, to benefit from the support others are willing to give, he does need to be forthcoming as well as remain aware of the views of those close to him. This also applies to those Horses enjoying the early stages of romance. This is very much a year to be attentive and careful.

The Goat

The Goat has a warm, friendly and understanding manner and gets on well with most people. He is generally easygoing, has a fond appreciation of the finer things in life and possesses a rich imagination. He is often artistic and enjoys the creative arts and outdoor activities.

However, despite his engaging manner, there lurks beneath his skin a sometimes tense and pessimistic nature. The Goat can be a worrier, and without the support and encouragement of others can feel insecure and be hesitant in his actions.

To make the most of himself the Goat should aim to become more assertive and decisive as well as more at ease with himself. He has much in his favour, but he really does need to promote himself more and be bolder. He would also be helped if he were to sort out his priorities and set about his activities in an organized and disciplined manner. There are some Goats who tend to be haphazard in the way they go about things and this can hamper their progress.

Although the Goat will always value the support of others, it would also be in his interests to become more independent and not be so reticent about striking out on his own. He does, after all, possess many talents, as well as a sincere and likeable personality, and by always giving his best he can make his life rich, rewarding and enjoyable.

Advice for the Goat's Year Ahead

GENERAL PROSPECTS

A challenging year. Delays, problems and increased pressures can lead to some frustrating times. However, while this may not be the easiest of years, it can be important *and* instructive. By rising to the challenges, the Goat can learn a great deal and this can be of considerable value later on, especially in the more progressive times that await in 2010.

CAREER PROSPECTS

The Ox year is a hard taskmaster and the Goat will be uneasy with some of the pressures it brings. However, by keeping alert, concentrating on his priorities and taking any chances to extend his skills, he can make progress that will prove important in the long term. Also, he needs to work closely with colleagues and be wary of possible disagreements or fraught situations. A year requiring skill and effort.

FINANCE

The Goat likes his pleasures and in the Ox year his travels and some home and personal purchases will particularly please him. However, this is a year for keeping a close watch on his spending and avoiding haste or risk.

RELATIONS WITH OTHERS

The Goat will be much in demand over the year and will often play a full and valued part in his home life. In return he will be grateful for and often reassured by the advice and support others are able to give, particularly in view of the awkward nature of some of the year. His personal interests could also have a good social element.

The Monkey

Lively, enterprising and innovative, the Monkey certainly knows how to impress. He has wide interests, a good sense of fun and relates well to others. He also possesses a shrewd mind and often has a happy knack of turning events to his advantage.

However, despite his versatility and considerable gifts, the Monkey does have his weaknesses. He often lacks persistence, can get distracted easily and also places tremendous reliance upon his own judgement. While his belief in himself is a commendable asset, it would certainly be in his interests to be more mindful of the views of others. Also, while he likes to keep tabs on all that is going on around him, he can be evasive and secretive with regard to his own feelings and activities, and again a more forth-coming attitude would be to his advantage.

In his desire to succeed the Monkey can also be tempted to cut corners or be crafty and he should recognize that such actions can rebound on him!

However, the Monkey is resourceful and his sheer strength of character will ensure he has an interesting and varied life. If he can channel his considerable energies wisely and overcome his sometimes restless tendencies, his life can be crowned with success and achievement. And with his amiable personality, he will have many friends.

Advice for the Monkey's Year Ahead

GENERAL PROSPECTS

A year for focus and dedication. Plans need to be thought through and the Monkey should be wary of spreading his energies too widely. Time spent on personal interests and specific projects can, though, often bring personal benefit, and travel is also favourably aspected. To keep himself on good form the Monkey would also do well to give some consideration to the quality of his diet and his general level of exercise.

CAREER PROSPECTS

The best results will come from the areas in which the Monkey is most experienced. This is not a year favouring radical change. It is, however, a good time to network and build connections. Progress may not be substantial and results *will* need to be worked for, but the lessons of the year can be positive and often far-reaching.

FINANCE

This is no year for taking risks, being lax in financial matters or over-spending. Time should be allowed to consider major purchases and, with travel well aspected, early provision for a holiday or break could be helpful.

RELATIONS WITH OTHERS

The Monkey always sets great store by his relations with others and over the year these can bring him a lot of pleasure. There will be excellent chances for him to make new friends and contacts and get himself better known at work. For some Monkeys, romance can add excitement to the year, although new relationships should be allowed to evolve in their own time. The Monkey's domestic life can go well this year, with joint activities and home projects favourably aspected. Quality time spent with others can reward him well.

The Rooster

With his considerable bearing and incisive and resolute manner, the Rooster cuts an impressive figure. He has a sharp mind, is well informed on many matters and expresses himself clearly and convincingly. He is meticulous and efficient in his undertakings and commands a great deal of respect. He also has a genuine and caring interest in others.

The Rooster has much in his favour, but there are some aspects of his character that can tell against him. He can be candid in his views and over zealous in his actions, and sometimes he can say or do things he later regrets. His high standards also make him fussy, even pedantic, and he can get diverted into relatively minor matters when in truth he could be occupying his time more profitably. This is something all Roosters would do well to watch. Also, while the Rooster is a great planner, he can sometimes be unrealistic in his expectations. In making plans – indeed, in most of his activities – he would do well to consult others. He would benefit greatly from their input.

The Rooster has many talents as well as commendable drive and commitment, but to make the most of himself he does need to channel his energies wisely and watch his candid and sometimes volatile nature. With care, however, he can make a success of his life, and with his wide interests and outgoing personality, he will enjoy the friendship and respect of many.

Advice for the Rooster's Year Ahead

GENERAL PROSPECTS

This is a year of considerable opportunity for the Rooster, although to benefit he does need to make the most of his ideas and skills. With determination, backed by the support and goodwill he will enjoy, he will be able to improve on his present situation.

CAREER PROSPECTS

The Ox year will bring some good chances for the Rooster to make more of his skills and experience and many Roosters will secure promotion or be able to further their career in more satisfying ways. For those who are feeling staid, dispirited and unfulfilled, this is a year for seizing the initiative and taking action. A lot is possible. Creative skills and interests can also develop in encouraging ways.

FINANCE

The Rooster's hard work and diligence can be rewarded with a financial upturn this year. However, this is a time for managing his money well, including, if possible, reducing borrowings and adding to savings as well as budgeting ahead for major purchases. Good financial management will pay off.

RELATIONS WITH OTHERS

Although this is a favourable year, the Rooster would do well to be more forthcoming and involve others in his plans. Domestically and socially, this can be a pleasing time, with the prospect of new friendships and, for the unattached, romance. Travel is also favourably aspected. However, in such a busy year it is important that the Rooster keeps his lifestyle in balance and gives some consideration to his well-being.

The Dog

Loyal, dependable and with a good understanding of human nature, the Dog is well placed to win respect and admiration. He is a no-nonsense sort of person and hates any sort of hypocrisy and falsehood. With the Dog you know where you stand and, given his direct manner, where he stands on any issue. He also has a strong humanitarian nature and often champions good causes.

The Dog has many fine attributes, although there are certain traits that can prevent him from either enjoying or making the most of his life. He is a great worrier and can get anxious over all manner of things. Although it may not always be easy, he should try to rid himself of the 'worry habit'. Whenever he is tense or concerned, he should be prepared to speak to others rather than shoulder his worries all by himself. In some cases, they could even be of his own making! Also, the Dog has a tendency to look on the pessimistic side and he would certainly be helped if he were to view his undertakings more optimistically. He does, after all, possess many skills and should have faith in his abilities. Another weakness is his tendency to be stubborn over certain issues. If he is not careful, at times this could undermine his position.

If the Dog can reduce the pessimistic side of his nature, he will not only enjoy life more but also find he is achieving more. He possesses a truly admirable character and his loyalty, reliability and sincerity are appreciated by all he meets. In his life he will do much good and befriend many people – and he owes it to himself to enjoy life too. Sometimes it might help him to recall the words of another Dog, Sir Winston Churchill: 'When I look back on all these worries I remember the story of the old man who said on his deathbed that he had had a lot of trouble in his life, most of which never happened.'

Advice for the Dog's Year Ahead

GENERAL PROSPECTS

The aspects may be challenging, but provided the Dog is careful, alert and prepared to adapt (rather than remaining stubborn or inflexible), what he experiences over the year can be to his long-term benefit. This is time for keeping expectations modest, avoiding rush and frequently consulting others.

CAREER PROSPECTS

A demanding year with new challenges and sometimes difficult situations to deal with. However, by concentrating on what needs to be done and using his skills to advantage, the Dog can prepare the way for future growth, particularly in 2010.

FINANCE

The Dog needs to be thorough and attentive in financial matters this year. Spending needs to be controlled and paperwork handled promptly and with care.

RELATIONS WITH OTHERS

In this mixed year the Dog will really appreciate his domestic life and despite the busy nature of the year he should make sure he spends quality time with those who are special to him. His interests and social life can also do him good .

The Pig

Genial, sincere and trusting, the Pig gets on well with most people. He has a kind and caring nature, a dislike of discord and often a good sense of humour. In addition, he has a fondness for socializing and enjoying the good life!

The Pig possesses a shrewd mind, is particularly adept at dealing with business and financial matters and has a robust and resilient nature. Although not all his plans may work out as he would like, he is tenacious and will often rise up and succeed after experiencing setbacks and difficulties. In his often active and varied life he can accomplish a great deal, although there are certain aspects of his character that can tell against him. If he can modify these or keep them in check then his life will certainly be easier and possibly even more successful.

In his activities the Pig can sometimes over-commit himself and while he does not want to disappoint, he would certainly be helped if he were to set about his activities in an organized and systematic manner and give himself priorities at busy times. He should also not allow others to take advantage of his good nature and it would be in his interests to be more discerning. There will have been times when he has been gullible and naïve; fortunately, though, he quickly learns from his mistakes. However, he possesses a stubborn streak and if new situations do not fit in with his line of thinking, he can be inflexible. Such an attitude may not always be to his advantage.

The Pig is a great pleasure-seeker and while he should enjoy the fruits of his labours, he can sometimes be self-indulgent and extravagant. This is also something he would do well to watch.

However, though the Pig may possess some faults, those who come into contact with him are invariably impressed by his integrity, amiable manner and intelligence. If he uses his talents wisely, his life can be crowned with considerable achievement and he will also be loved and respected by many.

Advice for the Pig's Year Ahead

GENERAL PROSPECTS

Ralph Waldo Emerson, born under the sign of the Pig, once declared, 'Be an opener of doors,' and for the Pig this is a year to open doors and set plans in motion. If he takes action, a lot will now be possible. In addition he will be helped considerably by drawing on the support of others. A year of great possibility and promise.

CAREER PROSPECTS

With his experience, capacity for hard work and the positive relations he has with many of his colleagues, the Pig will have a lot in his favour this year. This is a time when he should look to move forward and make his abilities count. Promotion and new responsibilities may beckon, while for those Pigs who are keen to take their work in new directions, this is a year for exploring possibilities.

FINANCE

The Pig's efforts over the year will be well rewarded and he may also be helped by his enterprising and sometimes entrepreneurial streak. However, he should make the most of any upturn by managing his finances well, being disciplined in his spending and, if possible, making some provision for his future.

RELATIONS WITH OTHERS

Genial and good-hearted, the Pig has a happy knack of getting on with most people and during the year he will enjoy great support. Domestically and socially, this can be a rewarding year, with some personal celebrations possible. There will also be plenty of chances to get to know others, although where matters of the heart are concerned, the Pig would do well to let any new romance develop in its own time. Overall a busy, eventful and pleasing year.